The New Wave Cinema in Iran

The New Wave Cinema in Iran

A Critical Study

Parviz Jahed

BLOOMSBURY ACADEMIC
NEW YORK • LONDON • OXFORD • NEW DELHI • SYDNEY

BLOOMSBURY ACADEMIC
Bloomsbury Publishing Inc
1385 Broadway, New York, NY 10018, USA
50 Bedford Square, London, WC1B 3DP, UK
29 Earlsfort Terrace, Dublin 2, Ireland

BLOOMSBURY, BLOOMSBURY ACADEMIC and the Diana logo are
trademarks of Bloomsbury Publishing Plc

First published in the United States of America 2022
Paperback edition published 2024
Copyright © Parviz Jahed, 2022

For legal purposes the Acknowledgements on p. xiii constitute
an extension of this copyright page.

Cover design: Eleanor Rose
Cover image: *Gav* (The Cow), 1969, Iran, Dir. Dariush Mehrjui © Iranian
Ministry of Culture / Alamy

All rights reserved. No part of this publication may be reproduced
or transmitted in any form or by any means, electronic or mechanical,
including photocopying, recording, or any information storage or retrieval
system, without prior permission in writing from the publishers.

Bloomsbury Publishing Inc does not have any control over, or responsibility for,
any third-party websites referred to or in this book. All internet addresses given
in this book were correct at the time of going to press. The author and publisher
regret any inconvenience caused if addresses have changed or sites have
ceased to exist, but can accept no responsibility for any such changes.

Library of Congress Cataloging-in-Publication Data
Names: Jāhid, Parvīz, author.
Title: The new wave cinema in Iran : a critical study / Parviz Jahed.
Description: New York, NY : Bloomsbury Academic, 2022. |
Includes bibliographical references and index. |
Summary: "The Birth of the Iranian New Wave Cinema is an historical and
analytical study of the Iranian New Wave Cinema (Mowj-e No) as an artistic
and intellectual movement that came to its best early productions between
1958 and 1978. As the movement has a long history, Parviz Jahed focuses on the
development and the early progression of the movement in the 1960s and
explores its emergence and development in the context of the cultural
and social conditions of Iran during this period"– Provided by publisher.
Identifiers: LCCN 2021052962 (print) | LCCN 2021052963 (ebook) |
ISBN 9781501369124 (hardback) | ISBN 9781501369094 (paperback) |
ISBN 9781501369117 (epub) | ISBN 9781501369100 (pdf) | ISBN 9781501369087
Subjects: LCSH: Motion pictures–Iran–History–20th century. | New wave films–Iran.
Classification: LCC PN1993.5.I846 J34 2022 (print) | LCC PN1993.5.I846 (ebook) |
DDC 791.430955– dc23/eng/20220208
LC record available at https://lccn.loc.gov/2021052962
LC ebook record available at https://lccn.loc.gov/2021052963

ISBN:	HB:	978-1-5013-6912-4
	PB:	978-1-5013-6909-4
	ePDF:	978-1-5013-6910-0
	eBook:	978-1-5013-6911-7

Typeset by Integra Software Services Pvt. Ltd.

To find out more about our authors and books visit www.bloomsbury.com
and sign up for our newsletters.

For my wife Roya and my son Barbod

Contents

List of figures ... ix
Acknowledgements ... xiii

Introduction ... 1

1 The Iranian New Wave (*Mowj-e No*) ... 5
   Recognition of and challenging *Mowj-e No* ... 7

2 The internal factors ... 19
   Cinema and the negotiation of modernity in Iran ... 21
   The emergence of national cinema ... 26
   Nativism vs. Westoxication (*Gharbzadegi*) ... 31
   The enablement and obstructionism of the state ... 35
   The mechanisms of censorship ... 40
   The establishment of cultural institutions and film centres ... 44

3 Looking for an alternative cinema in Iran ... 51
   Status of critical film discourse in 1960s Iran ... 52
   Intellectual cinema and challenging *Filmfarsi* ... 68
   Mowj-e No, the lost identity and manifestation of utopian cinema ... 77

4 *New Wave* and the literary tradition ... 91
   Adaptation from Persian classical literature ... 91
   Later fantasy and folktales ... 93
   Interaction between *Mowj-e No* and modern literature ... 95

5 The external influences ... 101
   The footprint of Italian neorealism ... 102
   The global impact of the French *Nouvelle Vague* ... 109
   The French *Nouvelle Vague* and the Iranian *Mowj-e No* ... 115
   Fereydoun Hoveyda, the auteur theory and Iran's New Wave ... 119

6 The forerunners of the New Wave cinema in Iran ... 137
   Ebrahim Golestan and writing with a camera ... 137
   The legacy of Farrokh Ghaffari ... 153
   Fereydoun Rahnema and his self-reflexive cinema ... 169

7	New Wave successors and new film aesthetics	185
	Formalistic approach	186
	Social realism and the street film genre	204

Afterword	215
Bibliography	218
Index of names	225
Index of films and books	230

Figures

2.1 Ezzatolah Entezami as Naser al-din Shah Qajar in Mohsen Makhmalbaf's *Once Upon a Time, Cinema* (1992) — 20
2.2 Ovanes Ohanian's *Haji Agha, Actor-e Cinema* (Haji Agha, the Cinema Actor, 1932) — 26
2.3 *Dokhtar-e Lor* (The Lor Girl, 1933), the first Iranian talkie directed by Abdolhossein Sepanta — 28
2.4 *Gav* (The Cow, 1969) by Dariush Mehrjui — 43
2.5 Ezatollah Entezami, Farrokh Ghaffari and Ali Nassirian at the Shiraz Festival of Arts, 1968 — 49
3.1 Naser Malek Motiee and Christine Paterson in Nezam Fatemi's *Mehdi in Black Suit with the Girl in Hot Mini Pants* (Mehdi Meshki va Shalvarak-e Dagh, 1972) — 53
3.2 Original poster of *Lat-e Javanmard* (1958), directed by Majid Mohseni — 55
3.3 Siamak Yasemi's *Ganj-e Qarun* (Qarun's Treasure, 1965) — 66
3.4 Parviz Davaei, a veteran Iranian film critic – photograph by Parviz Jahed — 71
3.5 *Khesht va Ayeneh* (Brick and Mirror, 1965) directed by Ebrahim Golestan — 75
3.6 *Shab-e Quzi* (The Night of the Hunchback, 1965) directed by Farrokh Ghaffari — 81
3.7 *Aramesh dar Hozour-e Digaran* (Tranquility in the Presence of Others, 1969/73) directed by Nasser Taghvai — 83
3.8 *P Mesle Pelican* (P for Pelican, 1972) directed by Parviz Kimiavi — 88
4.1 *Nasim-e Ayyar* (1967) directed by Esmail Koushan — 94
4.2 Behrouz Vosoughi in *Tangsir* (1973), Amir Naderi's epic and realistic adaptation from Sadegh Choubak's novel — 96
4.3 *Shohar-e Ahu Khanoom* (Ahu Khanoom's Husband, 1968) directed by Davoud Mollapour — 100
5.1 Taji Ahmadi in Ebrahim Golestan's *Brick and Mirror* (1963) — 106
5.2 Fereydoun Hoveyda in Éric Rohmer's *The Sign of Leo* (*Le signe du lion*, 1962) — 121

5.3	Mehri Vedadian in *Shohar-e Ahu Khanoom* (Ahu Khanoom's Husband, 1968) directed by Davoud Mollapour	124
5.4	Akbar Meshkin in Nasser Taghvai's *Tranquility in the Presence of Others* (1969/73)	126
5.5	*Gav* (The Cow, 1969) by Dariush Mehrjui	128
5.6	The original poster of Masoud Kimiai's *Khaak* (The Soil, 1973) based on Mahmoud Dowlatabadi's *Owsane-ye Baba Sobhan*	130
5.7	Bahman Farmanara's *Shazdeh Ehtejab* (Prince Ehtejab, 1974) based on Houshang Golshiri's modern novel	131
5.8	Parvaneh Masoumi in Bahram Beyzaie's *Ragbar* (Downpour, 1971)	133
5.9	Parviz Sayyad's *Bonbast* (Deadend, 1977), loosely based on a short story by Anton Chekhov	134
6.1	Ebrahim Golestan – photograph by Parviz Jahed	139
6.2	Ebrahim Golestan on the set of *Brick and Mirror* (1963)	142
6.3	Forough Farrokhzad on the set of *The House is Black* (1962)	143
6.4	Zakaria Hashemi and Taji Ahmadi in *Brick and Mirror* (1965)	147
6.5	Taji Ahmadi in *Brick and Mirror* (1965)	149
6.6	Parviz Sayyad in Ebrahim Golestan's *The Secrets of the Treasure of the Jinn Valley* (1974)	152
6.7	Farrokh Ghaffari – photograph by Parviz Jahed	155
6.8	Farrokh Ghaffari as the art director of the Shiraz Festival of Arts	160
6.9	Mohammad Ali Keshavarz in Farrokh Ghaffari's *The Night of the Hunchback* (1965)	165
6.10	The corpse works just like a Hitchcockian McGuffin in *The Night of the Hunchback* (1965)	167
6.11	Fereydoun Rahnema, one of the forerunners of the New Wave cinema in Iran	170
6.12	*Siavash in Persepolis* (1965), directed by Fereydoun Rahnema	175
6.13	*Siavash in Persepolis* (1965), a modern adaptation of Siavash's story from Ferdowsi's *Shahnameh*	176
6.14	*Iran's Son Has No News of His Mother* (1974), an alienated character searching for his identity by confronting the past	178
6.15	*Iran's Son Has No News of His Mother* (1974), a self-reflexive film consistent with the style of essay films	181
6.16	*Iran's Son Has No News of His Mother* (1974), Fereydoun Rahnema's last film	184

7.1 *A Simple Event* (1973), an outstanding New Wave film directed by
     Sohrab Shahid-Saless   189
7.2 In *Still Life* (1974) Shahid-Saless shows the boredom, despair and
     loneliness of the repetitive and monotonous lives of his characters
     through continuous and fixed long takes   191
7.3 *Bread and Alley* (1970) introduces Kiarostami's minimalist style 194
7.4 Kiarostami's *Gozaresh* (Report, 1977), a family drama focused
     on a marital crisis of a middle-class couple in modern Tehran
     in the late 1970s   195
7.5 Parviz Kimiavi's *Mogholha* (The Mongols, 1973), a modern
     self-reflexive film dealing with the notion of anachronism   197
7.6 Mohammad Reza Aslani's recently rediscovered film
     Shatranj-e Baad (The Chess of the Wind, 1976), a gothic
     thriller that was never given a chance to be screened in
     Iran publicly   199
7.7 Arby Ovanessian's *Cheshmeh* (The Spring, 1972), a stylistic
     New Wave film   201
7.8 Marva Nabili's *Khake Sar Beh Morh* (The Sealed Soil, 1976)
     which focused on the dichotomy between tradition and
     modernity in Iran   203
7.9 Behrouz Vosoughi as an iconic figure and a rebellious character in
     Masoud Kimiai's *Qaysar* (1969)   207
7.10 Saeed Raad, the anti-hero of Amir Naderi's *Tangna* (Deadlock, 1973) 210
7.11 Fereydoun Goleh's *Kandu* (Beehive), one of the best examples
     of street cinema in Iran   212

Acknowledgements

Writing about the New Wave Cinema in Iran has often been a challenging experience and I am very thankful for the support and relief offered by my family and friends. I would like to thank the School of Modern Languages at the University of St Andrews for allowing me to undertake this research project. I would like to express my boundless and hearty gratitude to Dr Saeed Talajooy at the University of St Andrews for generously providing me with his thoughtful insights and advice. I am also grateful to Catherine Mary Cobham for her advice and support. I would like to thank my friend and archivist Saman Bayat for providing me with the film stills.

I am extremely grateful to the wonderful people at Bloomsbury Publishing, particularly to Katie Gallof for her patience, support and enthusiasm for this project and giving me this fantastic opportunity. I also need to thank Sarah Norman for the copy-editing and Deborah Maloney for her rigorous proofreading of the book.

I wish to thank Mr Ebrahim Golestan for being so very welcoming to me and for sharing his brilliant knowledge, experiences and opinions with me. I consider him to be a great personal friend whom I am very lucky to have met.

I am also very thankful to the dear, departed Farrokh Ghaffari whom I never had the opportunity to share the results of my interviews with, but I am so pleased to have had the opportunity to be his guest and interview him on two occasions.

I am also thankful to these pioneers (Golestan, Ghaffari and Rahnema) for their extremely important role in the history of Iranian cinema and culture, particularly in paving the way when it comes to New Wave cinema in our country. Likewise, I wish to thank countless other brilliant filmmakers, critics, scholars and enthusiasts who have helped inform and provide the conditions necessary to produce this book.

I have a deep debt of gratitude to my beloved son, Barbod, who edited this book from the early drafts to its final release, and was so magnanimous in providing his input and thought-provoking discussions. I am very proud of him, and I hope I've made him proud with the outcome.

And finally, I need to thank my lovely wife Roya for her patience and for the encouragement she has given me that was so essential to the completion of this book. It was a rewarding, but also highly challenging project, and I am very thankful for the support and relief offered by my family.

Introduction

Iranian cinema has attained worldwide recognition over the last three decades. This recognition is largely due to the initial successes of Iran's New Wave (*Mowj-e No*) filmmakers, such as Abbas Kiarostami, Sohrab Shahid-Saless, Amir Naderi, Bahram Beyzaie, Nasser Taghvai and Dariush Mehrjui. The achievement of these filmmakers helped to pave the way for many contemporary Iranian filmmakers such as Kianoush Ayyari, Jafar Panahi, Aboulfazl Jalili, Mohsen Makhmalbaf and Asghar Farhadi who emerged after the 1979 Islamic Revolution in Iran. However, this book does not focus on this post-revolutionary period of Iranian cinema, which is currently a topic of immense interest for Iranian and Western film studies. Instead, this is an examination of the origins and early development and functions of Iranian New Wave cinema in the context of the wider national cinema of the late 1950s and early 1960s. This period was a significant turning point in the history of Iranian New Wave cinema: it was a time when innovative, controversial films were being made by a small group of intellectual filmmakers, who were countercultural and modernist in their approach, and yet had strong ties with the creative font of classical and modern Persian literature, Iranian theatre and documentary film tradition.

A major incentive in choosing to cover this subject is that, although there is some critical material on New Wave Iranian cinema, the period in question has to a large extent been overlooked, or merely covered in broad strokes. I hope to reflect on this era in more detail, exploring and explicating the works of the most prominent filmmakers of this era: Ebrahim Golestan (b. 1922), Fereydoun Rahnema (1930–75) and Farrokh Ghaffari (1921–2006) as a way to provide depth, and to cover the history and critical discourse centred around this early period. In addition to these key figures, whom I consider undercredited for the impact they have had on this movement, I made substantial efforts to at least pay some regard to the creatives who played a role in the formation of the movement, including some who were perhaps too obscure for me to be able to credit sufficiently due to the sources of research available and for this I can only apologize. I have concentrated on the rise of the New Wave and examine the socio-political forces, the influential tendencies in film criticism and also the external factors such as the influence of Italian neorealism and the French New Wave that contributed to the formation of this movement.

To this end, in the first chapter I set the stage by providing a general overview of the meaning and origins of the term 'New Wave' (*Mowj-e No*) in Iran's cinematic and cultural context through exploring the writings of both Western and Iranian film historians and scholars. I review the material on the Iranian New Wave (both in Persian and in English) written between 1958 and 1968. I argue that despite the recent scholarly interest in Iran's New Wave cinema, these original sources have remained under-explored by cultural scholars. The review of these writings serves to suggest that certain areas, including the intellectual framework of New Wave cinema and the role of the three prominent modernist filmmakers of the time, have not been investigated with sufficient depth. It also seems that the origins, sources, motivations and objectives of New Wave cinema and its forerunners have been left unassessed or misunderstood to a great extent, and I attempt to help shed light on these and provide some much-needed clarification.

A deeper delve into New Wave Iranian cinema entails the undertaking of a thorough investigation of its historical roots and the socio-political and cultural situation of Iran that paved the way for its emergence and development. In Chapter 2, therefore, I conduct a review of Iran's political, cultural and intellectual climate in the 1950s and 1960s to identify and analyse the underlying factors that led to the rise of Iranian New Wave cinema and its impact on Iran's cultural environment in the period of study. In this chapter I also underline how Iranian intellectuals in general, and Iranian intellectual filmmakers in particular, responded to the cultural and socio-political transformation within their society from the early years of the creation of cinema in Iran. I initially examine the Iranian intellectual movement in relation to the project of authoritative modernity in Iran. This is crucial because Iranian intellectuals, as creators and narrators of contemporary culture, played a vital role in mediating the encounter between Western culture and Iran's Islamic heritage (Boroujerdi 1996, p. xiv).

I track the socio-political activities of the intellectuals associated with the project of modernity from the early 1940s to the late 1960s and early 1970s. Through this lens I examine Iranian cinema in relation to the intellectual movement and in the broader context of the project of modernity in Iran. Sociopolitical topos such as nativism, Westoxication and going back to one's roots and national identity proposed by thinkers such as Jalal Al-e-Ahmad and Dariush Shayegan are examined in line with the quest for creation of this new cinema. I argue that their attempts to theorize and implement or to go against modernity had a great impact on and were in constant dialogue with Iranian cinema from its earliest days. I explain how Iranian cinema developed despite the practical, cultural and state-imposed restrictions and the broad conflict that this stirred between the proponents of modernity and the so-called traditionalists.

Chapter 3 examines the main critical debates on film and cinema in Iran during the period of the 1950s to 1960s. I found that much of the cinema-focused texts during that time were centred around issues of finding authenticity and breaking from *Filmfarsi*, and how cinema was labelled with adjectives such as 'intellectual', 'national' and the 'other'. By focusing on the main debates of critical film discourse during this period, the chapter demonstrates how Iranian film critics contributed towards the ideas that laid behind the formation of modern cinema in Iran. I consider evidence gathered from various sources, including archival materials, newspapers, film journals and magazines published during the 1950s and 1960s and also first- and second-hand interviews with several Iranian film critics and scholars.

In Chapter 4 I present the context to understand the interweaving of modern literature and the New Wave, as well as an outline of the strong tradition of literary adaptations which exists within Iranian cinema. The literary roots of Iranian New Wave cannot be overstated, and I examine the close connections that existed between modern writers and modern filmmakers in that period, and how their collaboration and their cinematic adaptation strategies were highly effective, leading to the creation of some of the most outstanding New Wave films such as *The Cow* (1969), *Aramesh Dar Hozour-e Digaran* (Tranquility in the Presence of Others, 1969/73), *Tangsir* (1973), and *Prince Ehtejab* (1974). My argument in this chapter is that in the modern atmosphere of Iran in the 1960s, modern Iranian cinema and literature moved together and the works of modern writers such as Gholamhossein Sa'edi, Mahmoud Dowlatabadi, Hushang Golshiri and Sadegh Chubak became a source of adaptation for the New Wave filmmakers such as Dariush Mehrjui, Masoud Kimiai, Nasser Taghvai, Bahman Farmanara and others.

Chapter 5 attempts to define the degree to which Italian neorealism and the French New Wave have contributed to the formation of New Wave cinema in Iran. By giving a Deleuzian reading of Italian neorealism, through the theoretical time-image framework put forward by French philosopher

Gilles Deleuze, I attempt to underline the neorealist aspects of the Iranian New Wave. In this regard, I explore the ways in which neorealist aspects of New Wave cinema in Iran are linked to Italian neorealism, particularly if one applies Deleuzean concepts to this filmic tradition, and how they fit within what Deleuze considered to be the main features of modern cinema. Upon a closer investigation of the relationship between the French *Nouvelle Vague* and Iranian *Mowj-e No* I review the many stylistic and aesthetic features exemplified within the works of Iranian New Wave filmmakers inspired by these French filmmakers.

I also argue that the influence of Italian neorealism and the French New Wave served as a kind of catalyst, rather than a reactant, for this movement. I identify how the cinematic shift could be considered a sort of by-product of modern Iranian literature and theatre developing concurrently in the 1960s and I provide the context around this phenomenon.

Chapter 6 is dedicated to the foundational decade from 1958 to 1968 and in this section, I look at the work and ideas proposed by the three forerunners of the New Wave that inspired me to write this book: Ebrahim Golestan, Farrokh Ghaffari and Fereydoun Rahnema. A primary objective of mine is to explore the historic significance of these artists and how their work pioneered much of what came afterwards. A brief biography and analysis of their films is given in chronological order – or sometimes logical order to aid clarity in terms of the wider scope – of their work in relation to the development of this new cinema.

In Chapter 7, I analyse the thematic and stylistic aspects of the New Wave successors. Many filmmakers who came on the scene later in the 1970s would build upon the potential and capacity of filmmaking demonstrated by the pioneers such as Golestan, Ghaffari and Rahnema. The main difference between the New Wave filmmakers was their approach to reality and the way that reality was represented in their films. Based on this notion, I recognize two major trends among the second-generation New Wave filmmakers, namely, formalism and social realism.

Beyond examining the historical, socio-political and cultural contexts in which the New Wave films were made, I was also concerned with the narrative-led innovations and the new stylistic aspects of these films. Methodologically and from a historical perspective, this is a fresh and novel approach which I believe differs substantially from the commonly accepted narratives surrounding the history of New Wave cinema in highlighting a number of unevaluated areas critical to the history of Iranian cinema.

1

The Iranian New Wave (*Mowj-e No*)

The term '*Mowj-e No*' (New Wave) first started to appear in critical literature of the early 1970s and was used to describe a body of controversial Iranian films that were then thought to have been made during the 1960s and 1970s by a group of young intellectuals, many of whom were foreign educated (Armes 1987, p. 191).

This would suggest that the *Mowj-e No* in Iran represented the desire of a younger, westernized generation to break free from the conventions of the mainstream and popular Iranian cinema (known as *Filmfarsi*) of the period. The situation in Iran, however, corresponded only partially to the French New Wave. The Iranian model of New Wave was a part of the modern flow that first appeared in the fields of literature, theatre, fine arts and music.

In his definition of the term, Ahmad Talebinejad points out this aspect of the movement when he explains that *Mowj-e No* is a trend aiming at a cultural objective. 'If it has not achieved the ultimate aim regarding film production, it has tried to depart from the swamp that is *Filmfarsi*' (Talebinejad 1993, p. 10).

Hamid Naficy suggests this New Wave cinema could be defined as a 'dissent cinema', a form of resistance not only against *Filmfarsi* (the dominant cinema) but also the Shah's authoritarian government:

> [The movement] constituted acts of resistance both against the dominant commercial film [F]arsi cinema and against the authoritarian political system. Undoubtedly, this cinema and its influence on the intelligentsia and the student population was one of the sparks that ignited the revolution. This influence did not occur in a vacuum. Rather, it was part of the emerging formations, dispositions, contingencies, discourses, and microphysics of power and protest that amplified each other rhizomatically.
>
> (Naficy 2011, p. 404)

Iran was almost certainly one of the offshoots of this scattered global trend; however, in contrast to some of the more well-defined interpretations assigned to the New Wave movements found in France and other Western cultures, there was no clear consensus amongst Iranian film critics as to what the term referred to.

Hamid Naficy and Roy Armes's points above would indicate that the Iranian cinematic understanding of the New Wave echoes the French notion of the term. This view suggests that the term New Wave (*Mowj-e No*) in Iran is a derivative of the French *Nouvelle Vague*. This belief is further supported by Iranian film critics such as Kambiz Kaheh and Ahmad Talebinjad who argue that the social, educational and cultural influence of France and Europe contributed to the style and approach of the New Wave Iranian filmmakers. Further still, in his introduction to *Yek Etefagh-e Sadeh*, Talebinejad points out that the New Wave in France was founded on the grounds that classical cinema was failing to intellectually satisfy the new generation. Similarly, in Iran *Filmfarsi* – which was the most popular form of cinema before the 1979 Islamic revolution – no longer captured the attention of the new generation who aspired to create a more stimulating and intellectually challenging cinema.

The goal of divergence from the mainstream and the conventional was a means unto itself; it was not an ambition that was approached in a strongly collaborative or strategic manner. These films can be categorized together, but there was no shared platform or manifesto-like statement linking them in a particularly cohesive fashion. In the face of challenges such as censorship and financing issues decimating the production and distribution cycles of these films, the total output was rather sporadic compared to many other movements of its kind outside Iran. Take for instance the arthouse cinematic output of Brazil, known as *Cinema Novo* (New Cinema), with a total of at least eighteen key films made between 1960 and 1970 compared to the eight New Wave films in total made in Iran in the same period (Stam and Johnson 1979, pp. 13–18).

Although this Iranian New Wave was never able to muster the same influence on global cinematic understanding and discourse as the French *Nouvelle Vague* or Italian *neorealismo* (neorealism), it was nonetheless a genuine and identifiable revolution in the course of Iranian cinema. Indeed, it was during this period that many prominent figures of Iranian modern cinema began to make their initial challenges to the thematic and aesthetic characteristics of the dominant *Filmfarsi* tradition. The introduction of new narratives, themes and genres managed to take hold to the extent that it came to greatly alter the course for not only arthouse but popular cinema as well. Rigidly held conventions such as shooting in studio lots, overly dramatic and exaggerated acting styles and happy endings were finally replaced with location shooting, use of non-actors and more nuanced actors from the theatrical tradition and much grittier narratives.

I posit that the Iranian New Wave had fully emerged by the early 1960s (in tandem with its counterparts in the rest of the world), often maintaining an intimate relationship with contemporary literature and theatre and the highly experimental documentary tradition, which included the works of filmmakers such as Ebrahim Golestan, Forough Farrokhzad and Fereydoun Rahnema.

I would also maintain that the vast and stylistically indigenous cinematic corpus that the pre-revolution filmmakers of this tradition left behind was hugely determinative of the future path and very essence of post-revolution arthouse cinema. This brought Iranian films to the fore of international spectators' attention in the successive decades, leading to the multitude of awards and recognition that these later films rightly received and continue to do so to this day.

Recognition of and challenging *Mowj-e No*

Despite evidence suggesting early engagement of these Iranian filmmakers with modern European cinematic spheres, a number of Iranian film critics, particularly those who were discussing the chronology of Iranian cinema from the early 1970s onwards, would not only argue against the existence of such an influence and reject any relationship between the Iranian *Mowj-e No* and the French *Nouvelle Vague*, but also would go as far as to deny the emergence of any sort of New Wave in Iranian cinema in the first place.

In her article '*Eshtebahat-e Tarikhi*' (Historical Mistakes), Gozaresh-e Film (a film journal), 2000, p. 55, Sabereh Kashi suggests that the New Wave is a confusing, misleading term, used to describe a movement that never truly took place within Iranian cinema. She states that the New Wave was just an illusion amongst Iranian film critics who wished to coin a fancy name for what was happening in Iranian cinema, and that there is no relationship between what happened in Iran and the New Wave in France, Brazil or any other country (Kashi 2000, p. 55). Kashi argues that, unlike French

Nouvelle Vague filmmakers, 'there are no relations or similarities between the aesthetic views of Iranian filmmakers', and that every film made by Iranian New Wave filmmakers has its own unique style, structure and content which differentiates it from others to the point that these works cannot be categorized in any single movement (Kashi 2000, p. 55).

Hassan Hosseini, another Iranian film critic, claims that the term New Wave was used to describe some distinctive Iranian arthouse films due to the critics' own desire to trigger a revolutionary reform in Iranian cinema. As he puts it, 'The possibility of creation/existence was impossible due to the specific societal and cultural weave of Iran'. and that 'the New Wave filmmakers in France changed the image of the French film industry in the world. In Iran, however, one finds major differences between the points of view and styles of the filmmakers of the time. Furthermore, they created new styles of filmmaking that never got a chance to emerge and influence the overall structure of Iranian cinema, as the rise of these distinctive forms did not and could not stop the continuation of the mainstream films known as *Filmfarsi* in Iranian cinema' (Hosseini 2002, p. 7).

In Hosseini's view, the New Wave films did not bear a marked difference to *Filmfarsi*; even the films of Haritash and Ranehma, from a technical perspective, were amateurish and weak, and of a lower grade than *Filmfarsi*. For example, in the same source about the subject of the New Wave, the critic draws comparisons between the fight scene in Amir Naderi's *Khodahafez Rafigh* (Goodbye Friend, 1971) and those that were found in *Filmfarsi* to indicate the level of technical shortcomings of the former film. Perhaps the very pointed characteristics of amateur techniques and more idiosyncratic styles that are universally emblematic of the New Wave movement went unnoticed by him and other critics who were very quick to lambast these New Wave films for weakness of technique. One aspect to which he does credit as a saving grace of the movement is 'these so-called new Mowj-e No allowed for the injection of youthfulness (fresh blood) to the film industry' (Hosseini 2002, p. 7).

Jamal Omid, in his *History of Iranian Cinema*, delineates the early European inspired arthouse films made by the likes of Ebrahim Golestan, Farrokh Ghaffari and Rahnema as 'one-off occurrences' that were the efforts of young and ambitious filmmakers looking to bring forth a new intellectual dawn, which nevertheless failed to 'spark' a coherent movement. Instead, Omid credits later releases by the likes of Dariush Mehrjui and Davoud Mollahpour for having created such a spark that had left a lasting impression and which he refers to as *Cinema-ye Motefavet* (a different cinema) (Omid 1995, p. 412).

The analysis of Omid in this book is based on quotes and contemporary sentiments from various sources, such as reviews found in journals and newspapers, and therefore provides a useful and generally objective amalgamation of such outputs, which would otherwise be difficult to find outside of first-hand research. His book especially features contradictory quotes from critics about various topics to show a breadth of opinions, rather than cherry-picking certain sources to support a certain viewpoint and disregarding others. However, there are conclusions that Omid makes, and in this book he draws a marked point of distinction from the cinematic release of films such as *Qaysar* (1969) and *Gav* (The Cow, 1969), reflecting a sort of consensus view held by many that to an extent discounts the films made before this point. He denotes a significant shift in how we categorize Iranian films which corresponds with this outlook, breaking the films down into three distinct classifications.

Firstly, 'commercial' films, which include Siamak Yasemi's *Ganj-e Qarun* (Qarun's Treasure, 1965), Samuel Khachikian's *Nare-ye Toofan* (The Cry of the Storm, 1969) and Ahmad Shirazi's *Donya-ye Por Omid* (A World Full of Hope, 1969). Secondly, 'intellectual' films including Golestan's *Brick and Mirror* (1965), Mollapour's *Ahu Khanoom's Husband* (1968) and Rahnema's *Siavash in Persepolis* (1965). And thirdly what he refers to as *Jebhe-ye Sevoom*/'the third front' cinema – a combination of commercial and intellectual films including Ali Hatami's *Toghi* (1970) and *Hassan Kachal* (1970), Soleyman Minassian's *Tolou* (Sunrise, 1970), Jalal Moghaddam's *Panjere* (The Window, 1970) and *Farar Az Taleh* (Escape from the Trap, 1971), Kimiai's *Qaysar* (1969) and *Reza Motori* (Reza Motorcyclist, 1970) and Mehrjui's *Gav* (The Cow, 1969) which were able to combine artistic originality and integrity with mainstream reach and box office success (Omid 1995, p. 522).

In the case of contemporary critics such as Parviz Davaei, Houshang Kavoosi, Fereydoun Rahnema and others, who were presented with such radical departures from the typical filmmaking that they were exposed to and would review, they opted to view these films through the lens of genre and indeed those very conventions and tropes which these filmmakers were oftentimes so consciously aiming to break away from. For the likes of Kavoosi, their understanding of which genre these films fall under, and drawing comparison to films made previously either in the West or domestically, were key in formulating their analysis. Alternatively, critics would simply omit to discuss them as a means of discrediting, or diminishing, their import.

Critics such as Davaei would oftentimes cite the early New Wave films as outliers, which did not belong within the broader scope of Iranian cinematic consciousness or, in the case of heavily impactful films (beginning with *Qaysar*), would identify them as the originators of major Hollywood film genres and set them against the independent films of other nationalities and perhaps later Iranian films which were derivatives of them.

For instance, Farrokh Ghaffari's *Shab-e Quzi* (The Night of the Hunchback, 1965) was compared to Hitchcock's offbeat, morbid comedy *The Trouble with Harry* (1955), whilst Ghafarri countered that Hitchcock himself drew inspiration for this narrative from *One Thousand and One Nights (Arabian Nights)* (Omid 1995, p. 368).

One critic, by the likely pen-name of Barham Bordbar, would describe *Shab-e Quzi* within the framework of a 'fantasy' film, and explain how it missed the mark as a product of that specific genre and that the grander themes are left unexplored. The hunchback is indeed a character often found in Iranian folk tales and also in *One Thousand and One Nights*. But he is also one of the main characters of Sadegh Hedayat's modern and nightmarish novel *Boof-e Koor* (The Blind Owl, 1937). Contrary to what Borbar suggests, as a socially conscious filmmaker, Ghaffari did not want to make a 'fantasy film' but instead he deploys a neorealist approach in his modern adaptation of the story of the hunchback in *One Thousand and One Nights*.

Such diversity of critical approach can be found in the contemporary treatments of Dariush Mehrjui's *Gav* (The Cow, 1969). For the critics who saw the film, it was not as much thought of as an encounter with a New Wave movement, but rather, an instance within the Iranian tradition of the rural genre. Yet in those same reviews, comparisons were drawn to American films being made at the time ranging from Arthur Penn's *Bonnie and Clyde* (1967) to Mike Nichols's *The Graduate* (1967), unintentionally prescient films in this context which would come to be known as a part of 'New Hollywood', a movement not entirely dissimilar to the *Nouvelle Vague* and other such national derivatives.

Fereydoun Rahnema drew the distinction that *The Cow* was 'far from the principles of *Filmfarsi* and day by day the difference between *Filmfarsi* and "Iranian film" is being brought to light and is close in form to the "independent films of the world"' (Omid 1995, p. 539).

Parviz Davaei would recognize *The Cow* as a forward step in filmmaking in Iran when he compares its technical aspects to the mainstream popular films of the time known as *Filmfarsi*, but still not at the level of being considered 'auteur cinema' (Omid 1995, p. 542). The reason for this was perhaps that the critics saw these films as too derivative of Western films and not grounded in authentic Iranain discourse.

It may have been difficult for these critics to parse true and fair analysis of the early Iranian arthouse films, as their deeper understanding of the nuances around the cultural specific intellectual debates taking place also entailed a strong entanglement with the concepts and notions being explored by these films. Perhaps these early *Mowj-e No* films did not align closely enough with the specific lines of thought to which these critics were attached. Their particular circumstances would not be applicable when reviewing arthouse films made in France or elsewhere from which they were emotionally and ideologically more distant.

On the more overtly negative end of the spectrum, critic Ali Shabani firmly placed *The Cow* within the *Filmfarsi* tradition and classified it as a part of the rural genre of films and one which 'in fact mocks and insults villagers' (Omid 1995, p. 368).

An apt example of placing a film within the framework of genre is Kavoosi's review of *Qaysar* (1969), in which he makes comparison to westerns and the feckless 'sheriff of Dodge City' who is powerless against the menace posed to the protagonist, forcing the latter to exact vengeance himself. In addition Kavoosi compares the presence of police to portrayals that would be found in a comedy, such as in their slapstick manner of running (Omid 1995, p. 534). This film was considered to be more 'authentically' Iranian than ones preceding it in the eyes of critics such as Davaei and Omid.

Similarly, Fereydoun Moezi Moghaddam places Amir Naderi's *Khodahafez Rafigh* (Goodbye Friend, 1971) in the police/heist genre. He also commends the strength of its novel cinematic techniques such as zoom, wide angle lenses and 'experimental mise-en-page' (Omid 1995, p. 595). Thereby he concedes that this is in stark contrast with the more mundane precedents which exist in Iranian cinema.

The critic Gholam Heidari (almost certainly a pseudonym of Abbas Baharlu) would look at the New Wave films as relying on the same taxonomy that was put forward by Omid, describing the films of this movement as possessive of 'romantic tendencies', indicating comparisons to nineteenth-century European Romanticists of the likes of Johann Wolfgang von Goethe and Lord Byron. He described this new loose film collective as an 'intellectual middle class reaction against the world and that these Romantics tried to achieve their ideals through 'retreating to nature or within their own minds (intellect)' (Heidari 1991, p. 42).

If not this type of analysis, then instead critics opted to make detail-oriented criticisms and nitpicks of films such as those of Fereydoun Rahnema from a historical point of view, pointing out historic anachronisms. Contrary to Kashi, Hosseini et al.'s perspectives on this matter, I would postulate that the New Wave in Iran was triggered by the same sweeping sentiments and notions as New Wave movements taking place in France and around the world. It might be fair to say that the New Wave cinema in Iran was not a particularly cogent and concentrated movement; it began in a very scattered way, with sporadic early productions.

Iranian New Wave films were not united in their thinking and no manifesto or outline was commonly agreed upon or ever put in place. Although it was not an integrated effort and one wherein all the filmmakers followed the same style, politics or sensibilities, it would be impossible not to concede that their films had common elements and similarities in form and content, most notably a concerted effort to create depictions of objective reality, incorporate strong use of symbolism and poetic iconography, create ambiguity in narrative and atmosphere, and almost all of them feature highly alienated characters. These are common elements that Iranian New Wave films shared not only with one another but also with many of the French *Nouvelle Vague* films. It is also true that the Iranian New Wave filmmakers were unanimous in having been strongly influenced by the European New Wave, but they did not follow exactly the same path as French filmmakers, with Golestan, Ghaffari, Rahnema, Beyzaie, Mehrjui, Taghvai, Kimiai, Hatami, Shahid-Saless, Farmanara and Kimiavi each taking a different approach and their differences being immeasurable from one another.

The films of the Iranian New Wave were dissimilar to one another both in how they came to be and what they strived to do differently. The filmmakers appeared not to have widely supported each other's work, and would often be dismissive of others' works in a way that was not as prevalent in France, for example the writers of *Cahiers du Cinéma* magazine were widely encouraging of their peers. The radical and leftist views of Jean-Luc Godard and the moderate romantic approach of François Truffaut result in altering stylistic worlds, yet both are classified as prominent filmmakers of the French New Wave.

The same diversity or strands of cinematic styles, ideologies and broader political and sociological differences were commonplace amongst other movements such as the French and German New Wave filmmakers or the Italian neorealists. But in all such instances there was some kind of unification effect apparent which, for various reasons, was less acutely present in Iranian New Wave, especially within its early stages. There was no similar magazine or platform available to these Iranian intellectual filmmakers as *Cahiers*.

David Bordwell draws an interesting comparison between the New German cinema and the French New Wave:

> New German cinema is not a stylistic movement in the sense that Italian neorealism and the French New Wave were. That is, it did not consist of a group of filmmakers using comparable formal and stylistic traits. Rather, the term was coined to describe a surprising revival in the largely moribund German cinema by a number of young filmmakers who had begun working outside the traditional industry in the 1960s.
>
> (Bordwell and Thompson 1994, p. 453)

The same is true of Italian cinema, where Roberto Rossellini – a Christian democrat – and Vittorio De Sica – a social democrat – whose political and ideological views were worlds apart, would collaborate on films together (De Sica starred in the Rossellini directed film *General Della Rovere*, 1959). The writers of *Studying Film* (2000) point out the differences between the ideas and political visions of the Italian filmmakers. The neorealist directors (chief among them Rossellini, De Sica and Visconti) came from different backgrounds and did not share the same political views: Visconti, although from an aristocratic family, was a Marxist, whilst Rossellini later had difficulty denying his links with Christian Democrat ideology, and De Sica was a Social Democrat. Nevertheless, their films were similar in significant ways (Abrams, Bell and Udris 2001, p. 261).

These differences between Iranian intellectual filmmakers could be regarded as teething issues, with divisions lessening and comparisons to other such movements becoming more identifiable, with a declining rate of repudiation from the conservative-minded Iranian film critics. With more films being made, there even came a degree of monetary success, emboldening producers and allowing for an industry-supported continuation of this Iranian New Wave. Artfilms and derivatives of those films started being produced after the relative success of certain productions such as Masoud Kimiai's *Qaysar* (1969), which spawned its own derivative national trend, taking over from *Ganj-e Qarun* (Qarun's Treasure, 1965) inspired films made up to then, as the prominent sub-genre of domestic cinema in the 1970s. Despite this, many critics refused to make the concession that this was indeed a cohesive moment until the very end of the pre-revolutionary period.

For the Iranian New Wave, a key divisional point was political in nature. Left-wing thought played a formative role, with many filmmakers such as Ghaffari, Golestan, Shahid-Saless, Naderi, Shirdel and Taghvai displaying various Marxist leanings in their films. Golestan and Ghaffari were affiliated with the Tudeh Party, the prominent pro-Soviet Union Communist Party, although both of them later made a departure from the party before the revolution.

Sohrab Shahid-Saless was a proponent of Marxism and the Tudeh Party throughout his life, although indications of Marxist ideology were not as explicit or frequently espoused within his filmography. Mehrjui was an existentialist filmmaker with mystical tendencies, but he wrote the scripts for some of his films, such as *The Cow* and *The Cycle*, in collaboration with Gholamhossein Saedi, a Marxist playwright and story writer.

Other *Mowj-e No* participants such as Masoud Kimiai, Amir Naderi, Fereydoun Goleh and Kamran Shirdel were never affiliated with any leftist movement, but the influence of leftist ideas in their social realist films could be observed as an indicator of their political leanings. But even within this left wing, which was the predominant outlook of the New Wave, there were also another group of filmmakers like Fereydoun Rahnema, Bahram Beyzaie, Arby Ovanessian, Parviz Kimiavi, Bahman Farmanara, Ali Hatami and Mohammad Reza Aslani who had no affiliation with the left and were not as interested in social realism.

Despite such cursory differences, it is very easy to spot the underlying similarities between these films, social realism being among the most critical and recurrent. The use of social realistic techniques has a near omnipresence when it comes to Iranian cinema for good reason, as it allows the uncovering of previously enshrouded layers of reality and life in that time and period. It has become a staple for many filmmakers who deal with stories that are microcosmic in scope, but with the very clear intention of revealing the grander stories of society at that same time and locale.

Fereydoun Rahnema and Bahram Beyzaie were more liberal intellectuals with nationalist tendencies and an interest in creating a theatrical/mythical cinema based on Persian rituals and mythologies. Their films, particularly Rahnema's filmography and Beyzaie's pre-revolutionary *Gharibeh va Meh* (The Stranger and the Fog, 1974) and *Charike-ye Tara* (Ballad of Tara, 1979), were more epic in nature and did not aspire to social realism. However, Beyzaie's other films such as his debut film *Ragbar* (Downpour, 1971) and his short film *Safar*

(The Journey, 1970), as well his post-revolution films such as *Bashu, Gharibe-ye Koochak* (Bashu, the Little Stranger, 1989), do fit the social realism mould whilst focusing on the same themes he explores in all of his films.

The key shared attributes of their work are on-location shooting; use of non-professional actors or lesser-known theatrical actors such as Jamshid Mashayekhi, Mohammad Ali Keshavarz, Fakhri Khorvash, Pari Saberi, Akbar Meshkin and Parviz Fannizadeh in Ebrahim Golestan's *Brick and Mirror* and Farrokh Ghaffari's *The Night of the Hunchback*; mystification, thematic ambiguity and non-linear narratives.

Furthermore, I think it is fair to say that the core rallying cry of the Iranian New Wave filmmakers was to liberate Iranian cinema from the mainstream cinema known as *Filmfarsi*, and traditional cinematic conventions, and for many this resulted in a grounding in reality. The stylistic and narrative innovations of the likes of Golestan, Rahnema, Mehrjui, Kimiai and Shahid-Salles would easily grant them the same 'auteur' status which their *Nouvelle Vague* counterparts are credited with. Their films were starkly different to anything made before, infusing new blood in the veins of a long lifeless national cinema.

Although influenced by Italian neorealism and French New Wave, the Iranian New Wave emerged in response to the cultural and intellectual climate of 1950s and 1960s Iran. Therefore it could be thought of primarily as the outcome of internal rather than external factors. This is also the view held by Ahmad Talebinejad: 'the factors leading to the rise of the New Wave in Iran were, in part, the result of internal conditions, particularly the intellectual or even political movements that came into existence at the time' (Talebinejad 1993, p. 10).

Since I have come across a great deal of evidence supporting this general perspective, including writing from the period and later interviews by the very filmmakers in question, my primary focus will be on exploring the domestic cultural and political factors which led to the flourishing of this movement and its intellectual roots. When it comes to identifying the first films of New Wave cinema, my perspective is different from most critics in the field. Looking at those same sources gives veracity to the placement of films firmly within this galvanizing environment, films that were made prior to the commonly accepted timeline for this movement.

In line with the thinking of Jamal Omid, one encounters an almost ubiquity amongst film critics, historians and scholars that credit Dariush Mehrjui's *Gav* (The Cow, 1969), Masoud Kimiai's *Qaysar* (1969) and sometimes Nasser

Taghvai's *Aramesh Dar Hozour-e Digaran* (Tranquility in the Presence of Others, 1969/73) as the very first films of the New Wave in Iranian cinema. For example, Masoud Mehrabi in *The History of Iranian Cinema* considers *The Cow* and *Qaysar* as the forerunners of a new trend in Iranian cinema (Mehrabi 1984, p. 126).

Ahmad Talebinejad also argues that the Iranian cinema entered a new era with the making of three films: *The Cow*, *Qaysar* and *Tranquility in the Presence of Others*. From his perspective, before the production of these films, some other filmmakers such as Fereydoun Rahnema and Ebrahim Golestan tried to produce distinctive films but nothing of significant consequence was realized in their work: '[...] prior to this time, cinema had no fruit to be approved of by experts, except for a number of failed efforts' (Talebinejad 1993, p. 10).

Hamid Naficy examines the history of Iranian cinema in the context of socio-political changes in Iranian society and identifies five important periods: the flickering years (1900–26); the fledgling beginnings (1930–37); years of experimentation (1938–65); towards a national film industry (1966–76); and the era of decline, turmoil and new opportunities (1977–79). Naficy attempts to examine the institutional aspects of the development of Iranian cinema. He offers a list of factors that paved the way for the emergence of New Wave cinema in Iran, but since he believes this ground was first paved in 1969 by Mehrjui's *The Cow* and Kimiai's *Qaysar*, he seemingly neglects the importance of the precursors of the New Wave. Naficy argues that the New Wave filmmakers' success in realistically depicting the life of ordinary Iranians and reflecting the psychological conditions of the characters in films that feature high technical qualities distinguishes these films from the rest of Iranian films (Naficy 1979, pp. 443–64). He also approaches the Iranian New Wave from a thematic and cultural perspective with a clear point of origin in the late 1960s.

Although Naficy's analyses played a considerable role in the dissemination of the Iranian New Wave movement, his articles fundamentally fall short in terms of tracing the roots of the New Wave to its true sources and in providing sorely needed details of these early developments which the purpose of this book is to elucidate upon. Naficy, like other Iranian researchers and scholars, overlooked the intellectual grounds and the formational evolutionary steps of the New Wave and the role of certain early intellectual filmmakers in developing an Iranian cinema that was radical in terms of structure and language, in dialogue with modernist European cinema, and acutely responded to the concurrent intellectual atmosphere and modern literary developments of Iran.

Naficy also argues that 'at the end of the 1960s, the local film industry, which had been producing low-quality melodramas, comedies and tough guy (*luti/ laati*) films, was suddenly jolted into a new era from the release of two films which set a new trend, later coming to be known as the New Wave: Kimiai's *Qaysar* and Mehrjui's *The Cow*' (Naficy 1979, pp. 443–64).

In contrast to this, I intend to highlight earlier films such as Ghaffari's *Shab-e Quzi* (The Night of the Hunchback, 1965), *Siavash Dar Takht-e Jamshid* (Siavash in Persepolis, 1965) and *Khesht va Ayeneh* (Brick and Mirror, 1965), made in the years prior, with the specific intention to change the Iranian cinema and indeed were successful in doing that to the same degree as those films credited by Naficy and other scholars. Therefore, my argument here is that the year 1969 was not the true birth year of New Wave cinema, but rather was a flourishing point of this movement in Iranian cinema building on an earlier true emergence.

As to the social and political roots of the New Wave, I would argue that intellectuality is a major component shaping New Wave cinema in Iran. Film critics such as Ahmad Mir Ehsan and Behzad Eshghi argue the same point but maintain that the same intellectual roots contributed to the failures of these films to take hold.

Eshghi examines Iranian intellectual cinema in the early 1960s and separates it from the New Wave and *Filmfarsi*. He praises intellectual works due to their avoidance of obscenity (which was evident in *Filmfarsi*) but simultaneously criticizes their elitism. Discussing the intellectual qualities of Golestan, Rahnema and Ghaffari's works, Eshghi argues that these filmmakers, due to their complicated intellectual language, could not attract attention, so they failed to create any positive cinematic convention to produce a sustainable movement. Even the critics' support could not have avoided their definitive failure (Eshgi 1988, p. 35).

Likewise, Mir Ehsan examines the films of these forerunners of the New Wave with both praise and criticism. He admits that these intellectual works provided the grounds for artistic and thoughtful cinema in Iran but finds their cinematic language 'stammering and crude'. Nevertheless, he does not explain how it is possible for this so-called stammering and crude cinema, which could not communicate or impress the audience, to contribute so much to the growth of Iranian artistic cinema. Mir Ehsan acknowledges the importance of intellectual films made by Rahnema, Ghaffari and Golestan, but he believes they were 'imperfect, insufficient and unable to communicate' (Mir Ehsan 2000, p. 84).

In reviewing the books and articles on Iranian cinema, whether in Persian or in English, one can observe that these works, especially those about New Wave cinema and its filmmakers, have insufficiently acknowledged and often completely failed to identify the true historical roots and the true founders of the movement. To fill this gap, in the following chapter, I will offer an overview of the cultural configuration of Iran's society in the 1950s and 1960s and explore the ways it played such a seminal role in the formation of Iranian New Wave cinema. As Hamid Dabashi puts it, 'this is essential for a proper understanding of the movement as an artistic response to the conflicts between tradition and modernity in a turbulent era of the history of Iran' (Dabashi 2001, p. 43).

I will first analyse the diversity of Iranian intellectual filmmakers' approaches to socio-political and cinematic modernity in Iran. In the late 1950s a number of political and cultural discourses – including Jalal Al-e-Ahmad's *Gharbzadegi* (Westoxication), anti-westernization, modernization and nativism – predominated Iranian intellectual thought (Boroujerdi 1996). These ideas are highly critical to the shaping of this movement and I attempt to provide a supplementary understanding of them.

By putting the question of national and cultural authenticity on the agenda, in the face of an era that was perceived to threaten the very existence of such notions, a nativist alternative was articulated in late 1950s Iran that posited a number of binary oppositions, including the East versus the West; tradition versus modernity; the domestic versus the imported, in order to challenge the dominant discourse of modernization in Iran. In this regard, some key concepts such as 'otherness' and 'nativism' characterized the political and cultural discourse of the 1950s and 1960s in Iran. Examining the importance of these arguments for the growth of early New Wave cinema, I will attempt to present a key intellectual framework for understanding this movement, with particular attention paid to how the discourse transpired between 1958 and 1969.

2

The internal factors

It is at this point essential to situate Iranian cinema in the broader context of modernity and the socio-political and cultural struggles that have characterized twentieth-century Iranian history.

Iran's Constitutional Revolution (1906–9) and modernization movements commenced close on the heels of the debut of cinema in Iran. In fact, cinema theatres appeared in Iran in concurrence with the rise of modern thought, so much so that the fate of cinema has been somewhat intrinsic to the historical fate of modernity. In addition to typical market interests and preferences, Iranian cinema and its critical discourses have, over many different periods, reflected the tendencies and common discourses prevailing amongst contemporary Iranian intellectuals, thinkers, filmmakers and film critics.

From the early years of the 1900s to the 1960s, cinema, kicking off in Iran in 1904, went through the final years of Qajar despotism; the 1906–9 Constitutional Revolution; Reza Khan's coup d'etat and subsequent reign from 1921 to 1941; a period of occupation during the Second World War, 1941–6; the American-British engineered 1953 coup d'etat (28 Mordad coup d'état); the implementation of authoritative modernization policies of Mohammad Reza Pahlavi; the formation of a commercially profitable domestic film industry (*Filmfarsi*) from the early 1950s and culminated in the New Wave cinematic movement.

During this sixty-year period – investigation of which is beyond the scope of this book – cinema as one of the most important inventions of the twentieth century and the most influential form of media, saw many ebbs and flows in the nation. In the still religious and non-democratic society of the early twentieth century, cinema was constantly denounced by clerics and religious classes on the one side, and censored and pressured by the state and occasionally military bodies from the other. The intensity and the types of pressures imposed on Iranian cinema changed over time. But, by the early 1960s, it was undeniable that cinema was one of the most important spaces for the negotiation of the new modalities of Iranian identity and was able to transcend social, political and religious censorship tactics by creating new forms of expression.

The case of Iranian cinema in the early days after its debut is somewhat paradoxical. The cinematograph was first purchased on the orders of a rather ignorant king, Mozaffar ad-Din Shah Qajar, who did not really have a proper plan for modernizing Iran. He wanted the camera for his personal entertainment and status boosting purposes, limiting its use and propagation to a small elite group of people in his court.

The person responsible for the purchase and first use of the cinematograph was a well-educated individual with the title of royal photographer, Iran's first cameraman, Mirza Ebrahim Khan Rahmani, known as Akkas Bashi (1874–1915). His first exposure to the cinematograph was at the Exposition Universelle in Paris (1900), culminating in some documentary type pieces he made such as the visit of the Shah to Belgium. These works are certainly interesting from a historic point of view, but the outcome of his work was unfortunately of very little import on a larger scale.

Figure 2.1 Ezzatolah Entezami as Naser al-din Shah Qajar in Mohsen Makhmalbaf's *Once Upon a Time, Cinema* (1992).

Disregarding this early stumble, the actual arrival of cinema and the true impact of its progressive gaze did not occur until much later. There were a number of drastic events (as mentioned above) which impeded its establishment. For example, with the coming to power of Reza Shah Pahlavi, the state exerted a tight grip over much of the arts and likely deliberately implemented harsh restrictions on the development of a national cinema, under the rationale that it could fall into the hands of the Marxist revolutionary forces or other oppositional threats. Such factors, in addition to the prohibitive expenses involved in early cameras and other equipment, meant domestic film productions were not a viable prospect until the mid-1930s.

Cinema and the negotiation of modernity in Iran

Cinema was a means of acclimatizing Iran's traditional society with Western life and urbanization and had a tremendous impact on Iranian social and individual behaviour and thoughts. Many traditional customs and views were questioned and reformed when people came into contact with the new worlds that cinema depicted. However, in the absence of a domestic film industry, representation of Iran on the silver screen consisted of foreign filmmakers often affiliated with state entities like Russia, producing biased documentaries, presenting slanted and stereotype-filled portrayals.

The films made in Iran before 1932 were either newsreels showing the activities of the royal court or orientalist documentary films about Iran made by non-Iranian filmmakers such as Merian C. Cooper and Ernest Schoedsack who made *The Grass*, which concerned the migration of the Bakhtiari tribe in 1925. Documentary films such as *Iran's Railroad* produced by the German Railroads Syndicate provided an orientalist picture of the daily life of Iranian people with an emphasis on the country's backwardness, to the point that it was severely criticized by Iranian spectators and the local newspapers at the time (Mehrabi 1996, p. 9).

The focus of the commercial cinematic output of this period can be seen as an attempt to cater to a society that was shackled by superstitious beliefs, cynicism and a general mistrust of any new phenomena. The general public were quick to exhibit aggressive reactions and hostility towards new practices they perceived as threats to their status quo. This was especially true of cinema which – owing to its openness towards showing facets of modernism that were being publicized and forcefully exponated by the state, such as women's liberation and general fraternization between the sexes – was diametrically opposed to the views and principles cherished by the traditionalists, who time and again voiced their opposition to any and all symbols of modernity.

In an article in *Ettela'at* daily newspaper published in 1932, Q. Moghaddam declared his opposition to cinema, enumerated the disadvantages of this industry, and called on the government to curb and control it:

> What is the benefit of importing different types of movies that have no use other than shattering the peoples' morality and mentality? Upon leaving these theatres, our youth normally get nothing out of the films but a love tale or nonsensical stories and narratives. This is while in Europe today they are making utmost use of cinema. A nation that has only recently stepped into the realm of progress and civilisation definitely needs to acquire good ethics, customs, and morals. Such a nation does not need evil influences and deviation from the path of the truth from the very first step. When a person spends his time mostly in cafes and theatres, he will naturally become lethargic, lose his physical power, and get nothing out of theatre and cinema other than what is detrimental to ethics.
>
> (Omid 1995, p. 48)

Moghaddam's article shows that the resistance to modern phenomena, including cinema, was not only a reaction by the *ulama* (religious scholars) and fundamental religious figures, but was also evident in the writing of secular journalists, who were supporters of the Shah's establishment, and relayed their concerns about the impact of cinema on the changing face of public norms and behaviours.

During the early years of Reza Shah's reign, government-sponsored journalists and the press were proponents of censorship and government control over films, and as a result of such demands, and the fear of cinematically propelled social upheaval, rigorous laws were imposed on filmmaking. As indicated by Hamidreza Sadr:

> [All such demands] became the perfect excuse for Reza Khan to tighten censorship laws governing filmmaking. In 1938 a bill passed by parliament, which included the punitive measures.
>
> (Sadr 2002, p. 45)

In addition, foreign films which in any way portrayed any disparagement of monarchy or promoted unrest in the eyes of the regime, would have those scenes cut out, such as the 30 minute sequence of the second trial of Carl Theodor Dreyer's *Joan of Arc* (1928) in which she incites the public to riot or a scene in Sidney Olcott's *Monsieur Beaucaire* (1924) where the king calls for his court barber to shave him which was censored.

(Sadr 2002, p. 125)

When, in the 1920s, Reza Shah ascended the throne and began to implement the plans his advisors had drawn for modernization, cinema was no longer a venue for the nobility monopolized by the Qajar court. It had become entertainment for the masses and assumed the responsibility of teaching Iranian people how to act and think like Westerners. Iranian film critic Ahmad Mir Ehsan explained how cinema played the role of a guide and vanguard in the early years of its debut in Iran:

Since its debut, cinema, as a symbol of reform, modernism, and a break with tradition, essentially adopted a critical stance against the traditions and old standards dominating Iranian society and became a prominent galvanising force for this. In this period, cinema, consciously or unconsciously, conformed with the Shah's anti-traditionalist policies and likewise, instead of grasping the true spirit and essence of modernity, zoomed in on modernity's superficial manifestations. Cinema inherently serves as a mirror held up to the modern world. Even in an underdeveloped cinema, in an underdeveloped country, cinema was in a way guiding and directing the lives of people, creating role models, and being used from the top as an instrument for the project of modernisation. What type of 'modernism' that was and how different it was from real modernity is a separate issue. The traditional outlook was that cinema was a means to promote prostitution and vulgarity, that is to say, it was thought to encroach upon traditional ethics.

(Mir Ehsan 2002)

More religious and traditional sectors of Iran's society opposed cinema as a blasphemous phenomenon that served the purpose of the government's bid to corrupt and westernize the country by destroying Iranian ethics and traditional values. As Hamid Dabashi states, 'Religious opposition to the cinema was immediate and emphatic. The efforts to introduce cinema to Iran drew strong opposition from the Muslim fanatics who despised the idea of recreating the human face and human body on the screen' (Dabashi 2001, p. 14). This opposition was so intense that it led to the denunciation of cinema.

Despite this, venues still managed to draw the necessary audience wherever their location and venues continued to spread in populated areas. In the early stages of transformation, there were even some venues in the late 1920s that had screenings exclusively for women; later these disappeared and were no longer commonplace due to the normalization of mixed audiences at the cinema.

Ovanes Ohanian's *Haji Agha, Actor-e Cinema* (Haji Agha, the Cinema Actor, 1932) was the first Iranian film to consciously reflect on the clash between tradition and modernity in early twentieth-century Iranian society. Ohanian was a young Armenian Iranian who lived most of his life in Russia and studied film at the Gerasimov Institute of Cinematography in Moscow and returned to Iran in 1925. He established a film school in Tehran under the name '*Parvareshgahe Artisiti-ye Cinema*' (The Cinema Artist Educational Centre). The training of actors and actresses to use in his films, rather than film production, was the cornerstone of the school. After a few months, Ohanian directed his first Iranian film, *Abi va Rabi* (Abi and Rabi, 1929). It was an imitation of comic performances by Danish comedy duo, Patte and Patachon (Issari 1989, p. 97).

Abi and Rabi was the first silent feature film in the history of Iranian cinema. The only copy of it burnt to ashes two years after its release in an accidental fire in cinema Mayak, one of the first film theatres in Tehran. After *Abi and Rabi*, Ohanian made his second film that was also a comedy: *Haji Agha, Actor-e Cinema*. The film set its sardonic gaze on the rise of cinema as a modern media blossoming within the fold of Iran's traditional society. It confronted the cinemagoers, and especially the intellectuals, for the first time with a serious and fundamental question: how could cinema, as a modern phenomenon, grow in a closed and traditional society that is hostile to it? How has the dominant fanatic, dogmatic mentality dealt with cinema and to what extent will it tolerate and approve of it? By astutely portraying this pivotal contradiction – namely the clash between the traditional mindset and that of films – *Haji Agha, the Cinema Actor* consciously and illuminatingly defended cinema and offered a logical and clear answer to the questions posed above.

Haji Agha, the Cinema Actor depicts a director who struggles to find a story for his film. Two of his students suggest that he make a film about their father (Haji Agha) who staunchly opposes the notion of cinema. He makes a film about the old man and shows it to him upon its completion. Haji Agha ultimately admits that cinema is beneficial and allows his daughter and son-in-law, the director's students, to carry on working in the film industry. Ohanian took the pioneering step of utilizing an actress for the first time ever in Iran. This happened in a society which, according to Mir Ehsan, was at the time on the verge of modernization and discarding of the hijab but was still facing powerful opposition towards such developments.

The first representative of professional cinema and the founder of the industry in Iran was a non-Muslim of Armenian and Russian heritage, in a country with a majority Muslim population. Highly infatuated with the modern world, he brought his interest in this modern and disruptive force to an underdeveloped and traditional country in which the pro-modernization forces had only recently come into power.

Nevertheless, he was acutely aware of the prevalence of the traditionalist view that cinema was a blasphemous phenomenon that aimed for complete disruption, and he addressed the topic in one of the most interesting films of 1930s Iran.

Haji Agha, the Cinema Actor laid the foundation of critical reflection in Iranian cinema. This film, which marked the onset of an intellectual approach towards cinema, naturally did not perform well at the box office and did not set forth any major trends in the Iranian cinema as a result. As Tahaminejad states,

> [...] one must also consider the establishment of *Parvareshgah-e Artisti* a valuable enterprise, it seems that history has not been very kind to us. It sends Sergei Eisenstein to guide the Mexicans in cinema, Jean Renoir to India to assist Satyajit Ray and Ovanes Ohanian to Iran. This is historical luck.
>
> (Tahaminejad 1976–7, p. 116)

After the commercial failure of his second film, Ohanian could not find the support for any more cinematic endeavours. He left Iran for India and continued his academic career in Calcutta. Subsequently he returned to Iran in 1947, where he died fourteen years later in 1961, having not produced anything further.

Figure 2.2 Ovanes Ohanian's *Haji Agha, Actor-e Cinema* (Haji Agha, the Cinema Actor, 1932).

The emergence of national cinema

In the 1930s, a number of sound films were made in the Persian language in India by Abdolhossein Sepanta (1907–69). Sepanta, a Zoroastrian Iranian pioneer filmmaker who was interested in studying ancient Iranian culture and literature travelled to India in 1927 and started to make films with Ardeshir Khan Irani, a film director of the Persian Zoroastrian Society and the founder of the Imperial Film Company in Bombay. In 1931, Sepanta made *Dokhtar-e Lor* (The Lor Girl, 1933), the first Persian talkie with the help of Ardeshir Irani.

The Lor Girl is an adventure movie about a teahouse maid Golnar (played by Roohangiz Sami-Nejad), who falls in love with Jafar (played by Sepanta himself), a government agent. As a child, Golnar was kidnapped and raised by Gholi Khan, the leader of a group of bandits in Khuzestan, south of Iran. Gholi Khan terrorized the area and let no caravan pass through with any wealth. Jafar is placed there as an undercover agent working for the government, tasked with bringing down the organization. Jafar meets Golnar at a local teahouse and they fall in love. Jafar eventually kills a number of the bandits and arrests Gholi Khan. Fearing retribution from the bandits, the couple flee to Bombay.

Later they return to Iran to get married after the 1921 coup, to live happily ever after.

Sepanta was a man with nationalistic sentiments but, having spent the majority of his time outside of Iran, he was less familiar with the social conditions of the country. He was the first Iranian filmmaker who, motivated by a search for national identity and an urge to revive the glorious past of Iran, embarked on filmmaking with this goal in mind.

By creating a hero (Jafar) who physically resembled Reza Shah, Sepanta implicitly praises Reza Shah's rule. In addition, the events of the 1921 coup are painted in a positive light within the narrative, allowing the couple's return to their home to be safe from former hostilities and, in one scene in the film, Golnar addressing Jafar says, 'I see that a star is shining in the dark, and it will brighten this country one day'. This is a symbolic allusion to Reza Shah's proclamation that he was to be the saviour of the Iranian nation.

According to Behrouz Tourani, Sepanta 'was easily duped by the official propaganda about the country's "great progress and the establishment of order and social justice"' (Jahed 2012, p. 60).

The Lor Girl was first screened in two cinemas, Mayak and Sepah, in Tehran in 1933 and then in India. It was well received by Iranian cinemagoers and was very successful at the box office (Omid 1995, p. 5). Roohangiz acted very well in the titular role and became the first female star in the first Persian talkie, though only starring in one more film after this role. Encouraged by the success of the film, Sepanta decided to make some more films in India. With the help of the Imperial Film Company of Bombay he made *Ferdowsi* (1934), *Shirin o Farhad* (Shirin and Farhad, 1934) and *Cheshman-e Siah* (Black Eyes, 1935) but none of them were as successful as his first endeavour (Issari 1989, p. 108).

After completing his last film *Leily va Majnoun* (*Leily and Majnoun*) in 1936, Sepanta returned to Iran to continue his filmmaking activities in his home country but the Iranian government was not interested in supporting cinema. Sepanta was a talented artist and a dedicated filmmaker who wanted to make Persian films about his favourite subjects which were mainly adaptations from Persian classic literature, but there were too many obstacles in his way. His efforts to establish a national cinema under Reza Shah's conditions reached a deadlock, paralysed by government bureaucracy. He was among a group of Iranian intellectuals who sought to find a cultural and national fulcrum in the turning point of the establishment of a new nation and government in Iran after the elimination of the Qajar dynasty.

Figure 2.3 *Dokhtar-e Lor* (The Lor Girl, 1933), the first Iranian talkie directed by Abdolhossein Sepanta.

As Mir Ehsan puts forth: 'Cinema, at the turn of the twentieth century, did not represent a genuine intellectual depth, arising from the context of life, production, creativity, and thought. We had a long way to go to arrive at an intellectual cinema' (Mir Ehsan 2002).

The intense competition from European and American films that were screened in Iran in the 1930s, and the screening of Persian talkies being made in India, which were technically far superior to the domestic silent products as well as the lack of state support for the local film industry, all caused stagnation of film production activities in Iran, which were unable to resume until after the Second World War. In 1947 Dr Esmail Koushan, a pioneering young Iranian who studied film production in Germany, returned to Iran and established his Mitra Film Studio. Koushan is known as the father of Iranian cinema because it was through his endeavours that local film production in Iran gained life after the Second World War.

Iranian cinema was almost completely inactive between 1937 and 1948, coming out of dormancy with the film *Toofan-e Zendegi* (Storm of Life) in 1948, a sentimental romantic melodrama written by Nezam Vafa and directed by Ali Daryabaigi, a theatre actor/director without prior experience in filmmaking. It was a social drama about the pitfalls of arranged marriage with a happy ending but it failed in the box office 'due to its poor quality and technical shortcomings' (Issari 1989, p. 130).

However, Koushan was undismayed by the commercial failure of his first film and made some more films in his newly established film studio Pars Film including *Zendani Amir* (The Prisoner of the Emir, 1948). According to a report by John Crume the film was superior to *Toofan-e Zendegi* in terms of sound, lighting, photography and direction, and acting, but was subject to poor box office performance (Issari 1989, p. 131).

Koushan's most successful commercial endeavour was *Sharmsar* (Ashamed, 1950). One of the reasons behind the success of the film was that it starred Delkash, a famous pop singer at the time, who would go on to act in several other films. Because of the film's ability to draw in audiences, there was a marked effort to expand the domestic film industry and many new film studios were established. As Behrouz Turani put it, 'until 1953, anybody with some money could launch a film studio and produce films sometimes with no previous experience in the area of filmmaking' (Jahed 2012, p. 57).

However, a few years after the end of the Second World War, by 1948, more systematic steps were taken in Iran to produce Persian language films and a national cinema. In the period between 1950 and 1958 (the year that, arguably, the first New Wave film *Jonub-e Shar/South of the City* by Farrokh Ghaffari was made) about one hundred films were made in Iran in different genres by a group of Iranian filmmakers including Siamak Yasemi, Hossein Daneshvar, Ahmad Shirazi, Mohammad Ali Jafari, Majid Mohseni, Mehdi Ra'ais Firouz and Samuel Khachikian. These films gained immediate and huge popularity and created a momentum for successive films made in the same style. Most were melodramas, musicals or pulp dramas based on theatricalized history and mythology, and would almost universally incorporate slapstick comedy, Persian song and dance numbers and other such crowd-pleasing elements. Although they were made to suit prevailing commercial tastes and were popular among Iranian audiences, such films were severely derided by Iranian film critics of the time for their poor cinematic quality and were branded as *Filmfarsi* by veteran film critic Dr Houshang Kavoosi.

Comparing these domestic productions to Hollywood and European cinema, Iranian film critics of the time argued that *Filmfarsi* neither meets the elementary technical standards nor the cinematic conventions, let alone possessing any artistic qualities. In the view of the politically oriented film critics, *Filmfarsi* was a vulgar and disposable cultural product. It diverted the attention of its audience from the crucial socio-political issues and contributed to apoliticization of the masses and the conservation of the status quo. More brazen leftist critics such as Fereydoun Jairani and Ali-akbar Akbari even went so far as to accuse *Filmfarsi* of being an organized machination of the Shah's government to manipulate and brainwash the nation. In his critical essay on the audiences of *Filmfarsi* productions, Jairani states:

> *Filmfarsi* had a great rule in manipulating the mass audience. In the films made between 1964 and 1968 in Iran, the hero was a defender of the status quo as well as supporting the traditional values of the society. According to Jairani, *Filmfarsi* products in this period of time supported the Shah's idea of the 'white revolution' and by their 'dream-making' contents, encouraged people to believe that idea.
>
> (Moazezinia 2001, p. 131)

This evokes what Adorno and Horkheimer refer to as the 'culture Industry' in their *Dialectic of Enlightenment* (1944). According to Adorno: 'Nevertheless, the culture indystry remains the entertainment business. Its control of consumers is mediated by entertainment and its hold will not be broken by outright dictate but by the hostiliry inherent in the principle of entertainment to anything which is more than itself. Since the tendencies of the culture industry are turned into the flesh and blood of the public by the social process as a whole, those tendencies are reinforced by the survival of the market in the industry' (Adorno and Horkheimer 2002, p. 108).

Like Adorno and Horkheimer, these Iranian film critics were influenced by the teachings of Marx and offshoot theories, and they would argue that *Filmfarsi* was a sort of mass culture created to ensure the continued obedience of the masses to market interests. As put forward by Robert Safarian, 'the leftist and revolutionary outlook which dominated the intellectual atmosphere in pre-revolutionary Iran, considered *Filmfarsi* as an organized plot of the government to distract people's attention from their real and fundamental problems' (Moazezinia 2001, p. 114).

Along with their disdain for the contemporary state of their national cinema, the idea of setting up a revolutionary artistic cinema to challenge this status quo occupied the minds of Iranian intellectuals for many years to come.

Nativism vs. Westoxication (*Gharbzadegi*)

Among the gradually emerging middle class in 1960s Iran, one would come across a strong tendency to imitate elements of the typical Western lifestyle. With this modernization came an opposing tendency, closely associated with Jalal Al-e-Ahmad, an influential literary figure and intellectual, who referred to this rejection of absolutist Iranian and Islamic values for embracing Western ideals such as *Gharbzadegi*, or 'Westoxication' in his seminal book of the same title.

Al-e-Ahmad in fact borrowed and developed his concept of 'Westoxication' from Ahmad Fardid's analysis of Martin Heidegger. The rather pejorative, yet commonly accepted, phrase *Gharbzadegi* was first coined in the 1940s by Ahmad Fardid, a professor of philosophy at the University of Tehran, and gained traction amongst intellectual discourse as well as entering the common parlance of political and nationalist Iranians after the publication of Al-e-Ahmad's book in 1962. As sociologist Ali Gheissari states:

> For Al-e-Ahmad the question was less philosophical and more political: Iranians as a Muslim community must begin from the point where they lost their cultural integrity and self-confidence. He believed that the nineteenth century liberal intellectual break with society's popular, mainly Islamic, traditions was a great mistake [...] He proposes a new and more genuinely indigenous movement of self-assertion to deal with all contemporary problems, from economic and political dependency to urban anomie.
>
> (Gheissari 1997, p. 89)

The term *Gharbzadegi* has been variously translated as 'Westoxification', 'Westoxication', 'Westernized', 'West-struck-ness', 'Westitis', 'Euromania' or

'Occidentosis', but I believe 'Westoxication' is closest to the exact meaning of the phenomenon. I propose that the Iranian films of the late 1950s to 1970s are impacted by or at times are cinematic manifestations of the above-mentioned discourse on Westoxication among Iranian intellectuals. Filmmaking thus served as a crucial platform for the corresponding socio-political conflicts spanning from the early twentieth century to the late 1960s.

The Iranian thinker Dariush Shayegan in *Asia dar Barabar-e Gharb* (Asia Versus the West) describes the effect of such toxification upon Iranians:

> Iranians among other oriental cultures, neither have been able to link themselves with the driving force of the Western thought nor to maintain their ancestral memory. Our inability to grasp the driving force and engine of the Western thought and our abandoning of our ancestral memory and our alienation from this legacy makes us to be rejected from there (ancestral legacy) and, at the same time, nor to reach there (the West).
> (Shayegan 1977, p. 56)

In the late 1950s, Mohammad Reza Shah's government embarked upon an extremely ambitious and highly intensive economic reform programme, seizing absolute control over the machinations of the state with the help of foreign powers, against the democratically elected Prime Minister Mohammad Mosaddegh. This was a massive, long-term project of industrialization and urbanization, accompanied by socio-political reforms and institutionalized hegemony in support of Western aspirationalism.

Describing his reforms as the 'white revolution', the regime made a misguided calculation that this could quell, or somehow even placate, the calls for revolution by the leftist intellectual, guerrilla and populist uproars led by Islamic leaders like Ayatollah Khomeini, whilst furthering the Shah's ideal vision for modernizing the country and its people. The attempt to modernize Iranian society was poorly implemented and lost its footing from the outset. Evoking a negative reaction from multiple sides, it led to a predisposition for returning to one's roots amongst some intellectuals and the traditional strata of the nation.

According to Mirsepassi, Al-e-Ahmad and other anti-Western intellectuals of Iran in the 1960s were opponents to

> the Westerned-backed Pahlavi state of the Shah who was violently forced into being through a military d'état in 1953 and terminated a decade of hopeful

experimentation with democracy. It was this above all that engendered a hatred for and mistrust of the 'West'.

(Mirsepassi 2010, p. 119)

The resulting anti-westernization backlash was pervasive in both secular and religious Iranian intellectual thought of the time, encouraging a form of nativism and a call for a return to an imagined self. The manifestation of the West and its influences in Iran from the turn of the twentieth century, in terms of its socio-political and cultural impact on Iranian society, has generated two opposing reactions within Iranian society: outright rejection or overt embracement, which I will be outlining in later chapters. As Iranian sociologist Jamshid Behnam stated: 'In the post-constitutional era, the Iranian intellectuals' strategy vis-a-vis the West was to "Master" it, while in the 1960s and the 1970s they began to advocate for its abandonment' (Behnam 1996, p. 157).

In his study of this cultural shift in Iranian society, Mehrzad Boroujerdi examines how the secular and religious Iranian intellectuals of the 1950s and 1960s confronted a dual sense of otherness with the state and the West, and the dissent and nativism that resulted from it. In Boroujerdi's words, Jalal Al-e-Ahmad's *Gharbzadegi* 'exhorted Iranian intellectuals to reassess their passive and servile embrace of Western ideas and culture and called for an awakening and resistance to the hegemony of an alien culture that increasingly dominated the intellectual, social, political, and economic landscape of Iranian society' (Boroujerdi 1996, p. 68).

Al-e-Ahmad's book depicts the 'westernized other' as shallow, illusory and distorted and the 'Iranian self' as honest, meaningful and forward-looking. This intellectual anti-Western, pro-sovereignty ideology attacked the westernized upper class and attributed to them a negative system of thought. At the same time, by associating the upper class with the alien West, it externalized, marginalized and trivialized them. On the other hand, by attributing positive values such as courage, solidarity, modesty, sincerity, self-sacrifice and piety to the lower, traditionally oriented classes, it elevated a particular type of Iranian identity. This approach can be traced in both popular films (*Filmfarsi*) and New Wave films of the 1950s and 1960s such as Ghaffari's *The Night of the Hunchback* (1965) and Yasemi's mainstream hit *Qarun's Treasure* (1965) as well as countless other examples.

Filmfarsi had served a contradictory function in this conflict. Despite its echoing of the anti-modernization discourses of society, its overall atmosphere, commercial goals and narrative themes and motifs contributed to the maintenance of the status quo. Thus, it served to deepen the divide between cultural traditionalism and modernism or nativism and pro-Westernism. Iranian cinema of the 1950s was in a fragile state. It was burdened with technical ineptitude and primitive narrative forms and performances. The films produced in this period praised sacrifice, decency, family values and class division and lashed out against unfaithfulness, deceit and the desire for wealth. Most of them were based on superficial, simply written drama-laden stories published in pulp magazines, such as *Sepid-o Siah* (*White and Black*) and *Setareh Iran* (*Iranian Star*), which included articles ranging from current events to celebrity puff pieces. Overtly oblivious to the turbulent political events that were taking place in Iran in the 1950s, Iranian cinema continued to purport its typical themes, such as conflict between the rich and the poor in a frivolous manner, with moralistic endings analogous to the Indian and Egyptian films of the 1950s. Other narrative themes that were ever present include the contrast between the urban and rural life, the migration of villagers into the big cities and exaggerated love stories rife with betrayal.

The iconography of *Filmfarsi* shows that one of the main intentions of Iranian filmmakers involved in this industry was to capture the traditional culture, lifestyles and customs that were disappearing due to modernization and westernization. The question of the opposition between nativism and Westernism is further complicated when one considers that, in depicting this question, *Filmfarsi* suffered from an acute and inherent contradiction. While *Filmfarsi* is not at ease with modern values and modernized and perhaps sexually liberated women, the whole film narrative revolves around the axis of the unification of a couple, in which the male protagonist represents elements of native and traditional culture, while the female protagonist is usually someone from an affluent westernized family. For example Habib, the illiterate hero of the film *Aghay-e Gharn-e Bistom* (Mr Twentieth Century, 1964) finds himself alienated from manifestations of modern life. He does not wear a suit and tie, does not listen to foreign music, and he ridicules westernization. But he drinks vodka like water and dances *Babakaram* (a traditional popular dance in Iran). Or in Nosratollah Vahdat's *Aroos Farangi* (The Foreign Bride, 1964) the protagonist Hussein Tormozi (played by Vahdat) is a cab driver taking a German girl, Maria (played by Iranian actress Pouri Banaie), to her relatives' home in Tehran, and they consequently fall in love. The female is attracted to him because of the sincerity of his religious convictions. He prays soberly and weeps, but in a later scene we find him in a cabaret encouraging a girl to dance with a stranger.

The persistence of the Shah's regime in implementing its white revolution alienated further the traditional conservative strata and increased the power of the westernized/modernized strata, leading to the grave cultural conflicts that Iran was embroiled in from the 1960s onwards. There emerged a wide gap between traditional and modernized sectors creating a standoff situation. This was mainly in the form of clashes and uprisings by the religiously affiliated groups, such as the 1963 demonstrations (*15 Khordad* uprising), establishing Ayatollah Khomeini as a political opponent to the Shah. It also led to guerrilla operations by Marxists motivated by the tactics and ideology of their southern American counterparts, such as the 1971 Siahkal armed revolt.

In both *Filmfarsi* and the New Wave films we can find the widespread influence of anti-westernization discourse among the Iranian intellectuals and the popular culture. However, the New Wave films challenged certain aspects of this discourse either implicitly or in a relatively straightforward and upfront manner. Understanding the ways these filmmakers reflected on this discourse suggests how this subject was at the forefront of the *Mowj-e No* (the New Wave).

The enablement and obstructionism of the state

During the pre-revolutionary period, Iranian cinema was not state run; instead the creation, distribution, importing and screening of all films was undertaken by the studios. This studio system was one of multiple privately owned operations including but not limited to Ariana Film; ParsFilm; Misaghiye; Poorya Film; Moulin Rouge; Asr-e Talai; Iran Film Studio; Mahtab Film; Jourak; Atlas Films. The first three listed were the largest in terms of revenue and output. Rather than fully fledged studios, some of these were merely individuals in rented offices and people who had close and friendly ties to the Iranian regime and as such were granted more access to bankrolling and financial annuities from the government for the purposes of film production, provided they were making content that was free of political elements or anything considered controversial by the censors of the time (Mohammadi, 2001, p.19).

Certain high-ranking officials within the Ministry of Culture and Arts and other bodies of the regime who had a hand in the network of film production, expressed a lack of enthusiasm towards the pursuit of cinema, failing to consider the potential upsides of this medium. A clear example of this is Abdol-Majid Majidi, a high-ranking minister in the regime of the Shah from the late 1960s, who had various responsibilities including being the head of the Director of Queen Farah Foundation and therefore a key player in matters of cultural budgeting and programming. By his own admission, he claims:

> We had a period of economic boom, and if we placed more support at the hands of the filmmakers of Iran the national cinema would have been greatly improved… All of us, both in the private and public sectors, did take good advantage of such opportunities. And we must therefore consider this period one of missed opportunities.
>
> (*Kayhan*, no. 474, London, 23 September 1993, p. 5)

Similarly, according to Mohammad Ali Issari:

> The film industry never enjoyed financial support during Reza Shah's rule and for several years into the reign of his son. On the contrary, the government, through naïve policies of protectionism, restrained this young industry from growing.
>
> (Issari 1989, p. 200)

By many accounts, the pre-revolutionary domestic film industry was undergoing a permanent state of financial deprivation. Iranian journalist and cinema venue owner Shahrokh Golestan addresses the topic in an interview with UK published Farsi language newspaper *Kayhan*: 'the financial difficulties of Iranian cinema are the lack of it!' (*Kayhan*, no. 474, London, 23 September 1993, p. 5).

Golestan identifies some of the challenges facing the industry. The import and screening of foreign films; cheap cinema tickets; extremely high tax rates; either indifference from the state, or over-intervention from figures who were unfamiliar with the world of cinema and filmmaking were all placing a heavy burden on the domestic film industry. In addition, Iranian films were not marketed to international markets and domestic revenue was extremely limited. Even those films that resulted in exceptional box office successes rarely had their proceeds put back into the industry and instead studios would try to replicate the success of the previous films through imitation of the previous successes with meagre budgets.

With the way things stood, producers were generally rather uninclined to put their capital at risk by funding artistic films which would have an even smaller potential audience when the profits to be had from mainstream productions was so limited.

A notable exception to this norm would be the case of *Ganj-e Qarun* (Qarun's Treasure, 1965) produced by studio Poorya Film. It grossed in excess of $1 million, beating a previous domestic record set by the Indian film *Sangam* (Confluence, 1964). The studio was able to create a number of productions of higher calibre than the typical Farsi titles put out by studios such as itself. According to Issari, this was a hit that 'gave prestige and impetus to the local film industry and became the forerunner of a new movement in Iranian cinema which later produced such prestigious films as Dariush Mehrjui's *Gav* (The Cow, 1969) and others that took the work of Iranian filmmakers beyond the boundaries of Iran' (Issari 1989, p. 155).

Dariush Homayoun, Minister of Information and Tourism, a related body to that of Arts and Culture, with responsibility for media outlets, affirmed this when he said:

> The country's ministers had no understanding of cinema, they paid little regard or were indifferent to cinema. We suggested [to them] that they increase cinema ticket prices and a tax on foreign imports to be collected in a chest to support Farsi film production. Also any collaboration with foreign film companies was suggested so that we could make improvements to the domestic film industry.

But, in the words of Homayoun, 'they did not act upon this nor take it seriously' (*Kayhan*, no. 474, London, 23 September 1993, p. 5).

What Homayoun refers to as 'working with foreign companies' was an interesting phenomenon but one that there are very few cases of. *Sahra-ye Tatarha* (The Desert of the Tartars, 1976) was an Italian film made in Iran by Valerio Zurlini, and *Carvan-ha* (Caravans, 1978) directed by James Fargo and starring Anthony Quinn, was released in Iran and America where it was heavily panned by US critics such as Gene Siskel and Roger Ebert for its superficiality and reliance on cliché (Ebert 1979, p.19; Siskel 1979, p. 5).

As Issari pointed out, with the exception of 1948 – when Iranian-produced films were exempt from taxes for a year – the government taxed local productions at the same rate as foreign films, that is, 20 per cent of box office revenue went to the local municipality and 5 per cent to the central government. Moreover, the government was always reluctant to permit theatre owners to raise ticket prices in accordance with inflation or even in line with the rise in price of other public services which were also state managed. This was a continuous source of friction between cinemas and the government, often causing theatre owners to go on strike and close their theatres for several days. The theatre owners formed a union of sorts known as *the Society of Cinema Owners of Iran* in 1968 to protect their common interests (Issari 1989, p. 200). The extent to which this was effective in achieving their goals is difficult to determine.

Golestan supposed that the opposition of the government towards raising cinema ticket prices was due to 'Security officials believing cinema to be the only means of entertainment for the masses, and thus should not be increased' and that 'the Ministry of Culture and Arts was never in favor of producers. Mainstream audiences went to watch Persian and foreign commercial films to escape from the pressures of daily life and troubles and for fun and entertainment, and they were not interested in watching art films' (*Kayhan*, no. 474, London, 23 September 1993, p. 5).

He considered the intellectual cinema to appeal only to a small subsection of society who would not be able to patronize such films due to the cinema ticket price. In addition, he asserted the majority of audiences were too involved in their daily life and would only watch commercial cinema for a means of escapism and entertainment.

According to Majid Mohammadi, 'pre-revolutionary intellectual cinema was not commercially successful because of its artistic and abstract aspects, as people had their tastes become far too entrenched through exposure to mainstream films' (Mohammadi 2001, p. 15).

Some New Wave films did, however, manage to infiltrate the mainstream through certain shared commonalities with *Filmfarsi*. Successful films included Masoud Kimiai's *Qaysar* (1969), *Reza Motori* (Reza Motorcyclist, 1970), *Dash Akol* (1971) and *Gavaznha* (The Deer, 1974) and Amir Naderi's *Tangna* (Deadlock, 1973) and *Tangsir* (1973) or *Sadegh Kordeh* by Nasser Taghvai. Whether this was due to the films' true-to-life representations; exciting narrative structure; quick-moving pace and suspenseful storytelling; that they fell into the engrossing crime, melodrama or comedic genres; or through reliance on the draw of famous actors such as Behrouz Vosoughi, Pouri Banai and Saeed Raad, they were more popular than others, which allowed them to attain relative, and sometimes unprecedented, levels of financial success. Less successful commercially were *Khesht va Ayeneh* (Brick and Mirror), *Mogholha* (The Mongols, 1973), *Gharibeh va Meh* (The Stranger and the Fog, 1974), *Cheshmeh* (The Spring, 1972), *Aramesh dar Hozour-e Digaran* (Tranquility in the Presence of Others, made in 1969 but released in 1973) and *Tabiat-e Bijaan* (Still Life, 1974), in which the narrative structure was more complex and abstract with a symbolic and allegorical language and a slower rhythm, and generally featured fewer mainstream actors.

Most widely known as an actor for his role as the highly successful recurring comedic character 'Samad', Parviz Sayyad had a distinctive position among New Wave filmmakers as, like John Cassavetes or Vitorio Decica, he would spend money earned from commercial films to bankroll independent and intellectual films. He was a prolific producer keen to support the production of intellectual films, and he had this to say of the tastes of Iranian viewers: 'People of different classes like Samad films and I had no problem filling the cinema halls that showed this kind of film. My problem was with films like Sohrab Shahid-Saless's *Still Life*, which had no audience' (*Kayhan*, no. 474, London, 23 September 1993, p. 5).

Sayyad even tried to incorporate the popular Samad character into a more intellectual context with the Jalal Moghaddam directed, Farrokh Ghaffari produced, and Sayyad written film *Samad va Foolad Zereh Div* (Samad and the Steel Armoured Ogre, 1971). But the alteration of Samad's familiar dialogue and personality to be more 'intellectual', as well as other stylistic changes, led to the film being a unique flop in an otherwise highly popular series (Kayhan, no. 471, London, 2 September 1993, p. 5).

The extent to which this was the only factor is a little surprising, as the film still contains much of the same comedic gags and tropes that exist in the other Samad films; however, the use of more absurdist and culturally unfamiliar elements such as scientific experimentation on the demon, unusual visual and sound mixing, as well as a cast of actors like Moghaddam and Ghaffari, who were not known to mainstream audiences, could go some way to explaining what put audiences off this film.

Sayyad admits to also having made a miscalculation in the potential audience for the grandiose and realistically made historical drama *Sattar Khan* (1972) directed by Ali Hatami: 'Our thinking was that people at least were familiar with the history of Iran and the personality of Sattar Khan, but then we came to realize that the Iranian audiences wanted Sattar Khan on the silver screen as a Spartacus like figure' (*Kayhan*, no. 474, London, 2 September 1993, p. 5).

The mechanisms of censorship

In addition to the obstacles imposed by financial and production difficulties, the hindrance of censorship on the development of Iranian cinema posed significant challenges. With the state taking a somewhat hands-off approach to film production, it inversely held a great amount of control over the release and distribution cycle of these films, with not unexpectedly negative consequences.

It would be of value to go over the complex mechanisms by which the censorship efforts of the Shah contributed to the political, ethical and religious content found within Iranian filmmaking, although Iranian filmmakers learned how to circumvent the censorship regulations by inventing indirect means of expressing their ideas and by creatively relying strongly on metaphors and symbolism. By examining the broad workings of the censorship system in Iranian cinema, we can get a sense of the impact and implications of political and ethical restrictions that were imposed, as well as the self-regulatory effect it had on the style and form of the *Mowj-e No* films.

Scholar Mahmoud Khoshnam claims that intellectuals living in despotic nations like that of Iran under the Shah would come to learn through experience how best to overcome the problems of censorship, especially when the censors were simple minded in their thinking, which allowed for the deployment of subversive trickery (Khoshnam 2003, p. 35).

The Iranian government exercised very strict control over the political content of Iranian films through its censorship code, with the first censorship regulation passed in 1950 by the Ministry of State, but the uncodified pressures of state censorship had been a formidable presence on the arts and media, particularly films, long before this date. Issari had this to say on the effects of censorship on the shaping of mainstream filmmaking:

> In the name of protecting the monarchy, the Shi'a religion, the central government, and the local traditions, artistic expression and experimentation in film subjects were stifled. Subjects permitted to be made into feature films were restricted to trite stories, slapstick comedies, and over-used comparisons of village and big-city life. Persian cinema was not allowed to examine the problems, weaknesses, and strengths of the society it served. Therefore, instead of cinema becoming a leader of public opinion, it catered to the uneducated tastes of the masses.
>
> (Issari 1989, p. 201)

According to Dariush Homayoun, Minister of Information and one of the officials of the Censorship Office in Iran, a machinated censorship operation began at Reza Shah's Ministry of Culture and was initially heavily concerned with censorship of newspapers and books. Later, during the reign of Mohammad Reza Shah, a department known as the Publishing and Publicity Office was created, which was run by the police and tasked with the censoring of books and the press, headed by Muharram Ali Khan, a censor famous for not allowing anything to slip past his sensitive radar when it came to subversive content (Khalaji 2003, p. 15).

After the National Organization for Security and Intelligence (SAVAK) was established, it became responsible for censorship and the police were no longer involved. The Publishing and Publicity Office gradually transformed into the Ministry of Information, which had a different role to the SAVAK. Until the 1950s, SAVAK was directly involved with the censoring of books, newspapers and films, but this baton was passed to the Ministry of Information. SAVAK was no longer directly responsible for the act of censorship but instead kept tabs on certain groups and individuals, and conducted related intelligence activities such as building cases for prosecution. Such strict restriction and censorship was not limited to cinema; Iranian literature and theatre also suffered greatly from these efforts.

According to Dariush Homayoun, the Shah took a personal role in the administration of censorship and carefully perused newspapers and magazines and watched movies (Khalaji 2003, p. 15).

Under Article 55 of the 1950 Censorship Law, the government was allowed to block the screening of films that were against Islam and the monarchy. Under the regulation, films containing content that incited people to revolt against the government or incite workers, students, farmers and other classes to confront the police and destroy factories, universities and schools were banned. It was also forbidden to show erotic scenes and nudity and to use vulgar words and themes that were considered to be the moral corruption of society.

This regulation was in place until 1966 when a new censorship law was passed with changes to twenty-seven articles, resulting in much stricter regulation than the previous iteration. By many accounts it was applied more rigorously and imposed more restrictions on Iranian filmmakers.

The new law prohibited the showing or encouragement of 'vulgarity' such as erotic, sexual and homosexual scenes, crude language, and the act of murder (this was interpreted loosely and there were many murders in Iranian films that passed censorship approval). It forbade the production and screening of films that were perceived to be disparaging to the country's military and administrative officials, and scenes alluding to the assassination of senior government officials or ideas promoting political subversion were also prohibited. Furthermore, it forbade the showing of ruined and backwards landscapes and the lives of poor people, described as 'humiliating the dignity of Iran and Iranians' (Rezaei 2010, pp. 32–4).

The government banned many New Wave films that were made with a realistic, critical approach or showed a less than positive or murky image of Iranian villages and cities and the poverty and immiseration of citizens. The censors would cite the 1950 Censorship Law to ban films outright or to force the filmmakers to make changes and remove subversive scenes in their films, often causing heavy re-edits and reshoots for films already constrained by tight budgets.

In addition to state censorship, the religious stratums were highly reactionary and particularly sensitive in regards to sex and eroticism, as well as insulting/anti-religious scenes in films. They would often conduct pressure campaigns on government officials to ban films with such content. In response to protests by Islamic ulama against the showing of erotic films, Nosratollah Moeinian, then Minister of Information, proclaimed in an interview in 1964 that the public consensus demonstrated a high level of concern over the screening of immoral films, and that this concern was to some extent justified, therefore the screening of films contrary to national goals and public morality would be prohibited (*Kayhan*, 17 April 1964).

In fact, the Censorship and Film Supervisory Department generally did not concern itself with the prevention of films containing erotic imagery, but it was highly sensitive to political and social commentary and insinuation, taking the over cautious approach when it came to banning the screening of films perceived to pose such unlawful content.

Farrokh Ghaffari's *Jonub-e Shahr* (South of the City, 1958*)* was confiscated after a few days of screening in cinemas by the order of SAVAK and its original version was destroyed and a modified version of it known as *Reghabat dar Shahr* (Rivalry in the City, 1963*)* was shown to the public that was significantly different from the original version. For this reason Ghaffari chose to remove his name as the director and producer of the film from the credits.

Gav (The Cow, 1969), *Aramesh dar Hozour-e Digaran* (Tranquility in the Presence of Others, 1969/73), *Berehneh ta Zohr ba Sorat* (Naked until Noon with

Speed, 1976), *Dayereh-ye Mina* (The Cycle, 1975–8), *Shatranj-e Baad* (The Chess of the Wind, 1976), *Asrar-e Ganj-e Darre-ye Jenni* (The Secrets of the Treasure of the Jinn Valley, 1974) and *Gavaznha* (The Deer, 1974) were among the films that fell victim to censorship. Dariush Mehrjui's *Gav* (The Cow, 1969) was banned by the government for its realistic and murky image of rural life that clashed with the progressive image of Iran that the Shah's government wished to project, despite it being sponsored by the Ministry of Culture and Arts. But Mehrjui was able to smuggle the film abroad and he showed it at international film festivals to the great annoyance of the government.

While censorship presented restrictions and pressures on Iranian filmmakers, it did not hinder them to the degree that state actors may have hoped. The very effects of self-censorship resulted in the powerful employment of symbolic and poetic constructs to artfully dodge the demands for obedience from establishment forces, putting such tactics at the very heart of the New Wave movement. By the 1970s, symbolism and allegorism became critical and ubiquitous to *Mowj-e No* films. In *The Mongols*, for example, Kimiavi would relate the Mongol hordes invading ancient Persia to the invading force of Western cultural influence through their entry from an oversized television into Iranian villages.

Figure 2.4 *Gav* (The Cow, 1969) by Dariush Mehrjui.

In Masoud Kimiai's *The Deer* (1974), there is a scene where Qudrat (Faramarz Gharibian), an anti-Shah guerrilla whose name literally translates to 'power', is a friend of Seyed (Behrooz Vousoughi) whom he has idolized since their teenage years as someone with a yearning for justice. In the final scene, Ghodrat lays his pistol down next to a flower pot as he exits his room in the final sequence of the film, providing further allusions to the growth and continuation of the guerrilla movement against the Shah's government.

Bahram Beyzaie is particularly adept when it comes to the symbolic and metaphoric; the names of his characters are also symbolic such as *Haghighat* (the truth) and *Ghena'at* (frugality) as well as his use of colours and some objects such as glasses. One of the iconic motifs of Beyzaie's films is an image of a large pair of glasses. It is a metaphor for the ever-present and watchful eyes of big brother (SAVAK), as the camera monitors people in public spaces and shows that we are living under the gaze of others. In both *The Crow* (1976) and *Killing Mad Dogs* (2001) we see a high-angle long shot of the pavement that the two main protagonists (Asieh and Kian) are passing by under a large advertisement of an optician featuring big watchful glasses.

The establishment of cultural institutions and film centres

The Ministry of Culture and Arts did not provide the necessary support to Iranian cinema; at the same time commercial conditions were suboptimal for the New Wave and intellectual filmmakers seeking to make their films different from dominant tastes and therefore they had no hope of being financed by the private sector.

Farrokh Ghaffari played a significant role in acquainting Iranian filmmakers and film critics with art films and masterpieces of world cinema at a film centre he established known as *Kanoon-e Melli-e Film-e Iran* (The National Iranian Film Centre). He continued his constructive role when he was appointed as the deputy of Reza Ghotbi, the manager of National Iranian Radio and Television (NIRT).

The National Iranian Film Centre should be considered as one of the main factors for the formation of New Wave cinema in Iran. It was first established in 1949 but shut down in 1951 and then reopened in 1959. It became a favourite gathering place of Iranian cinephiles and people who were interested in modern and arthouse films. In the 1960s many Iranian film critics and filmmakers were members of Ghaffari's *Kanoon-e Melli-e Film Iran*. Forough Farrokhzad, Ebrahim Golestan, Bahram Beyzaie, Fereydoun Rahnema, Dariush Mehrjui, Nasser Taghahi, Mohammad Reza Aslani, Kamran Shirdel and Bahman Farmanara often declared that it was at *Kanoon* that they had seen artistic films of European cinema including the Italian neorealist and the French *Nouvelle Vague* films for the first time.

I think it is fair to make the comparison between the role played by *Kanoon-e Melli-e Film* in the creation of the New Wave cinema in Iran and the one by Henri Langlois's *La Cinémathèque Française* in the formation of the French *Nouvelle Vague*. It was at this centre that, with the help of Ebrahim Golestan, Ghaffari managed to screen masterpieces of European and American cinema, including those of Ingmar Bergman and Orson Welles, and of modern French and British cinema. In his introduction to the aims of the centre, Ghaffari explained the intention of the National Iranian Film Centre to show real cinema to Iranian spectators and intellectuals who were fed up with imported American and Indian commercial films:

> The commercial cinema imported to Iran is not compatible with the needs and interests of Iranians, and it is the responsibility of intellectuals to fight against these vulgar and misleading films. *Kanoon-e Melli-e Film* hopes to take steps in the way of propagating and defending the real art of cinema, with the help of Iranian intellectuals, and pave the way for the creation of an artistic cinema in Iran.
>
> (Omid 1995, pp. 948–49)

In addition to the National Iranian Film Centre, the role of governmental bodies and institutions such as *Kanoon-e Parvaresh-e Fekri-e Koodakan va Nojavanan*, better known as Kanoon/the Center for the Intellectual Development of Child and Adolescent (CIDCA), and NIRT in the formation of the *Mowj-e No* should not go unmentioned. The placing of the likes of Firuz Shirvanlu, Farrokh Ghaffari and Fereydoun Rahnema at these centres allowed for highly agreeable conditions for experimentation with filmmaking outside of commercial goals and thus was invaluable to the creation of *Mowj-e No* films.

Such programmes were funded on behalf of the Shah's government, in an effort to whitewash their less-than-stellar record on human rights and politically motivated crackdowns on intellectuals on the international stage. They were in essence virtue signalling that they were supportive of intellectuals and creative freedoms, whilst providing the added benefit of bringing such efforts and activities 'in house', so that they could have closer supervision and exert a higher degree of control over the film production process.

As film critic Jamsheed Akrami put it:

> The new wave filmmakers' works were making an impact at international film festivals, and this was very much in line with the cultural campaign of the Shah's government, which was looking for artistic and cultural gains in order to counterbalance its debased political image on the international scene.
> (Akrami 1987, p. 132)

These films were born out of an environment that was closely affiliated with the regime and would thus often have to be muzzled when it came to taking any sort of critical tone towards the Shah's policies and other such matters. However, as the filmmakers were presented with no financing alternatives in the private sector, it was on the whole a very welcome and positive force.

Kanoon (CIDCA) was originally created with the intention of promoting literacy and literature to the youth and children of Iran in 1965 by the Shah's wife Farah Pahlavi. It originally operated as a book publisher for the most part, before Firuz Shirvanlu, the head of the centre in 1965, decided to establish a filmmaking wing for the organization, and invited Abbas Kiarostami to head the project. As Alberto Elena writes, 'the Centre... was to play such a definitive role in the hatching and development of the new Iranian cinema, both before and after the Islamic Revolution' (Elena 2005, p. 17).

This is where Kiarostami would make his first short *Nan-o-Kocheh* (Bread and Alley, 1970), a film that had some key stylistic and thematic features of Kiarostami's later films. Again with the idea of children and youth in mind: 'The idea of creating a filmmaking section at *Kanoon*... arose as an extension of the activities of some of its graphic artists such as Farshid Mesqali and Arapik Baghdasarian who were keen to try their hand at film animations' (Elena 2005, p. 17). They later developed a collective dedicated to teaching the practical and theoretical processes that go into filmmaking.

At the Tehran 5th International Festival of Film for Children and Young Adults, Kiarostami's work and the animation were bundled together to receive the top prize at the event (Elena 2005, p. 18). However, this was really the extent to which these films received publicity and they were only shown at Kanoon's various branches in the different districts of Tehran and other cities of Iran.

It was a validating moment for the institution and gave credence to an artist who would go on to have such a luminous career and profound impact on the reputation of Iranain arthouse cinema.

Many second-generation filmmakers of the New Wave of Iranian cinema, who began their filmmaking activities in the late 1960s, such as Bahram Beyzaie, Abbas Kiarostami, Sohrab Shahid-Saless and Nasser Taghvai, without any prior experience or training were able to make their first short films with the financial support of this centre. On a personal note, Kanoon is also the venue where I, as a teenage film enthusiast, received my first exposure to the process and world of filmmaking at the Shahi branch of Kanoon in the north of Iran, and so I appreciate firsthand the importance of such a unique and well-managed programme for the country.

Along with Kanoon, NIRT and its affiliated company known as Telfilm had a considerable role in the development of arthouse cinema in Iran in the late 1960s. The presence of influential figures such as Farrokh Ghaffari and Fereydoun Rahnema in key positions at NIRT was very decisive. Ghaffari, as the Cultural Deputy to Reza Ghotbi, Head of NIRT and Rahnema as one of the most important producers at NIRT, played a key role in supporting young modernist filmmakers and providing the necessary funding for their filmmaking.

Telfilm was established by NIRT in 1969 to produce artistic films for release on television. As Mohammad Ali Issari stated,

> within a few years from its inauguration, NIRT became the most important center of filmmaking, in particular documentary filmmaking, in the country, and many young filmmakers trained in Iran and other countries rushed to join it. In contrast with the past, these filmmakers were encouraged and given the freedom and facilities to explore and examine on film their society and its culture.
>
> (Issari 1989, p. 214)

In fact, the production of some of the most texually dense and controversial *Mowj-e No* films such as *Cheshmeh* (The Spring, 1972), *Mogholha* (The Mongols, 1973), *Bita* (1973), *Aramesh dar Hozour-e Digaran* (Tranquility in the Presence of Others, made in 1969 but released in 1973), *Zanburak* (1975), *Dar Ghorbat* (Far From Home, 1975), *Bagh-e Sangi* (The Stone Garden, 1976), *O.K. Mister* (1979), *Dayereh-ye Mina* (The Cycle, 1975–8), *Tabiat-e Bijaan* (Still Life, 1974) and *Shazdeh Ehtejab* (Prince Ehtejab, 1974) were enabled via the support of Telfilm, which provided 50 per cent funding for a 50 per cent stake in the film or complete funding in exchange for full film rights.

In 1966, Rahnema, as an employee of NIRT, started a group known as the *Iran Zamin* (Land of Iran) which supported filmmakers such as Nasser Taghvai, Parviz Kimiavi and Mohammad Reza Aslani to produce highly creative documentary films with an emphasis on poetry and theatrics rather than typical newsreel footage that was one of the main outputs of NIRT. This was fertile ground for these budding young filmmakers. 'A number of good documentaries on culture, art and folklore of the country were made under *Iran Zamin*'s Patronage' (Issari 1989, p. 214). These were nostalgic pieces, which looked to idolize the past and were in line with Jalal Al-e-Ahmad and Dariush Shayegan's nativist ideology that was centred around addressing the subject of 'Westoxification', for example the eradication of indigenous and traditional ways of life as the result of the Shah's modernization project and through the impact of technology and the influence of media. Thus, these filmmakers, while enjoying government facilities, were generally critical of the policies of the Shah's government, especially in relation to rural life and culture. As Issari pointed out, 'although documentaries made by and for NIRT covered various subjects, very few of them were propaganda films for the regime. One reason was that NIRT had a well equipped and well staffed news department through which the activities of the Shah, the Royal family and high government officials were photographed daily and shown on the evening news' (Issari 1989, p. 215).

With the support of NIRT, Rahnema not only made his final film *Pesar-e Iran Az Madaresh Bi Etella' Ast* (Iran's Son Has No News of His Mother, 1974) but he also supported other young filmmakers to make their films. He was in charge of this project until his passing in 1975.

Another means through which the development of the atmosphere of the New Wave was catalysed was the holding of various film and cultural festivals such as Shiraz Festival of Arts, Sepas Film Festival, and the most prestigious: Tehran International Film Festival. The Tehran International Film Festival, which was held from 1971 to 1976 on an annual basis under management of Farrokh Ghaffari and Hajir Dariush, soon became one of the six most important international film festivals in the world (Issari 1989, p. 203).

The motto of the festival was 'to recognize the notable films from East and West. To encourage humanity in the art of cinema. To create a better understanding between nations of the world. To produce an environment for exchange of constructive ideas about matters relating to filmmaking in the present time. And

Figure 2.5 Ezatollah Entezami, Farrokh Ghaffari and Ali Nassirian at the Shiraz Festival of Arts, 1968.

to facilitate the exchange of films on an international level' (Shoa'ee 1975, p. 167). The scope of the festival went beyond the borders of the country.

It was organized by the Ministry of Culture and Arts under the royal auspices of Farah Pahlavi and, like the Kanoon programme, it helped to acquaint foreign filmmakers with Iranian cinema. The festival served as the venue for arthouse films from America, Europe (particularly Eastern Europe), Africa, Latin America, the Arab world, Japan, Russia and Iran. It was a place for Iranian filmmakers to get acquainted with artistic world cinema, as well as meeting and exchanging views with some of the great world film directors. In addition, some important Iranian New Wave films were screened for the first time at this festival and were judged by international jury members most of whom were world-renowned filmmakers including Satiajit Ray, Arthur Hill, Delbert Mann, Frank Capra, Emmanuelle Riva, James Mason, Alain Robbe-Grillet, Miklós Jancsó, Jiří Menzel, István Szabó, Nikita Mikhalkov, Bert Haanstra and Alberto Lattuada.

This festival therefore had a fundamental role in introducing the New Wave filmmakers such as Sohrab Shahid-Saless, Parviz Kimiavi, Bahram Beyzaie, Arby Ovanesian, Kamran Shirdel, Bahman Farmanara, Khosrow Haritash and Mohammad Reza Aslani to international filmmakers and film critics who attended the festival every year. During the sixth year of this film festival, some important New Wave films were shown including Shahid-Saless's *A Simple Event* (1973), Beyzaie's *Downpour* (1971), Ovanesian's *Cheshmeh* (The Spring, 1972), Farmanara's *Prince Ehtejab* (1974), Kimiavi's *The Mongols* (1973), Haritash's *Divine One* (1976) and Kimiai's *The Deer* (1974). There were also retrospectives of great filmmakers such as Charlie Chaplin, Buster Keaton, King Vidor, Michelangelo Antonioni, Federico Fellini, Pier Paolo Pasolini, Rene Clair, William Wayler, Miklós Jancsó and François Truffaut (Omid 1995, pp. 978–84).

3

Looking for an alternative cinema in Iran

In this chapter, the main critical debates on film and cinema in Iran during the period of the 1950s to 1960s will be examined. This is an essential step towards understanding the reasons behind the formation of the New Wave cinema in Iran and its progression. The 1960s was a time when a new way of looking at films was advanced. It was a cultural and political climate that secured a new place for cinema and led to the creation of a group of films and filmmakers that broke new ground in Iran.

Critical to this study is how, during the 1950s, a group of Iranian cinema graduates and cinephiles returned to Iran after having lived and studied in European countries. Initially they became involved mainly in film criticism and advocated a more innovative approach to artistic quality and technical standards than would ordinarily be present in Iranian productions. Whereas the majority of active Iranian filmmakers were involved with the *Filmfarsi* industry, these intellectual filmmakers were intent on creating an alternative form of cinema that distanced itself from this mainstream product. The participating filmmakers simultaneously entangled themselves in the discourse on Westoxication amongst Iranian intellectuals and writers and the discussion on the need for an intellectual cinema and quality filmmaking amongst film critics. This artistic and politically charged description of what cinema could be would go on to be recognized as the New Wave.

Having identified the critical discourse among film critics, filmmakers and intellectuals, the challenge is to understand the nature of the New Wave movement and to trace the developments of the concepts of the art of cinema in the cinematic, artistic and political climate of Iran in the 1960s. This critical discourse played a fundamental role in the development of the New Wave movement and served as the arena where the dialogue between the film critics, intellectuals and filmmakers was conducted. The examination of this discourse offers the widest and most comprehensive basis for a better understanding of the movement in Iran.

Status of critical film discourse in 1960s Iran

Beginning in the 1950s, in the critical discourse of film in Iran many terms were coined and broadcast, all of which had aspirational connotations and described a cinema that was yet to be created or had not turned into a dominant trend within Iranian filmmaking. The goal of this critical discourse was the founding or promotion of such notions, with the adoption of terms such as national cinema; Iranian cinema; Iranian film; cinema for the public; noble cinema; and the industry of Persian films. There was still no unanimous understanding of these concepts among Iranian critics, who assigned to them their own preferential qualities, which were at times dissimilar or even contradictory to what another critic considered to be the case. In return, other terms were present in the discourse for the purposes of disparagement, dismissal or condemnation of the dominant output of Iranian cinema, which continue to be used in critical discourse today. Such terms are *Filmfarsi*; *Cinema-ye Farsi*; *Film-e Jaheli*; *Film-e Mobtazal*; and *Film-e Abgooshti* or *Cinema-ye Abgooshti* (Moazezinia 2001).

In this chapter I consider evidence gathered from multiple sources from this early period: archival documents and materials; newspapers; film journals and magazines which were published during the 1950s to 1960s, together with interviews with some Iranian film critics and writers. After an assessment of these sources, I will outline the foci and themes that were most evident during that time and explore issues such as '*Filmfarsi*', 'intellectual cinema', '*film-e ba keyfiat*/quality film', '*cinema-ye melli*/national cinema' and '*cinema-ye digar*/ other cinema'.

Focusing on the main critical film debates of those decades, we can see how the Iranian film critics contributed towards the idea of the formation of an alternative cinema that broke radically from the conventions of *Filmfarsi*.

I show how some controversial films of the 1960s such as Golestan's *Khesht va Ayeneh* (Brick and Mirror), Ghaffari's *Shab-e Quzi* (The Night of the Hunchback) and Rahnema's *Siavash Dar Takht-e Jamshid* (Siavash in Persepolis) were shortsold by those Iranian film critics of the period who had a different understanding of an 'artistic' or 'real Iranian' cinema.

Film critics such as Parviz Davaei, Parviz Nouri and Bahram Reypour believed in the reinforcement and rectification of *Filmfarsi* movies and supported those filmmakers who attempted to make a link between popular and artistic cinema.

Figure 3.1 Naser Malek Motiee and Christine Paterson in Nezam Fatemi's *Mehdi in Black Suit with the Girl in Hot Mini Pants* (Mehdi Meshki va Shalvarak-e Dagh, 1972). Whilst the values of Filmfarsi were distinctly traditional Iranian they would on occasion still use Western actors like Paterson who to the author's knowledge has only starred in Iranian films.

But on the other hand, it was a core group of critics/writers-turned-directors – in particular Hajir Dariush, Farrokh Ghaffari, Fereydoun Rahnema and Ebrahim Golestan – who had a mental image of new artistic cinema and argued that national filmmaking must undergo a fundamental transformation. These filmmakers were mostly educated in Europe and came to the scene with their new and original cinematic ideas in the early 1960s.

From the beginning of the 1950s, at the onset of film reviews written by critics such as Houshang Kavoosi, Farrokh Ghaffari and Hajir Dariush and the publication of film magazines such as *Setareh Cinema* (Cinema Star), *Peyk-e Cinema* (Cinema Courier), *Honar va Cinema* (Art and Cinema) and *Film va Zendegi* (Film and Life), opposition to mainstream Iranian cinema (*Filmfarsi*) intensified. Among them, Houshang Kavoosi expressed perhaps the highest level of contempt for *Filmfarsi*. With a harshly dismissive, almost humiliating tone, he attacked all the elements of Iranian film production, from the script to the directing and acting.

In this era the term *Filmfarsi*, which was coined by Kavoosi, turned into one of the most important topics of film critical discourse in Iran. It is a term that is the most important and famous non-translated word for film literature in Iran and is not derived from any Western film terminology. To emphasize the novelty of this term and to convey the meaning he had in mind, Kavoosi would write it with no space in between. By adjoining 'film' to '*farsi*' (Persian) into this compound word, he meant a cinema which according to him was neither film nor *farsi*, but an amalgamation of both. In a discussion in this regard, Kavoosi explains:

> Generally, the act of coining always creates a third meaning. For example, when we say rosewater, this word contains both rose and water, but we do not write it separately. So, this combination has a third meaning which is both rose and water and at the same time it is neither rose nor water. The same goes for *Filmfarsi*. *Filmfarsi* was both film and Farsi and at the same time neither film nor Farsi.
> (Moazezinia 2001, p. 6)

In response to the question what were the identifiable characteristics of *Filmfarsi*, he is quoted:

> Such films had no form, no syntax and no story. That is why I called them *Filmfarsi*... The French would call those types of films 'crotte de bique' meaning goat stool. Or to be more respectful, they call it 'navep', meaning *turnip*.
> (Moazezinia 2001, p. 7)

With regards to this specific term, many contemporary Iranian critics took umbrage, perhaps because it was seen as a conscious or unconscious slight to the quality of life in Farsi, or associated with Iranian culture. Some thought it wrong from a linguistic point of view and that it led to further misunderstandings rather than clarity (Moazezinia 2001, pp. 8–10). But such objections failed to prevent its traction and widespread usage.

The term has been used for several decades to both delineate and disparage mainstream cinema in Iran by film critics in a way that today has no theoretical

Figure 3.2 Original poster of *Lat-e Javanmard* (1958), directed by Majid Mohseni.

and conceptual meaning and has become like a swear word. On the other hand, although there has not been a unanimous understanding of this word among Iranian film critics, most of them have used the term to name the majority of popular products of Iranian cinema between the years 1958 to 1979. In fact, the term, right or wrong, has been repeated in thousands of pages of Iranian cinema texts and critiques for half a century and continues to do so (Moazezinia 2001, pp. 73–4, 190–91). It is important to mention that according to Kavoosi,

'*Filmfarsi*' does not refer to one special trend in Iranian cinema but encompasses all trends in Iranian cinema (Moazezinia 2001, p. 191).

As Kavoosi points out in his article about *Filmfarsi*:

> We say two types of films are made in today's Iranian cinema: *Filmfarsi* and Iranian film. *Filmfarsi* refers to that group of cinematic elements where in the cinematic technique and structure and the treatment and development of the story, we see obvious grammatical mistakes. So, if we consider a limit of point zero for value in cinema, because of the incomplete rhetorical technique and their contextual structure, they will be placed below this limit. That is why we call them '*zir-e film*'/undermovie(s), which is an English portmanteau. These two types of cinema are known in Iran, their viewers are known, their filmmakers are known, and their writers are known.... creation of a 'good' cinema in developing countries is a danger to the existing cinema, which has no value and is 'undermovie'.
>
> (Kavoosi 1969, p. 57)

What Kavoosi categorizes as *Filmfarsi* was a group of films that were made based on the clichés and conventional styles of Egyptian, Indian and Turkish popular cinema welcomed by the people due to their visual and narrative appeal (Kavoosi 1969, p. 57). In his review of *Shabha-ye Ma'bad* (The Nights of the Temple, 1953), directed by Nasser Kourehchian, Kavoosi wrote: 'Poor cinema, miserable people! Watching this film is torture and maceration. I tolerated this torture so that you readers interested in cinema do not have to go through it' (Kavoosi 1954, p. 52).

In fact, Kavoosi went as far as to object to people watching this film at all, but the audience did not pay heed and were more than eager to see it, with the film attaining sensational popular success. According to Houshang Ghadimi (one of the film critics of the same era), the reason behind the popularity of these films was that the typical audience of *Filmfarsi* were addicted to this type of moralistic melodrama (Ghadimi 1954, p. 24). In fact, the *Filmfarsi* audience appeared from the heart of the controversies concerning the semi-modern society of the Pahlavi period. Subsequent to political and social changes in Iranian society in the 1950s and the change in economic relationships and the gradual transition from a traditional feudal system to a modern and dependent capitalist one, the needs and demands of society had altered accordingly. The outcome of this was that the themes and genres of *Filmfarsi* were changing as well. The films were a combination of family melodramas and folk stories in which the contrast between good and evil was mainly based on class distinctions (rich and poor), value distinctions (nobility and villainy) and social distinctions (rustic and urban) (Kashi 1998, p. 140).

Namoos parasti (the preservation of female chastity), veneration of the noble poor and reproach towards the unscrupulously wealthy, and the problems of rural-urban migration are the most oft-repeated themes of *Filmfarsi*. These themes were influenced by the folk stories and pulp fiction pieces published in the popular magazines that were broadly familiar to the majority of the public. Exaggeration in set design and characterization, heroism, dancing and singing, dispensation of moral advice (e.g. peace of mind and wealth do not come hand in hand), traditionalism, believing in destiny, and clownery and lumpenism were the main characteristics of *Filmfarsi* (Barzin 1994, p. 24).

The cinemagoers in Iran were not a homogenous group and they came from different strata and social classes. A study of cinemagoers in Iran denoted two distinct groups that were distinguishable among the Iranian spectators during the years of this study: upper-class spectators (the elite audience), and lower- to middle-class spectators (Issari 1989).

The upper-class spectators aspired to be westernized and this was reflected in their viewing choices as they generally favoured American or European films. Conversely, *Filmfarsi*, Indian, Arabic and Turkish films were the typical preference of lower- and middle-class people going to the cinema.

From the early 1960s the migration of villagers to cities in pursuit of employment in factories and construction sites increased, to the extent that population growth in villages decreased to 1.6 per cent and increased in urban areas to 5.1 per cent. In 1966 Tehran's population had reached 2,712,944 (Barzin 1994, p. 24).

With the urban migration and expansion of cities, the number of urban workers increased. The middle and governing classes, who mainly established themselves in the richer quarters of the cities, stepped up rapidly to embrace modernity, most in its imitative West-obsessed forms and some in more creative and progressive forms. On the other hand, the urban workers who resided in the poor neighbourhoods or suburbs typically perceived this modernity as a threat to the preservation of their traditional way of life. In the capital of Tehran, this was defined in terms of rich districts in the north and poor districts in the south.

Most people resided in poor neighbourhoods, had a low income and were keen to maintain their faith, traditional customs and beliefs. Although they had accepted the general requirements of living in a modern society, and some had a westernized appearance, many had not been able to reconcile their religious beliefs with modernity at the most fundamental level. The trend in the formation of two different cultures led to the formation of the terms *Bala Shahri* (rich urban) and *Payeen Shahri* (poor urban) becoming a recognizable distinction of identity amongst residents (Barzin 1994, p. 25).

The audience of *Filmfarsi* were the great number of men and women who had migrated from the villages to poor neighbourhoods: urban workers, peddlers and a large number of the illiterate (Heidari 2000). In accordance with the class division of the audiences, the cinema houses would be divided into two groups. One group, small in number (and later classified as 'first-class' cinemas), catered mainly to the elite and upper-middle class, often showing European and American films made to a higher calibre. The other group of cinemas, much larger in number (and later classified as 'second-class' and 'third-class' cinemas), catered to the lower-class and primarily undereducated masses. They generally screened only Farsi, Indian and Arabic films (Issari 1989, p. 64).

> The cinema houses frequented by the elite and sophisticated audience, located mostly in the centre and the northern part of Tehran, normally would not show *Filmfarsi*. In an interview with the BBC Persian, Arsham Yesians, the owner of Radio City Cinema (A 'first-class' cinema in the centre of Tehran, which was burned down in the course of the 1979 Revolution) explained: 'We thought that if we put on *Filmfarsi*, a number of viewers would come to our cinema who were not our steady customers, which would end in the loss of a number of our permanent customers, particularly women. That was why we tried not to show *Filmfarsi*.'
>
> (Golestan 1993, p. 77)

This situation changed in 1963 when, after the success of *Ganj-e Qarun* (Qarun's Treasure, 1965) and upon the request of *Filmfarsi* filmmakers, the Shah ordered Dr Pirasteh, then Minister of Interior, to screen *Filmfarsi* films in the northern cinemas. Despite this particular intervention from the government (*Kalameh*, no. 12), as Issari noted, the division of audiences and cinema houses remained strong in Iran and had a direct impact on the local feature film industry (Issari 1989, p. 65).

Though the warp and woof of Iranian cinema was determined by political conditions, cinema attendees were determinative of success in the domestic market. The further back we go, the more these audiences for *Filmfarsi* on average were illiterate or low literate, whose expectations from films were easy-to-follow action, romance, dancing and singing, and content suggestive of sex. Following the tendency of *Filmfarsi* towards sex-appeal, the stars of such films would gain a huge following and the adoration of filmgoers, particularly amongst the younger audience, and thus they generated a lot of success and money for such films. Iranian cinema's policy towards displays of sexual imagery and a focus on reinforcing notions of these stars as sex symbols conformed to the government's modernization policy. The official policy in the field of art was to encourage a highly westernized and modern art. Along with modernization and westernization in Iran, the scope of film production changed and the filmmakers' attitude towards sex became more liberal. In order to be able to compete with the imported American and European films, *Filmfarsi* was obliged to resort to new methods and approaches, to attract a younger and more educated audience while retaining its traditional audience. Statistical investigation of film audiences in Iran shows that education has always been an important factor. According to Ali Assadi, most of the audiences of *Filmfarsi* were illiterate whereas educated people were the audiences of Western films. In a study carried out in Bandar Abbas (a small town in the south of Iran) in 1968, it was found that 62.9 per cent of the illiterate and just 16 per cent of educated spectators chose Farsi films (Assadi 1973, p. 13).

Thus, it can be said that highly educated people had a minimal interest in *Filmfarsi* because of their poor technical quality and superficial approach. According to Issari:

> With the exception of a small number of locally produced feature films that did fairly well with both audiences, the educated cinema goers for a long time did not accept Persian films as a substitute for the high-quality foreign films to which they had grown accustomed. This rejection drove the Persian feature films into second and third-rate cinemas, where the profit margin was small and audiences were content as long as the film was Iranian in nature and spoken in Persian.
>
> (Issari 1989, p. 65)

The need to preserve a high level of communication with the audience of *Filmfarsi* has come to determine the simplistic content and form of this cultural product. Like Indian films, actors would start singing out of the blue and just moved their lips while someone else would sing. They would run among flowers, hold each other's hands and turn round and round, peek through trees and bushes and chase each other. The sad tone of some of these songs stemmed from another characteristic, which was the tendency towards pain and sorrow, and this too came from Indian cinema. It is undeniable that social and economic pressures had an important effect on the aesthetics of *Filmfarsi*. Being extremely sensitive towards social divisions and inequalities can be considered one of the outstanding features of *Filmfarsi*. It has been influenced by the widespread anti-westernization discourse in Iranian culture, which, in turn, has contributed to the enhancement of this discourse. The point, however, is that in the 1960s *Filmfarsi* served a dualistic and rather contradictory function. That is to say, besides echoing and amplifying anti-rich and anti-westernization discourse, its overall atmosphere has contributed to the maintenance of the status quo. Based upon the underlying theme of social inequalities, the films have more or less the same narrative structure which is repeated with variations ad infinitum. The story typically revolves around either a heterosexual love affair/familial relationship or a family (not necessarily nuclear) whose unity and integrity are placed under threat from some external danger. In most cases the couple/collective becomes united in overcoming destructive forces. *Qarun's Treasure* (1965) is a typical example of *Filmfarsi* which addresses this issue. It is the story of a poor man who at the end of the film becomes united with his wealthy father.

With these characteristics, *Filmfarsi* had no place of importance among the Iranian film critics who mostly regarded it with a snobbish attitude. In the discussion over the artistic or commercial value of *Filmfarsi*, critics, like Houshang Kavoosi, not only denied any artistic value for these films, but also denied their commercial value: 'The question is if this cinema, as a producing unit, has any value or not. In my opinion, unfortunately the answer is disappointing' (Kavoosi 1970, p. 17).

Kavoosi does not regard *Filmfarsi* cinema as a business from an economical point of view. He calls it 'shop keeping', arguing that a *Filmfarsi* maker, just like a shopkeeper, wants to gain benefit using the most immediate and illogical ways. In contrast, a businessman has more foresight in this regard and tries to reach his goals via logical and correct means (Kavoosi 1970, p. 17). Kavoosi does not even believe in reforming this cinema and argues that its construction had been wrong from day one: 'I never call this cinema the cinema of Iran and prefer to call it Farsi cinema. Because the only sign of its being Iranian is that its films are made under the sky of Iran' (Kavoosi 1970, p. 18).

Hajir Dariush, too, is among the critics who along with Kavoosi criticized *Filmfarsi* as a vulgar (*Mobtazal*) trend. His film articles were regularly printed in *Omid-e Iran* (Iran's Hope) magazine in the years following the 1953 coup. In one of his articles he writes:

> Regarding Farsi cinema one should note that now it is the time to fight against artlessness, vulgarity (*Ebtezal*) and pure commercial benefit gaining in the country's cinema. This lies with the smart critics of our country to try and beat those who try to ridicule our ancient culture and civilisation with their vulgar films.
>
> (Dariush 1954, p. 23)

In his article 'A Discussion on *Filmfarsi*', Dariush claimed that real cinema had not been yet formed in Iran: 'Critics should seriously fight the repulsive rubbish that is fed to the people in the name of "cinema" and "recreation". This is how one can be hopeful towards the formation of real cinema in Iran' (Dariush 1954, p. 21). In response to critics who believed in supporting *Filmfarsi* he wrote: 'Anyone who just declares he supports Farsi films and calls any worthless rubbish the best Farsi film, its director the Alfred Hitchcock of the country and its star the Marilyn Monroe of Iran, is the person who is knowingly or unknowingly demolishing the cinema of the country' (Dariush 1954, p. 21). Dariush considered there was no artistic value to *Filmfarsi* productions and in his articles he talked of the need for the formation of an artistic and original form of cinema. In his article 'A *Filmfarsi* is Not a Farsi Film', he declared:

> If people of my type have nothing to do with Farsi cinema, it is just because we consider it a pure business, like producing vegetable oil and do not find anything worth discussion and comment (as an artistic genre and way of expression) in its products... Farsi cinema has tried to develop a thin and easily liked taste among people, for the past 20 years, to gain commercially from it. Men who have made our Farsi films did not have the required level of subtlety and elite taste. *Filmfarsi* today is a cinema that stupefies people. One can summarise the common points of the context of Farsi films as such: First: This will pass too. Second: The way it passes is not bad at all. The reason: In the framework of *Filmfarsi* the more stupid, illiterate, poor and carefree you are, the more successful you will be. [Pointing] to Ali Bigham (Sorrowless/carefree Ali), the famous and typical character of *Filmfarsi* in Siamak Yasemi's *Ganj-e Qarun* (*Qurun's Treasure*, 1965). This is how *Filmfarsi* kills the tendency towards progress and improvement in its viewers by means of cinema to gain more benefit just like an addictive drug. We should declare our hatred towards this cinema, not as a film critic, but as an ordinary Iranian citizen.
>
> (Dariush 1968, p. 12)

In examining the published film material of this period, we find that Iranian film critics did not pay much consideration to the social and cultural influence of *Filmfarsi* on ordinary cinemagoers. This lack of accurate recognition of the cinema audience in Iran was a disconnect on the part of many Iranian film critics of this period, who were incapable of understanding the particularities of *Filmfarsi* and the mechanism of its influence on Iranian spectators. The impression of *Filmfarsi* on its audience was so intensive that it made them sympathize with the characters of the film and contribute to their own happiness and sorrow. The characters and music of the films would enter the mainstream consciousness and would be recited by people long after leaving the cinema. It is apparent that these spectators who had got used to the conventions and styles of *Filmfarsi* and to their simple, attractive and relatable worlds, would not be able to maintain this sense of relatability with the serious, multifaceted and less familiar worlds one would find within European and Iranian intellectual films. And so the agitated reaction and angry protests to Jean Renoir's *The River*, which was screened in 1953, makes sense within this context as to why such attitudes were displayed by the public against the screening of artistic films. The backlash was intense enough to lead to a ban on *The River*'s performances. It caused film critics of that time to publish a declaration, in which it was said:

> Last Wednesday when Cinema Iran was showing the artistic masterpiece 'The River', which portrays the life of Indian people, some spectators who are ignorant of the art of cinema, and tend to show their sordid preferences for the sensational spectacles of commercial films that are full of provocative displays and savage violence and to impose them on to cinema screens, resorted to ugly demonstrations. We hereby express our repulsion to the behaviours of such persons, and demand Cinema Iran and Screening Department of the Ministry of the Interior to screen this artistic masterpiece for real film audiences, and not to show weakness vis-à-vis demonstrations of these persons.
>
> (Tahaminejad 1986, p. 132)

In most film reviews of this era, we see a kind of disbelief towards the technical ability and cinematic skills of *Filmfarsi* directors. Kavoosi claimed that the directors of *Filmfarsi* had no film knowledge at all:

> Filmmakers blame their illiteracy, tastelessness and lack of talent on problems with the equipment. Do not listen to them! Know that even when we put the best equipment at their use, they still make these stupid products. It is like putting the best stationery at the service of an illiterate. When some claim, 'People don't

understand, we have no choice but to lower the value level of the films', it is a pure lie. They put most of their cinematic knowledge in the films. As a rule, they are not able to make anything better.

(Kavoosi 1961a, p. 15)

Kavoosi, who had studied cinema in Paris at the Institute for Advanced Cinematographic Studies (IDHEC), had a dogmatic belief in academic education in cinema and did not believe it was possible to learn cinema empirically: 'So, I only believe in the work of filmmakers who have learnt cinema in countries who have had an invention or own a style in the field of cinema. I never believe in the gentlemen who have learnt cinema here, by themselves' (Kavoosi 1970, p. 17).

Farrokh Ghaffari, like Kavoosi, presented a similar sentiment in his film reviews and writings. In his review on Nosratollah Mohtasham's *Agha Mohammad Khan Qajar* (1954), he wrote:

The scriptwriter, producer and director have not even involved a historian in their work and they themselves have no knowledge of our literary, artistic and historical heritage and do not have enough familiarity with Iranian painting to provide the décor and accessories... One who has not studied history and does not know the people who lived in that era, and has not seen what they wore or used and has not even bothered to do research about it, puts some things together and with a series of *Chale Meydani* (bookish words) and out of the mouths of the actors preaches history and wants to teach patriotism and adversity with foreign forces.

(Ghaffari 1954, pp. 121–27)

Gradually Kavoosi's opposition towards *Filmfarsi* became so intense that he considered even discussing it as a futile endeavour and referred to it as a 'national disgrace': 'Discussing *Filmfarsi* is torturous to me, as it forces me to momentarily think about the incoherent and vain pictures presented in such films. I wonder how the art and culture authorities have tolerated this "national disgrace"' (Kavoosi 1961a, p. 27).

Others, such as Parviz Davaei, another film critic of the 1960s, took a much more favourable approach towards *Filmfarsi*. His pragmatic outlook meant that he regarded it as an inextricable social and cultural phenomenon. In an interview with *Mah-e No* (New Moon/Month) magazine, he said:

I have to say that *Filmfarsi* is not separated from Farsi life, and now this *Filmfarsi*, with whatever characteristics you attribute to it, indirectly, talks about the innovations, tastes and mental needs of our people. By indirectly I mean that the film itself does not reflect the life of our people, but the fact that people like these films and appreciate them makes a bond between the films and the people. In the course of time and with no force, people have accepted *Filmfarsi*. Now, based on the people's understanding and liking, *Filmfarsi* has found its place [...], when we condemn *Filmfarsi* for its lack of mental content, we are in fact condemning people, who mostly out of their own control have not been able to gain enough mental power.

(Davaei 1969, p. 26)

Davaei argued that there exists some aspects of Iranian identity in *Filmfarsi* that attract the masses towards it. The films continue to garner their audience's attention and are found amusing by them despite all their technical shortcomings and problematic rhetoric:

It is an undeniable fact that *Filmfarsi* (in any shape) has opened its place amongst the majority of people (we don't have anything to do with the elite and intellectuals who do not recommend this cinema for people. In any case, they have nothing else to recommend in its place). *Filmfarsi* is among the few goods which has been welcomed by people for what it is and with little external encouragement (such as governmental imposition, heavy advertising etc.) The truth that this fact reveals is that *Filmfarsi* gives people what they need.

(Davaei 1969, p. 14)

In this era, other terms such as *film-e mobtazal* (literally, vulgar or obscene), *film-e Jaheli*, *film-e Abgooshti*, which essentially referred to variations of *Filmfarsi*, entered the critical lexicon. Some of these terms, such as *film-e mobtazal*, were simply more derisive ways of saying *Filmfarsi* and likewise attribute low taste to the majority of the mainstream cinema in Iran. But others, such as *film-e Jaheli* and *film-e Abgooshti*, refer to the appearance of new trends and subgenres within *Filmfarsi*.

I have expounded upon some of these terms in my previous writings, including in my directory of world cinema:

Film-e Jaheli was a popular film genre in the 1960s and '70s Iran. It is also known as *kolah makhmali* (velvet capped) in Iranian film literature. This genre is attributed to a typical character called *Jahel* (literally means ignorant), who is historically rooted in the tradition of chivalry and the manliness of an Iranian, and in the past referred to chivalrous and altruistic persons and those who defended the weak and oppressed in the face of bullies and oppressors. In the contemporary culture of Iran and with the development of modernism and extermination of traditional values and institutions, *Jahel* has lost its former significance and is now applied to ruffians who do not belong to any class or social strata, and who lead a parasitic life and benefit from other people's toils.

(Jahed 2012, p. 26)

As for *film-e Abgooshti*, the term is derived from *Abgoosht* (literally, meat broth) which is among the most traditional Iranian foods associated with the working class, composed of simple, heavy ingredients. In the *Abgooshti* film genre, important sequences often take place inside a tea-house, where the main character of the film, who is usually from the lower class of society, would order this low-cost, yet hearty meal. The films would emulate, and sometimes themselves formulate, the patriotic and cultural affectations of the working classes. They were made with the amusement of such an audience in mind, again featuring lots of dancing, slapstick, comedic sidekick characters, heroic displays of strength and other crowd-pleasing elements.

It is a genre of *Filmfarsi* that came into prominence with Siamak Yasemi's *Ganj-e Qarun* (Qarun's Treasure, 1965), which was about a lower-class boy Ali Bigham (Mohammad Ali Fardin) who rescues a suicidal man from drowning, whom he later learns happens to be his own estranged father Qarun (played by Arman). Ali understands that Qarun had thrown out his mother, a housemaid that worked for him, onto the streets after impregnating her.

The tale is both inspired by religious texts – Qarun is an arrogant wealthy character who appears in the Torah and Quran – and the issues of class division. However, their division is resolved by the end of the tale and Ali Bigham attains the wealth and respect of upper society through his noble and heroic deeds, getting the upper-class girl of his dreams (Forouzan).

Film critics who looked at mainstream Iranian cinema from a political and moral leftist/revolutionary perspective which dominated the intellectual atmosphere of Iran society would denigrate *Filmfarsi* with the term *mobtazal* (vulgar). This attitude mainly stemmed from a populist form of Marxism that considered such recreations as a harmful pastime and a scheme by the government to distract people from important issues. They bore an outlook in which recreation, free time and entertainment were almost sinful (Moazezinia 2001, p. 110).

In a seminar on Iranian cinema, Jalal Sattari gave a definition of the word *ebtezal* (vulgarity) as follows:

Figure 3.3 Siamak Yasemi's *Ganj-e Qarun* (Qarun's Treasure, 1965), the most popular film of the early 1960s Iran that features the iconic elements of Filmfarsi.

> Defining *Ebtezal* is a difficult task as at times it has been defined in particular ways that give it new meanings. But, as you may know, it is easy to draw a clear line and distinguish between *Mobtazal* and *Ghair-e Mobtazal* (non-vulgar). Nevertheless, if we look at Farsi films from this perspective, we can agree on one fact: what is the necessity of showing films that have scenes of sex or violence in them [...] These vulgar films always depict the rich as one against people and the poor as a kind-hearted, mellow and at times stupid person. What kind of psychology is this? This psychology is to some extent vulgar (*Mobtazal*).
>
> (Sattari 1975, p. 18)

Houshang Kavoosi believed *Filmfarsi* to be the very embodiment of *Ebtezal* and considered most of the products found in Farsi cinema to be *Mobtazal*, as he would write in an editorial in *Honar va Cinema* (Art and Cinema): 'If only one *Mobtazal*, idiotic film made would contain 10 minutes of value in its runtime, I would raise my hat to its maker and hail their talents as a unique case example in this country' (Kavoosi 1961a, p. 32).

Farrokh Ghaffari was also keen on the *Ebtezal* moniker, which he used to cite the superficiality and indigence of these films: 'The alert (conscious) viewer sees that the *Filmfarsi* maker imitates the most vulgar (*Mobtazal*) and indigent cultural manifestations in making their so-called popular film... Unfortunately, not only in Iran, but all across the world people demand indigent and facile things... This facile affinity should be eliminated in all aspects' (Ghaffari 1966, p. 19).

In his review of Iranian films, to much the same effect, Ghaffari opted to use the adjective '*Band-e Tonbani*' (doggerel) instead of *Mobtazal*: 'This is a very important term. The person who has made it has done a fine job. A "*Band-e Tonbani*" civilisation, a "*Band-e Tonbani*" artist and a "*Band-e Tonbani*" cinema' (Ghaffari 1966, p. 19).

According to these and many other critics, *Filmfarsi* bore no connection to the real life of Iranian people nor any resemblance to their material concerns or socio-political conditions; instead *Filmfarsi* opted to paint a superficial and unrealistic image of Iran. Kavoosi criticized *Filmfarsi* for its obscenity to the extent that he compared it to a prostitute who earns her living by selling herself: 'The current *Filmfarsi* is like a prostitute who earns her bread through selling her body and maybe that is why it has attracted some of these women to itself' (Kavoosi 1961a, p. 33).

When appointed as one of the censor officials in the Ministry of Culture and Arts, Kavoosi added an act to the Film Censorship Regulations to stop making vulgar films: 'Showing worthless films that propagate *Ebtezal* and facile liking among the masses is prohibited' (Kavoosi 1968, p. 11). He insistently defended his theory that a worthless and vulgar (*Mobtazal*) film had to be rejected with no fear or notice, so that people would not dare to make such films (Kavoosi 1968, p. 11). As a critic, he published fifty-two volumes of *Film va Honar* magazine, but he still argued that Iranian cinema was in need of publications that informed people about the vulgarity (*Ebtezal*) in Iranian films: 'These publications should write about the facts with no fear and have no caution or reserve in these issues' (Kavoosi 1968, p. 11). A few years later, in a conference about Iranian cinema, in defence of his conduct Kavoosi said:

> Regarding censors, the most positive thing done was this campaign against *Ebtezal*. My point was, by inserting act 20, we would be able to stop some of these films and the work of some of these filmmakers. Now, unfortunately, we have reached a point where they ask what *Ebtezal* is! I believe if they act right, it is possible to distinguish between a *Mobtazal* and *Ghair-e Mobtazal* film. Because, the work is mostly in the hands of *Mobtazal* filmmakers, those who

produce superficial films designed to meet the minimum standards of market profitability. This is a facile and *Mobtazal* type of cinema, as its filmmakers need not be literate or possess cinematic knowledge.

(Kavoosi 1975, p. 24)

But Parviz Davaei went against Kavoosi and all those critics who were demanding censorship and restrictions on the creation of *Filmfarsi* in order to facilitate a better cinema. In opposition to such preventative measures he wrote:

Restrictive measures which are imposed with no thinking, like the bans which the office of censor has recently placed on *Farsi* films, will be no good for improving *Filmfarsi*. Reforming Farsi cinema is not a one-night job and will not be done through *Filmfarsi*. The point is, these small films, even though lacking any sign of the life of our people except for some superficial characteristics, are welcomed by the majority of our people much more than important foreign films. One cannot reform *Farsi* films by eradicating its makers and confiscating and shredding the films. These things will not change the level of thought and culture of people.

(Davaei 1969, p. 18)

From this we can perceive that amongst the differing mindsets concerning *Filmfarsi* there was a very clear sense that something was amiss within the industry as it stood. The deviation arose when it came to proposing a solution and this can be broadly split into two bands: those so contemptuous that they chose to dismiss *Filmfarsi* outright, finding it to be irredeemable and unworthy of being considered a national cultural output and an embarrassment on the world stage; and those with a more sympathetic outlook, who perceived this still fledgling cinema as being made to suit a specific audience, and perceived the industry as a fertile base that with the injection of deeper introspective and creative agency could be reformed and guided towards more noble cinematic pursuits.

Intellectual cinema and challenging *Filmfarsi*

The most commonly used and widely recognized terminology for describing cinema that stood opposed to *Filmfarsi* was '*cinama-ye roshan fekri*' (intellectual cinema) and '*film-e roshanfekri*' (intellectual film). Supporters of intellectual cinema were considered outsiders in many respects, whilst the Iranian state had its own intellectual supporters and promoters. Intellectual films, even those made by pro-government intellectuals, often had critical perspectives and prescriptions that aspired to improve the status quo. Nevertheless, intellectual cinema, more often than not, was supposed to be dissenting in its political gaze. Criticism of the status quo of society was one of the characteristics of intellectualism and a point of differentiation from other groups. The intellectuals of the 1950s to 1960s in Iran were not only preoccupied with attacks on the monarchy and Shah's project for the modernization of the country, but also with criticizing the customs and traditional foundations of society (Hajjarian 2000, p. 9).

As a consequence, at the time, Iranian intellectuals faced pressure and oppression from two opposing sides: the semi-modernist government and the fairly powerful traditional forces. In this era, there was a sharp divide between the state and the intellectuals in Iran. As Mehrzad Boroujerdi points out in his *Iranian Intellectuals and the West*, despite their dependence on the state for their economic livelihood, these intellectuals did not perceive themselves as part of it (Boroujerdi 1996, p. 32). According to Boroujerdi, 'having observed the corruption, inefficiency, waste, and mismanagement of the Iranian bureaucracy- in addition to the repressive nature of the political infrastructure, they became further alienated from the state' (Boroujerdi 1996, p. 32).

The Shah's pro-Western policy and its non-democratic repressive nature placed the regime at odds with many intellectuals. On the one hand, there was a kind of cynicism and distrust towards intellectuals amongst the ordinary populace. Jalal Al-e-Ahmad, in his book *Dar Khedmat va Khayanat-e Roshanfekran* (On the Service and Betrayal of the Intellectuals, 1979) evaluated Iranian people's perception of the term 'intellectual' as follows: 'For the ordinary people of the streets and villages, "intellectual" at first was equivalent to *"Fokoli"* (dandy) and neologist and *"Mostafrang"* (one who has been to the West and educated there) and to some extent *"Gherti"* (sissy), *"Makosh Marg-e Ma"* (effeminate)' (Al-e-Ahmad 1979, pp. 45–6).

This type of position against the intellectuals was a reflection of the widespread divide, between traditional versus modern lines. On a superficial level and in critical discourse, the general outlook was the separation of Iranian intellectuals from common people. The inference existed that in the course of the contemporary history of Iran, the intellectuals had propagated discussions or supported ideas that were neither related to the realities of their society nor a point of reference by the majority of people (Saghafi 2000, p. 30).

This public assumption about intellectuals was reflected in *Filmfarsi*. If we consider urban literates and technocrats as one of the nurturing points of intellectualism, *Filmfarsi* directly condemns and belittles this demographic. From the beginning of the 1960s onwards, *Filmfarsi* took a position against literacy by glorifying hardened, illiterate heroes. The literate were shown to be the villains and ridiculed.

In 1964, a survey revealed that the fathers of high school students in Tehran worked in the following jobs: 46.7 per cent clerks, 33.4 per cent freelance businessmen and 5.3 per cent labourers. Up until August 1973, only 2 per cent of urban workers' children and 1 per cent of all villagers attended university (Baharlou 2001, p. 94). So considering that its viewers were mostly from the illiterate, semi-literate or deprived urban or rural classes, it was natural for *Filmfarsi* to depict intellectuals and literate groups in a negative light. In *Aroos Farangi* (The Foreign Bride, 1964) Hasan Tormozi takes great pleasure from watching the dancers at a cabaret. However, when he sees his bride dancing the tango with strange men, he is overcome with jealousy, disrupts the wedding ceremony and addresses the guests: 'It's not bad for you to dance with each other's wives, but I am a driver, I don't like a macho man hugging my wife and dancing with her. I don't like my wife's hand clasped in another man's hand. You might have open minds, but we close minded people are like this...' (Baharlou 2001, p. 95).

On the face of it, this is about a clash of cultures, but in fact this speech and the stance that the film adopts is very much against what was perceived to be the world of intellectuals – indeed, the speech serves as a snide remark against intellectual attitudes. The term *cinamaye-roshanfekri*, like *Filmfarsi*, has been subject to many misunderstandings. Foreign educated intellectuals were ridiculed and caricaturized in many *Filmfarsi* productions. Film critics of the time would also deride intellectual films as pretentious and unrelated to the lives and worlds of the everyday Iranian. Kavoosi criticized the intellectual attempts of Iranian filmmakers as much as he criticized *Filmfarsi* productions: 'I do not like intellectual-like cinema and believe its existence is a sociological phenomenon. The evolution of intellectual cinema in Iran was only an antithesis for vulgar Farsi cinema' (Kavoosi 1975, p. 62).

Many of the critics and opposers of *Filmfarsi*, like Houshang Kavoosi, Shamim Bahar and Parviz Davaei, who believed in creating a different and inventive type of cinema, regularly declared their opposition to Iranian intellectual filmmakers and intellectual films of the era. These critics refused to support any of the early films of the Iranian New Wave such as *Khesht va Ayeneh* (Brick and Mirror, 1965), *Jonoob-e Shahr* (South of the City, 1958), *Shab-e Quzi* (The Night of the Hunchback, 1965), *Siavash dar Takht-e Jamshid* (Siavash in Persepolis, 1965) and *Khane Siyah Ast* (The House is Black, 1962) and denigrated them in their writings. Parviz Davaei's critique of Golestan's *Khesht va Ayeneh* and Kavoosi's

Figure 3.4 Parviz Davaei, a veteran Iranian film critic – photograph by Parviz Jahed.

critique of Ghaffari's *Shab-e Quzi* reflect this anti-intellectual trend among critics. Davaei hammered *Khesht va Ayeneh*:

> No! *Khesht va Ayeneh* is not the film of these people; just as (*Filmfarsi* like) *Ganje Qaroon*, *Delhore*, *Dozd-e Bank* and *Shamsi Pahlewoon* are not. To compare these works with Golestan's works is not completely fair, but in a general sense *Khesht va Ayeneh* defames the intellectuals among the ordinary *Filmfarsi* audience just as *Ganje Qaroon* defames the ordinary viewers among intellectuals… No, Mr. Golestan! Our miserable and semi-literate people, towards whom you have held up your nose and passed by, do not really want a film on the scale of Antonioni (at least not yet…). If you make films for these people, you should know them first… *Khesht va Ayeneh* shows in every part that you do not know them.
>
> (Davaei 1965, p. 27)

In Davaei's opinion most of the filmmakers educated in the West lacked consideration, a nobility that was required for them to truly reflect the national identity within their cinema:

> I have to say that our friends may know the mechanism and technique of filmmaking and have talent, but they have not been good Iranians. They have gone abroad and studied in the West and then come back but remained relegated in the zone of *Filmfarsi* and began to make films. One cannot talk about the lives

of people while standing somewhere far from people's lives. When they speak, what we see them do, and their words do not reflect these issues. This is not a simple depiction of the lives of our people.

(Davaei 1970, p. 17)

It is under such reasoning that Davaei refused to accept any of the intellectual films of that era and criticized them severely. To improve the output of intellectual filmmakers he suggested that they live among people to get a better sense of everyday Iranian culture and society: 'Our intellectual filmmakers should rent a house and get to know the problems of a rented house. They should go to teahouses, among peddlers and swindlers and spend some time with them to get to know their mentality and standpoint' (Davaei 1970, p. 17). However, Hajir Dariush held a more positive view of such intellectual efforts:

> Some of our intellectuals have made certain attempts at direction of feature films in recent years: Farrokh Ghaffari with *Shab-e Quzi*, Ebrahim Golestan with *Khesht va Ayeneh* and Fereydoun Rahnema with *Siavash dar Takht-e Jamshid*. Apart from stylistic issues, all these three films were of a much higher standard than our usual domestic cinema on an intellectual level. But we must note that these works have no practical or mental connections with *Filmfarsi* and were made outside of the framework of this industry or business or whatever you want to name it.
>
> (Dariush 1968, p. 11)

Dariush was among the few critics who recognized and lauded this newly formed cinema. Most critics of this era and even later eras denied the artistic and cinematic value of these works. Esmail Nouriala, another film critic of the time, categorized Iranian cinema into three groups: 'The first group is the pure business-like and commercial cinema. The second group is the peripheral cinema and avant-garde which is not a real cinema. The third group is the real cinema that makes both the critics and learned and ordinary people content' (Nouriala 1969, p. 34). In his review of Golestan's *Khesht va Ayeneh*, he claimed the film was of a high quality but was unable to concede that it displayed the right qualities:

> ... It is too early for us to have an avant-garde cinema in Iran. It is too soon for *Khesht va Ayeneh* – without talking about it being good or bad – to be shown here. *Khesht va Ayeneh* needs an atmosphere which we do not have and it is still a peripheral film. If Golestan had selected a more popular subject, instead of that

of *Khesht va Ayeneh*, he would not face this loss. But he has done an innovative job. If we want to judge him individually; *Khesht va Ayeneh* was much better than *Qaysar*, and the beginning of the real Iranian cinema was that film.

(Nouriala 1969, p. 17)

The New Wave filmmakers were disappointed by the harsh criticism and negative attitudes they received from the Iranian film critics concerning the intellectual and controversial characteristics of their films. For this reason, when Ebrahim Golestan supported a film like *Qaysar* (1948) for its realistic approach to cinema, his support encouraged filmmakers such as Masoud Kimiai, who was heavily discouraged by the cruel criticism of film critics such as Kavoosi. Kimiai explains this sense of frustration and isolation among his generation of New Wave filmmakers very well:

> When we got together, we realised how lonely we were. Iranian cinema was dominated by *Filmfarsi* products with dancing and singing scenes and colourful negatives, while our films were black and white and bitter. But we put it like this from the first. We lived like that, but each of us stood on our own feet independently.
>
> (Talebinejad 1993, p. 82)

Many early stage New Wave films were branded as 'intellectual gesturing'. The works of Golestan and Ghaffari in particular were widely dismissed as being made to pretentious ends with the moniker of 'intellectual' by those who took the term to carry negative connotations. In response to such criticism, Ghaffari said:

> I do not think that having intellectual films is the problem of our cinema. The main problem is that the average standard of filmmaking is low and we do not even make good films by those standards. If we take a poll, I am sure we find that our few intellectual films did not lead our people astray. The problem lies somewhere else…
>
> (Ghaffari 1975, p. 19)

Ghaffari wanted to help close, or to draw attention to, the wide gap that existed between Iran's and other, more developed cinemas. By exposing his compatriots to more challenging and complex films he was showing what lies in the realm of the possible for Iranian filmmaking, rather than imposing self-censorship on his work or simplifying his cinematic ideas and ambitions. He further explained his position:

> When they say our intellectual films estrange people, I believe it to be an inevitable thing. Consider the name of those who make intellectual films now. Consider their pasts and the reason they make such films. You will see they have no other choice.
>
> (Ghaffari 1975, p. 19)

Jalal Moghaddam, the director of *Farar az Taleh* (Escape from the Trap, 1971) and the co-writer of the script of *Jonoob-e Shahr* (1958) and *Shab-e Quzi* (1964) with Farrokh Ghaffari, was of the belief that the game-changing issue facing intellectual cinema was the distance between it and a message that would be digestible for the public. He said in an interview:

> I believe that intellectuality does not mean building a private world for ourselves. I do not think trying to run away from people, the people we live amongst, would be a beneficial thing to do. Escaping from society and people reminds me of those who take refuge in drugs… Just to put a space between themselves and the people. I particularly believe that being an intellectual is not something one can bury oneself in; on the contrary, it is something one should grow in.
>
> (*Moghaddam* 1968, p. 22)

The most scathing criticism of intellectual cinema was carried out at a time when these films had the minimum possibility of attaining engagement from the general public. Some of them, like Farrokh Ghaffari's *Jonoob-e Shahr* (1958), were banned permanently after a few days of public viewing. Golestan was forced to rent a cinema privately for a few nights to show his film *Khesht va Ayeneh*, as none of the nation's cinemas were willing to show it. Fereydoun Rahnema's *Siavash Dar Takht-e Jamshid* (Siavash in Persepolis, 1965) was met with the same fate. As Mohammad Reza Aslani, one of the second generation of New Wave filmmakers put it, 'everyone, from the censorship office of the regime, to *Filmfarsi* producers and critics had united in their desire to hinder the rise of intellectual films' (*Film va Cinama*, 1998, p. 26).

Based on the arguments put forward in this chapter, I conclude that terms such as *Filmfarsi* and *film-e roshanfekri* (intellectual film) were key terms of distinction that were made in film critical discourse in Iran from the 1960s onwards. According to Iranian film critics of the era *Filmfarsi* referred to a vulgar (*Mobtazal*), unrealistic and manipulative style of cinema produced to appeal to the public for commercial purposes. On the other hand, *film-e roshanfekri* as a term referred to a more artistic, realistic and poetic cinema that was not well received by the average filmgoer and was regarded by many critics as pretentious,

Figure 3.5 *Khesht va Ayeneh* (Brick and Mirror, 1965), a masterpiece bashed by the Iranian film critics of the time for its intellectuality, directed by Ebrahim Golestan.

snobbish and pseudo-intellectual. Although there were some controversies among critics about the meaning of these words and their applications when it came to the categorization of Iranian films into two main groups, *Filmfarsi* and *film-e roshanfekri*, there was uniformity in their views.

It is unfortunate that these ground breaking films were not fully comprehended or appreciated in their own time. This was partly because their intended audience at the time were unable to relate the films to any other form of modern cinematic aesthetic or philosophical framework that they were familiar with. Outside of the regular arthouse film screenings hosted by Farrokh Ghaffarri at *Kanoon-e Melli-e Film-e Iran* (the National Iranian Film Centre), which were not widely attended and often led to walkouts and heated arguments, there were very few opportunities for Iranian film critics to view anything other than mainstream Hollywood cinema and *Filmfarsi* and its Egyptian and Indian counterparts. Therefore, the benchmark that they held about what forms cinema should take had been shaped by this. Had they been more receptive to the modern language and controversial forms of new cinema that had emerged in France and Italy after the Second World War, they would have been in a much better position to make their judgements.

Although at the heart of things a strong theoretical framework did not exist that would have served to prop up the momentum of the Iranian New Wave, the filmmakers were united in their antithetical approach to *Filmfarsi*, and in challenging it thematically and stylistically. Their shared aspiration was to create conditions for effective authorial intervention in the process of film production in Iranian cinema. In this sense, they succeeded in creating an alternative cinematic movement mainly influenced by the auteur theories that were originally developed by Italian neorealism and the French *Nouvelle Vague*. The primary driving force behind all of these films was the director's vision. That is not to diminish the artistic and technical abilities of their collaborators, as without the ingenuity of cinematographers such as Soleyman Minassian (who was more of a jack-of-all-trades) and Nemat Haghighi, talented sound recordist Mahmoud Hangval, the brilliant scriptwriting abilities of Jalal Moghaddam and the innovative film composers Esfandiar Monfaredzadeh and Ahmad Pejman, these exceptional filmic visions could not have been realized.

Cinema in Iran began with extremely low creative and technical standards. *Toofan-e Zendegi* (Storm of Life, 1948), which was the first sound film made in Iran, came at a time when European and American cinema had already surpassed many film genres, cinematic styles and film movements such as German Expressionism, French Impressionism and Italian neorealism. Thus the emergence of the New Wave Iranian filmmakers in the 1960s was all the more impressive because they managed to bridge the huge gap that existed between the low-quality forms of national cinema and a modern and developed universal cinema almost simultaneously.

By the 1960s, the propagandized atmosphere of Iranian society portrayed the nation as highly optimistic and this resonance was seen in the form of fairy-tale like narratives and dreamlike fantasies with happy endings that were all-encompassing elements and norms of *Filmfarsi*. A considerable number of New Wave filmmakers such as Golestan, Ghaffari, Kimiai, Naderi, Taghvai and Mehrjui held a much less optimistic view of culture and society writ large than these crowd-pleasing *Filmfarsi* productions, choosing to distinguish their work by setting them against dark, dreary backdrops with extremely harsh and bitter worlds featuring desperate and alienated characters, and often bringing films to sad and tragic ends.

In its first phase, intellectual cinema tried its best to build up new aesthetical standards to contrast with the thematic and stylistic traits that are typical of *Filmfarsi*, disregarding the tropes of reconciliation between the classes, heroism, dancing and singing and instead favouring more nuanced tales of dejection, alienation, pessimism and identity seeking set against realistic, gritty backdrops. However, it could be considered that this modern phase in cinema in Iran did not go in the same direction as its European or American counterparts, most likely as a result of the above-mentioned socio-political factors, which were unique to Iran, rather than a conscious repudiation or suppression of Western influences.

It would be a great mistake, however, to think that the nativist/anti-Western Iranian intellectuals and filmmakers were immune from Western cultural influence. On the contrary, most of them had been inspired by modern European and American philosophers, writers and filmmakers such as Albert Camus, Jean-Paul Sartre, Ingmar Bergman, Ernest Hemingway, William Faulkner, John Ford, Michelangelo Antonioni and Jean-Luc Godard.

The dualistic impact that modernism had on Iranian cinema led to a tension which echoed the development of cinema into a distinct national artform. Serving as both a positive catalyst for change, and a source of great discourse, struggle and active resistance, has come to typify and embody what makes Iranian cinema unique and noteworthy.

Mowj-e No, the lost identity and manifestation of utopian cinema

An element of thought that penetrated the Iranian New Wave was centred around an underlying utopian ethos. Most of the pre-revolutionary filmmakers were in pursuit of a lost sense of identity through which they could portray an idealistic vision of the nation's future, laying out a culturally and nationally tinged cinematic blueprint.

The loss of one's identity is considered an important crux of modern Iranian literature and cinema. The emphasis on this concept is apparent in various media and particularly in the works of writers and filmmakers such as Sadegh Hedayat, Jalal Al-e-Ahmad, Fereydoun Rahnema, Bahram Beyzaie, Dariush Mehrjui and Parviz Kimiavi. For Hedayat, this would take the form of extreme affinity for a supposed pure Persian nationalism and the desire to go back to a period of pre-Islamic 'corruption' by Arab culture. For example, in his three-act play *Parvin*,

Dokhtar-e Sasan (Parvin, Daughter of Sasan) about a girl who is taken forcibly from her family by Arab invaders and chooses to commit suicide rather than to be defiled by her kidnappers, we see this viewpoint very clearly. Similarly, another of his plays *Maziar* is about an Iranian warrior who fought to repel the Arab invasion.

Bahram Beyzaie, whose cinematic and theatrical works also centre on the theme of identity seeking to pin down an Iranian national and historical persona, treated the subject differently. In his film *Ragbar* (Downpour, 1971), the cultural and political identity of Iranian society is shown to be under threat as it is subjected to modernizing forces and driven further away from its traditional roots. A young and intellectual teacher, Hekmati (Parviz Fannizadeh), is transferred to a school in a traditional neighbourhood in the south of Tehran where his modern ways and ideas lead to conflicts between him and the local people. The film takes a highly remonstrative tone when addressing the breakdown of traditional society and newly formed social dynamics. According to Saeed Talajooy, 'at a psychological level, the film manages to reflect on the retrogressive nature of many of the events that form our identity' (Talajooy 2012, p. 121).

Ragbar introduces a new and different type of heroism to Iranian cinema. Hekmati is a stranger who is stuck in a hostile and unsympathetic environment. According to Talajooy, 'the competition of an intellectual and a wealthy roughneck over the love of an intelligent but poor woman may become the allegory of the Iranian cinema or the Iranian society of the late 1960s' (Talajooy 2012, p. 121). In *Charike-Ye Tara* (Ballad of Tara, 1979), the historical man represents the national and historical identity of Iran.

In *Bashu, Gharibe-ye Koochak* (Bashu, The Little Stranger, released 1989), Beyzaie expresses nationalist sentiments while maintaining identity concerns. The eponymous boy has had his home ravaged by war in the south of Iran and has fled from the conflict to a northern part of the country where people judge him for his dark complexion. At one point, he reads aloud from a textbook, which emphasizes the cultural and national unity of Iranians regardless of their religious, ethnic, linguistic or racial differences, to children of his age in order to gain their sympathy.

Ayat in Beyzaie's *Gharibeh va Meh* (The Stranger and the Fog, 1974) is an example of someone with an identity crisis. He is a landless man who one day suddenly comes ashore and knows nothing of his identity and historical past. He stays in the village for a while, but the villagers refuse to accept him. For this reason, in search of his historical identity, he is wounded again and returns to the sea alone. As Saeed Talajooy stated in his Freudian reading of the film, 'Like all of us, Ayat comes from the unknown and returns to the unknown. Like a newcomer, a child, he is surrounded by the gaze of a social "other" that reconfigures his life at every step by placing him in the middle of questioning circles of people' (Talajooy 2012, p. 135).

The oppressive political environment arising from the 1953 coup and the Shah's modernization project in the 1960s not only led to a rift between the state and the nation (especially the intellectuals) but also deepened social and class divisions and contradictions. The New Wave filmmakers were universally opposed to the Shah's government and his modernization policies and social reform implemented in the framework of the so-called *Enghelab-e Sefid* (White Revolution) principles, such as land reform, the *Sepah-e Danesh* (Literacy Corps) and *Sepah Behdasht* (Health Corps). The modernization of society, dictated and systemically implemented from above, created resistance among the traditional strata of society that fought against modern cultural values and caused a crisis of identity and alienation, the impact of which can be seen in many Iranian films of the time.

The migration of traditional-minded and rural people who left their agrarian lifestyles behind in the hopes of a better life and greater prosperity led to a large influx into the capital Tehran and several other cities which continues to take place today. They had no choice but to endure a meagre subsistence living in tightly packed slum areas of the city. The gap between their traditional lifestyle and the modern lifestyle of the urban middle class widened and caused a dichotomy of identity between the 'self' and the 'other'.

Although, to paraphrase Peter Fitting, there is no accepted, fixed definition of 'utopian cinema', one can still reach a specific definition of the genre based on examples from documentaries and films available to us, and one can list the shared features between these films. Fitting defines 'utopian cinema', similar to 'utopian literature', as a work of art that aims to portray or deal with a non-existent world or a world from the past that no longer exists. This aspect of 'utopian cinema' makes it a cinema of nostalgia that idealizes the past and laments the disappearance of values (Fitting 1993, pp. 1–17).

Most of the *Mowj-e No* films had a sharply critical view of the social and political situation in the 1960s and 1970s. For this reason, many of these films, such as *South of the City* (1958), *The Secrets of the Treasure of the Jinn Valley* (1974), *Tranquility in the Presence of Others* (1969/73) and *The Cycle* (1975–8), because of their critical tone and frankness in showing the bitter and dark realities of society, were censored and banned during the period when the slogans of the 'Great Civilization' (*Tamaddon-e Bozorg*) and the 'White Revolution' of the Shah chanted. The expressionist and melancholic image of a remote and impoverished village in Iran in the 1960s shown by Mehrjui in *Gav* (The Cow) was in stark contrast to the propaganda of the Shah's regime and neutralized the messages of his 'Great Civilization' and 'White Revolution'. The village that was portrayed in *The Cow* bore no resemblance to the villages shown in the rural genre of *Filmfarsi*, films such as *Bolbol-e Mazraeh* (The Nightingale of the Farm, 1957), *Ahang-e Dehkadeh* (The Song of the Village, 1961) and *Parastuha be Laneh Barmigardand* (The Swallows Return to Their Nest, 1964) made by Majid Mohseni.

New Wave films, such as *The Secrets of the Treasure of the Jinn Valley* (1974), *The Cycle* (1975–8), *Safar-e Sang* (Journey of the Stone, 1978), *The Mongols* (1973) and *O.K. Mister* (1979), all have a prophetic nature and show a transforming society that promises a new era in stark contrast to the promises made by the Shah. The idea of changing the political situation of the country is depicted implicitly in a symbolic way. The stone that fell from the mountain in Kimiai's *Journey of the Stone* and destroys the tyranny of the lord of the village, the fake palace that the hero of *The Secrets of the Treasure of the Jinn Valley* builds with the treasure he found (an allegory of Iranian oil) which eventually collapses, and the revolt of the people of the village of *O.K. Mister* against the British agents, all predict the possibility of an uprising that was in line with the anti-Western discourse of the time and anticipated the 1979 Islamic Revolution.

Farrokh Ghaffari's *Shab-e Quzi* (The Night of the Hunchback, 1965), set shortly after the 1953 Iranian coup d'état, opens with the performance of a traditional comedy theatre troupe who have been hired by a modern Hollywood-inspired femme fatale character. In another scene we are presented with a westernized antagonist who is throwing a rock and roll party on the rooftop, whilst in the traditional house next door, a man is forcing his daughter to accept an arranged marriage proposal to a much older man, a direct juxtaposition of the concurrent lifestyles of these people and the conflict that has arisen from such differences. Ghaffari criticizes the ethical and traditional values of a society that aspires to move so rapidly towards modernization.

Ghaffari's *Shab-e Quzi* was the first Iranian film in which the identity crisis of Iranian urban people was portrayed. In this film, which was a modern and free adaptation of one of the tales of *One Thousand and One Nights* (*Arabian Nights*), the corpse of a traditional performance actor becomes an object that is passed from hand to hand, creating a suffocating and repressive atmosphere which

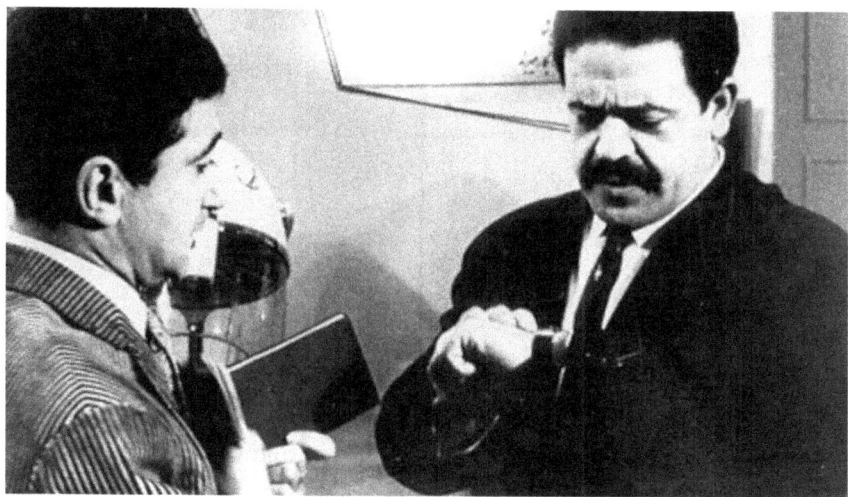

Figure 3.6 *Shab-e Quzi* (The Night of the Hunchback, 1965), an absurd Kafka-esque portrait of 1960s Iran, directed by Farrokh Ghaffari.

resonated with the country's political suppression after the 1953 coup, the rapid pace of modernization of a traditional backwards society and the identity crisis of the nation. We see westernized (Westoxicated people in Jalal Al-e-Ahmad's language) rich people who set up a party with rock and roll music but are in fact swindlers whose job is to smuggle antiques and use the members of a traditional theatre troupe for their wicked purposes.

We also see social distress and identity crisis in the city in *Brick and Mirror* (1965). An abandoned infant becomes a MacGuffin like object, similar to that of the hunchback's corpse in Ghaffari's film, which serves to take the character and audience on a grim tour of the terrain wherein they await the widespread confusion and distress that is about to reveal itself. The main characters' feeling of vulnerability are amply demonstrated as they become deeply traumatized by the dysfunctional bureaucratic system and the widespread immorality, irresponsibility and lies of people they encounter. None of the social institutions such as the police, the judiciary and the orphanage work as intended, and the intellectuals are engaged in endless abstract debates and are of no help in their Kafka-esque predicament.

One of the most interesting examples of juxtaposing the motifs associated with the conflict between the extremes of traditionalism and Westernism can be found in *Brick and Mirror* where a picture of Ayatollah Khomeini was intentionally placed by Ebrahim Golestan in a shot of the copper workshop in *Bazaar-e Mesgarha*. According to Golestan:

It was June 1963 – 10 days after Khomeini's uprising. I took a picture of Khomeini and placed it in the copper workshop, the coppersmith working in the shop asked me, 'Who is this man?' I told him 'He's Mr Khomeini'. – This was in the heart of the south of Tehran, but even the religious people were still not familiar with Khomeini. He again asked me 'who's he?' I told him that he's a Sayyid (descended from Imam Ali) and so am I, that's why I'm putting his picture up. Thus, we established the atmosphere thusly.

(Jahed 2005, pp. 186–87)

For even further emphasis, in the shot where his picture is visible, large metal sparks fly out of the oven. 'I told him to increase the flames as we shoot this part' (Jahed 2005, pp. 186–87). In this way, the director symbolizes the heating up of political tensions and civil upheavals taking place within Iran at the time, and is a foreboding allusion to future events in Iranian society including the 1979 Islamic Revolution.

In the rural genre of *Filmfarsi*, a villager who migrates to the city with dreams of improving his condition is blindsided by the wicked city dwellers, falling victim to their deceptions. The bitter and cruel realities of the city life are at odds with the villager's fantasies of a prosperous and happy life in the city. Their imaginary paradise had turned into a nightmarish and dizzying hell, and left them lonely, helpless and struggling to survive in the filth of the city, dreaming of the good days of life in the village. Such idealistic portrayals of simple pastoral village life that served as a common backdrop to so many *Filmfarsis* were later deconstructed by *Mowj-e No* filmmakers such as Mehrjui in *Gav* (The Cow, 1969) and Beyzaie in *The Stranger and the Fog* (1974) who painted a grimmer and absurdist picture, with much more poverty-stricken, fractious realities.

Daruish Mehrjui's *Gav* (The Cow, 1969) addresses social tensions within a rural setting where a humble man with a deep affection for his cow is driven to financial and emotional ruin after its accidental death. The protagonist becomes so deeply troubled with his impending identity crisis that it manifests itself in a dramatic and haunting fashion as he breaks down and believes himself to have become a cow in front of the whole village.

In Davoud Mollapour's *Shohar-e Ahu Khanoom* (Ahu Khanoom's Husband, 1968) the film centres on two wives of the same husband, one of whom is completely modern and out of her element. A scene of her walking through the town dressed in fashionable Western clothing with an umbrella in hand – as opposed to the hijab – is shot in a way that can be comparable to a tense horror film. As she garners the attention of the men of the town, we see her

Figure 3.7 *Aramesh dar Hozour-e Digaran* (Tranquility in the Presence of Others, 1969/73), a melancholic depiction of the alienated middle class Iranians of the 1960s, directed by Nasser Taghvai.

frantically pass through corridors. Shots from her point-of-view are intercut with close-up shots of an enlarging group of men's feet as they chase after her. The scene ends with what could equate to a jumpscare if not for the light-hearted soundtrack. The sense of threat that she is feeling, from the men of the town, could be seen as representative of society at large not being able to handle such rapid modernization and openness towards female sexuality.

Nasser Taghvai's *Tranquility in the Presence of Others*, one of the first New Wave films, showed a critical approach to the life of the middle and upper classes of Iranian urban society in the 1960s and revealed their loneliness, alienation, emptiness and moral decline. The film was made in 1969 but was banned for its critical view of a distressed society and the futility of life as a high-ranking officer in the Shah's army, therefore it was not shown until 1973. Besides their different film styles and cinematic approaches, Iranian New Wave films show the critical approach of their directors towards modernity through their social aspects which go hand in hand with the political and intellectual discourse of nativism and root-seeking tendencies that were prevalent in Iran in the 1960s and offer their critical view of Western modernity that intellectuals such as Jalal Al-e-Ahmad and Ali Shariati were also criticizing. As Ali Mirsepassi remarks, there was a desire amongst Iranian intellectuals to reconfigure modernity in the national context – nativism in Mehrzad Boroujerdi's analysis (Mirsepassi 2010, p. 117).

The 'Westoxification' (*Gharbzadegi*) discourse put forward by Al-e-Ahmad was reflective of the suffocating, meaningless and empty outcome of the transition to modernity in the worlds of *Mowj-e No*. Al-e-Ahmad's anti-Western sentiments had a significant impact on a whole generation of Iranian intellectuals, writers, artists and filmmakers by offering an emotionally charged 'nativist' ideology that goes against the 'universalist' ideology of the Iranian leftists, which was a dominant framework of many filmmakers of that period.

Parviz Kimiavi was a director that aligned with such thinking. However, whilst Kimiavi's films often grappled with these ideas, his critical approach, unlike Al-e-Ahmad or Shariati, was not directed as attacks on the government and those in power. In a similar way to Dariush Shayegan or Ehsan Naraghi, he wishes to examine and bring to the fore the detrimental aspects of modernity and the dissemination of westernization on Iran's native culture without turning his attention towards political power relations.

In his book *Asia dar Barabar-e Gharb* (Asia Versus the West), Dariush Shayegan, a writer educated in Paris who was highly involved in the worlds of Persian classical literature and mysticism, wrote scathingly on Western modernity and expressed lament for the collapse of traditional ways of life. From this perspective, and in a different reading, it can be claimed that Kimiavi's films were made with a utopian mindset.

When the villagers in Kimiavi's *O.K. Mister* (1979) come face to face with the culture of the colonizers, represented by a semi-fictional character named Darcy (an exuberant performance by Farrokh Ghaffari), it has a hugely detrimental effect on their way of life, as they completely forget not only their traditions and customs but even their mother tongue, and they start speaking gibberish.

Peter Fitting has referred to the representation of a simpler, happier world in 'utopian films' as an alternative prescription to the sad and complex world in which we actually live. According to Fitting, 'hope for a better life and for happiness in the world exists in utopian characters as they wait for a better future'. Utopian films such as *Lost Horizon* (1937) are optimistic and offer salvation and a breaking free from the pain of the modern world, unlike 'dystopian films' such as *A Clockwork Orange* (1971), *1984* (1984), *Lord of the Flies* (1963), *Metropolis*

(1927) and *Brazil* (1985), all of which paint a bleak and pessimistic picture of the world in the future (Fitting 1993, pp. 1–17).

Fitting believes that such films include not only science fiction and fantastical stories that create another world for us, set in unclear futures or alternative timelines, but also more naturalistic stories and even documentaries in which this non-existent world is discussed or shown, whether as a world that is long gone or one that we should aspire to create (Fitting 1993, pp. 1–17).

In his documentary film *Takht-e Jamshid* (Persepolis, 1960) Fereydoun Rahnema says:

> One of the reasons why I paid attention to *Takht-e Jamshid* was that the environment of Takht-e Jamshid and its ruins gave me the opportunity to express different ideas and thoughts about life and art […] Takht-e Jamshid is a ruin that was built thousands of years ago. We bring out imaginations and visions out of an objective reality […] cannot we talk again about the places that have been destroyed and ruined?

Rahnema's goal with his television project *Iran Zamin* was to record subcultures, the remains of the lost civilization, and the glory of ancient Iran through an archeological and ethnographic approach. This goal was similar to the Disappearing World project, a British documentary television series produced by Granada Television in the early 1970s in which documentarians and ethnographers went to different communities and societies to record the cultures that were being forgotten and destroyed, a style of documentary-making that was pioneered by the great American documentarian Robert Flaherty.

When Rahnema began the *Iran Zamin* project at the research department of National Iranian Television in 1970, he invited young filmmakers such as Parviz Kimiavi, Nasser Taghvai, Mohammad Reza Aslani, Manoochehr Asgari-Nasab, Manouchehr Tayab, Nasib Nasibi and Houshang Azadivar, equipped them with cameras and gave them complete freedom to travel to different parts of Iran and record subcultures and remains from the past. This became a series of exploratory, anthropological and ethnographic documentaries of priceless historical and cultural significance. Among the directors Kimiavi, Aslani and Taghvai followed a personal, subjective approach in their films, as opposed to other Iranian documentarists such as Tayab, Manouchehr Tabari or Gholamhossein Taheridoost, who followed an ethnographic and exploratory approach. For example, Kimiavi's vision in *Ya Zamen-e Ahu* (Oh Guardian of Deers, 1970) and *Tapeh-haye Qaytariyeh* (The Hills of Qaytariyeh, 1969) is not the vision of an archeologist or a traveller who is looking for ancient artefacts in the depths of the dirt or the viewpoint of a tourist who enters the Imam Reza shrine in Mashhad.

In many Iranian New Wave films there can be found a sense of yearning for the disappearance of cultures, characters and lost or forgotten worlds that reflect the collective melancholy of intellectuals in 1960s Iran, the nativist discourse of the time, and the idea of going back to one's roots and ideas of authenticity.

In his essay *Mourning and Melancholia* Freud makes a clear distinction between 'mourning' and 'melancholia' (Freud 1961). He considers mourning as a standard process of grieving for a lost object, and 'melancholia' as a refusal to give up on the lost object. For Freud, melancholia is linked to an unknown loss, a loss that doesn't know itself. Giorgio Agamben takes the Freudian concept of melancholia and puts it in a larger historical-geographical context in order to explore the link between melancholia and human existence. For Agamben, melancholy is a way of making connections with objects that are unreachable or even non-existent. Agamben emphasizes fetishism and its relation to melancholia when he describes:

> the fetish confronts us with the paradox of an unattainable object that satisfies a human need precisely through its being unattainable. Insofar as it is a presence, the fetish object is in fact something concrete and tangible; but insofar as it is the presence of an absence, it is, at the same time, immaterial and intangible, because it alludes continuously beyond itself to something that can never really be possessed.
>
> (Agamben 1993, p. 33)

The fetish objects contain experiences of loss and the melancholic mourning over this loss. One can follow Morad Farhadpour and Maziar Eslami's Agamben-Freudian reading in their book *Paris-Tehran* when they claim that the nativism and anti-colonial discourse is also a collective melancholy of Iranian intellectuals who are mourning for a glorious past and a golden age that has been looted throughout history (Eslami and Farhadpour 2008).

Accordingly, one can claim that the archeological tendencies of intellectuals such as Sadegh Hedayat and Fereydoun Rahnema and the anti-colonial root-seeking tendencies of thinkers such as Al-e-Ahmad and Shariati reflect this collective melancholy in different ways. They both defend a national and local identity that has been attacked by an outside culture. This invasive culture has an Arabic nature for Hedayat and a Western nature for Al-e-Ahmad and Rahnema, but all of them have tried to revive or retrieve a genuine local identity.

Grievance over the disappearance of past glory, sadness for the glorious ancient empire of Persia, and the stolen legacy and cultural sources serve to act as the proverbial 'lost object' in Rahnema's and Hedayat's works, which show the same collective melancholy that appears in different forms in the works of Iranian writers and filmmakers of the 1960s and 1970s such as Kimiavi, Beyzaie, Hatami and Aslani. If we look at the works of these filmmakers from the angle of utopian cinema we find both the resuscitation of an ideal utopian world and a longing for the disappearance and destruction of some once-glorious former utopia. Fitting believes that utopian films always contain hope for a new world to be created from within the ruins of the old. In Kimiavi's *The Hills of Qaytariyeh* the bones in the archeological site of Qaytariyeh belong to a world that no longer exists. The ruins of Arg-e Tabas collapse in this film and Aseyed Ali Mirza is its last guard. At the end of *P Mesle Pelican* (P for Pelican, 1972) there is another sign of this loss although the film offers a hope for a better future world to rise out of the desert and the ruins of Tabas. In *The Hills of Qaytariyeh* the bones scream 'swear on the sun that we will escape'. In *Oh Guardian of Deers* those who play the naqareh at the Imam Reza shrine promise cures to the ailing pilgrims who are waiting for a miracle at the shrine. The strange, frenetic dance of Darvish Khan in *The Garden of Stones* and the way he hangs himself from a tree can be a sign of his escape from the present situation and his expectations for all the unrealized hopes and dreams in this material world.

Peter Fitting states that within utopian cinema the madness and schizophrenia of individuals are representations of their attack against the social system, or an escape from the accepted societal norms – a utopian escape from a dystopian situation. Commenting on the portrayal of his otherworldly characters, Kimiavi says that 'my characters are not unique, but the society has turned them aloof and strange'.

P for Pelican is a poetic 30-minute cinematic short about an elderly nomadic hermit in the desert, Aseyed Ali Mirza, who is alienated from the city and urban civilization, having lived in the ruins of Arg-e Tabas for forty years without ever setting foot inside the city. To his chagrin the local village children come to surround and mock him for being crazy. But upon encountering one sympathetic boy he gradually comes to an epiphany that he must await the appearance of a deity in the ruins of Tabas. At the end of the film, the young boy leads him to his promised salvation, his foretold utopia manifests itself in the form of a white pelican in the Garden of Golshan, and he runs towards it whilst clad in white himself. After entering the pool inside the garden, he becomes one and the same with his spiritual beloved, the pelican, and is saved from all of the pain and suffering he had to encounter in the earthly realm. Likewise in *Bagh-e Sangi* (The Garden of Stones, 1976), the hanging stones are an entrancing form of folk art but also represent the connection of Darvish Khan Esfandiarpur, a deaf and mute shepherd living in the desert, with the other utopian realm. The film begins with Darvish Khan encountering a rock as though it is a godsend from the heavens, similar to the obelisk of Kubrick's *2001: A Space Odyssey* (1968). There is a secret in the perforated stones, and there is wisdom in Darvish Khan's stone garden that only he knows and that the audience never witnesses.

Kimiavi's semi-fictional documentaries and narrative films often imagined places with their own natural order and rhythm that was somehow threatened by unnatural and foreign elements, from something concrete such as technology to more intangible outside influences. The simple, primitive, mystic world of

Figure 3.8 *P Mesle Pelican* (P for Pelican, 1972), a semi-fictional documentary film about an isolated old hermit, directed by Parviz Kimiavi.

Aseyed Ali Mirza in *P for Pelican* is threatened by the residents of Tabas and their children, representing the younger generation in general.

In *The Hills of Qaytariyeh* archeologists unsettle the world of the dead and we hear the skulls in the dirt saying 'Now the days of freedom in the kind heart of dirt are going to end, and this is the beginning of captivity'. In *The Mongols* the swarm of television officials rushing to the villages of Iran is as invasive and destructive as the decision by the governor and the cultural heritage officials of Kerman to take Darvish Khan's stone garden in *The Old Man and His Stone Garden* (2004) so they can turn it into a tourist attraction. This destructive element in *The Garden of Stones* is shown in the form of technology or the disruption of village life by the forced recruitment of people into the military. If the invasion of Western culture in Iranian society is shown symbolically in *The Mongols* then it is presented more directly in *O.K. Mister* in the form of an oil-seeking Western colonizer William Knox D'Arcy. In this film, we also see how the locals in the village change and lose their identity after D'Arcy enters their lives and they encounter the swarm of Western culture and Western products such as radios and television sets.

Nature and non-urban places play a significant role in Kimiavi's films. Except for *The Mongols* and *Iran Sara-ye Man Ast* (Iran Is My Homeland, 1999), which feature a few urban scenes, Kimiavi's usual locations are nature and rural areas. I believe that this turn to nature in his films is another reflection of the nativist discourse of the 1960s in Iran, and based on the local monographs and studies conducted by Iranian writers and intellectuals on villages and faraway rural areas of Iran, by Al-e-Ahmad and Gholamhossein Saedi, amongst others (books such as *Orazan, Ahl-e hava, Ilakhchi, Kharg Island, The Unique Pearl of the Persian Gulf* and *Tat People of Block-e-Zahra*). In *O.K. Mister* the slogan 'Dirt, Flower, Flour' is presented as a way of fending off Western culture and technology, and as a way of 'going back to oneself' and the idea of Iranian authenticity.

These films narrate the romantic nostalgia of the Iranian intellectual, the revulsion that they feel towards impure urban spaces, their escape to the peaceful and pure rural areas, and work as one's invitation to go back to our roots, to tradition, spirituality and morality while also being a sign of the collective melancholy of Iranian intellectuals and filmmakers in the 1960s and 1970s.

4

New Wave and the literary tradition

Adaptation from Persian classical literature

Iranian cinema has always been indebted to literature since its inception. The first films in the history of Iranian cinema were adaptations of classical and epic Persian literature such as Ferdowsi's *Shahnameh* (The Book of Kings c. 977 and 1010 CE), *Hezar-o-Yek Shab* (One Thousand and One Nights), Niẓāmi Ganjavi's *Leyli o Majnun* (Leyli and Majnun, 584/1188), Vahshi Bafqi's *Farhad o Shirin* (sixteenth century) and Jami's *Haft Orang* (composed between 1468 and 1485). In fact, the tales from *One Thousand and One Nights* and the *Shahnameh* were the main literary inspirations for filmmakers from the early days of Iranian cinema with Abdolhossein Sepanta, Dr Esmail Koushan, Siamak Yasemi, and later on Farrokh Ghaffari and Fereydoun Rahnema all making films that adapted these narratives, which are not only myths and fairy tales, but integral to understanding the nation's chronology.

Abdolhussein Sepanta played a fundamental role in the formation and development of Iranian cinema and is regarded as the father of Iranian sound films. His film *Dokhtar-e Lor* (The Lor Girl, 1933; a.k.a. *The Iran of Yesterday and the Iran of Today*) was the first sound film ever to be produced in the Persian language, and a surprise domestic success (Mehrabi 1984). Sepanta and other early Iranian filmmakers such as Dr Esmail Koushan and Siamak Yasemi relied on the fondness of Iranian audiences for classical Persian stories and widely known mythology. Their aims – beyond the primary one of entertaining audiences – was to harken to the mythical past of chivalry and sacrifice, in an effort to promote the spirit of nationalism and patriotism and praise the accepted virtues and ethical values of a traditional Persian society that we ought to be striving towards. Abbas Baharlou, a film critic and historian of Iranian cinema, considers the lack of freedom of expression and censorship in films as the primary cause for the tendency of Iranian filmmakers of this era towards Persian classical literature (Jahed 2006).

In Baharlou's view, adaptations of these works were less challenged by censorship, though not free from it by any stretch. Sepanta's experience in Iran's cinema and the ban on his film *Ferdowsi* (1935) were early indicators that the government was uncomfortable with such films if they did not conform with the official versions of history. According to Issari, when Sepanta made *Ferdowsi* about the life of the great Persian poet played by Sepanta himself, the king of Iran Reza Shah ordered the sezure of his film because the poet did not bow before the Qaznavi king in the film (Issari 1989, p. 109).

Sepanta, in an interview with Jamal Omid in 1969, states he had to reshoot scenes involving Ferdowsi at the court of Sultan Mahmoud Qaznavi in order to have his film released in Iran (Issari 1989, p. 109).

Sepanta had a great gift for presenting modern perspectives on classical literature but his particular circumstances, including the absence of technical equipment and the political conditions of the country, presented an insurmountable obstacle. Despite the enthusiasm and efforts of Sepanta, Koushan and Yasemi in adapting these tales, their films were highly marred by technical weaknesses and defects in storytelling, directing, acting and costume design. It is undeniable that in this period, technical standards of Iranian cinema were still not good enough to create satisfactory adaptations of great Persian narratives. These films never succeeded in portraying the epic glory of the *Shahnameh* or the richness of Persian romantic poetry on the screen.

Ahmad Mir Ehsan, writer and film critic, argues that unlike Iran, cinema in the West appeared as a modern phenomenon amidst a modern society, whereas cinema grew in Iran in the heart of a traditional society. It was brought to Iran by the King of Qajar as a tool of entertainment for members of the monarchy and the royal court (Jahed 2006).

According to Mir Ehsan, cinema was created in the West in a period when modern literature had already established itself for many decades and there was exposure to it in fiction writing, but cinema in Iran began to find its way after only a decade of experimentation with modern literature. In Mir Ehsan's view, the many factors that made adaptation a meaningful practice in American cinema did not exist in 1950s Iran. As a result, Iranian filmmakers were in a situation that did not allow them to use modern Persian fiction as a source of film adaptations. Nevertheless many Iranian filmmakers looked at classical Persian literature as ready-made material for films, because the craft and technique that goes into writing a skillful screenplay was almost entirely absent from Iranian cinema at the time.

Later fantasy and folktales

Stories from the *Shahnameh* and other Persian classical poems were not the only literary sources for Iranian filmmakers of sound films, particularly during the 1950s. They also displayed great interest in a number of folktale collections that were popular among the general public, particularly *Shirin o Farhad*, *Amir Arsalan-e Namdar* (The Renowned Amir Arsalan), *Samak-e Ayyar*, *Hossein Kord-e Shabestari*, *Youssef o Zolaikhah*, *Leyli o Majnun*, and *Hassan Kachal* (Hassan the Bald).

Such interest was also extended to the stories of some popular writers of the 1950s including Hosseingholi Musta'an, Mohammad Hejazi, Iraj Mastaan, Arvenaghi Kermani and Kurous Baba'i because the adaptation of their writings all but guaranteed the success of these films and more spectators to fill the cinema halls.

The change in course for the types of adaptation in Iranian cinema was, in my belief, spurred by the profound changes in the social space of Iran in the 1950s. When we review the 1950s, adaptations began to focus more on modern stories almost alongside the same timeline as the shift to modernization among the broader populace. In this way, the themes and ethical values commonly used in Persian folktales and popular stories, adapted to time, are transmitted accurately to Iranian films. Between 1950 and 1952 literary adaptations of popular folktales were serialized in periodicals. The most important film adaptations based on these stories were *Parichehr* (1951) by Fazlullah Baygan based on Mohammad Hejazi's serial story, *Hakem-e Yek Rooz-e* (Ruler for a Day, 1952), which was directed by Parviz Khatibi based on his own play *Jonon-e Hokoumat* (The Madness of Power, 1951), and *Gonahkar* (The Guilty, 1953) directed by Mehdi Gerami based on a short story by Hosseinqoli Mosta'an. Nevertheless, even these new adaptations suffered from the same lack of technique and weakness in narrative structure that plagues all *Filmfarsi*.

The 1960s and 1970s saw a resurgence of adaptations based on Persian folktales and oral literature including *Amir Arsalan-e Namdar* (The Renowned Amir Arsalan, 1966) and *Nasim-e Ayyar* (1967) by Esmail Koushan; *Hossein Kord-e Shabestari* and *Youssef va Zolaikhah* (Joseph and Zuleika, 1968) by Mehdi Ra'ais Firouz; *Shirin o Farhad* (Shirin and Farhad, 1970) by Esmail Koushan; *Leyli o Majnun* (Leyli and Majnun, 1970) by Siamak Yasemi; and Ali Hatami's *Hassan Kachal* (Hassan the Bald, 1970).

Figure 4.1 A poster of *Nasim-e Ayyar* (1967) directed by Esmail Koushan.

Among these, Ali Hatami's *Hassan Kachal* was the most creative adaptation of a very famous Persian folktale. Hatami was fascinated with Iranian traditional performances, folk and classic literature and history, especially the history of the Qajar dynasty, although his renditions of this era failed to satisfy Iranian critics who were quick to fault the verisimilitude or supposed historical accuracy of his films as well as his personalized and extravagant narratives and takes on history. Critics failed to see the authenticity of his creative expression and his attempts to tap into the strong dramatic capacities that reside in Iranian classic and folk literature, and had hitherto not been realized in cinematic form. A playwright and scriptwriter himself, Hatami managed to create linguistically complicated and culturally intricate worlds, so it seems the critics and audience of the time were unfair in not crediting the director for his powerful formalist approach towards cinema and the strong affinity he had for symmetrical compositions and tableaux-style *mise-en-scène* influenced by Iranian coffee-house paintings and miniatures. He made films in different genres including comedy, history, melodrama and musical. The varied styles and genres in *Hassan Kachal* made him a unique figure among his New Wave peers. Hatami's *Hassan Kachal* and later *Baba Shamal* (1971) bore significant differences from other adapted films of this era and earlier.

Interaction between *Mowj-e No* and modern literature

The 1960s was the 'golden era' of Iranian literature, drama and art, a period in which cinematic, dramatic and literary discourses enriched each other, but this strong interaction between modern literature, theatre and cinema that is an important feature of the movement has never before been investigated. So, in the section that follows I explore the interactive relationship between the New Wave movement (*Mowj-e No*) and its literary and dramatic sources. One notable characteristic of the 1960s was the expansion of the cultural and artistic spheres of society, despite the crackdowns on political activism and the shutdown of parties which stood against the Shah and the dictatorship. At the beginning of the 1960s, starting with the students' movement, the younger generation began to show signs of a major shift in mentality. The struggle between the givens of tradition and the new modes of life suggested by modernity was entering a new stage with new forms of hybridity – progressive, retrogressive, revolutionary, Islamist, Marxist, etc – evolving among the people.

After experiencing defeat on political and military fronts during the 1953 coup, the Iranian intellectuals of the 1960s tried to express their dissatisfaction through the medium of literature and cinema, and relied on heavy utilization of metaphorical and allegorical language as means to evade censorship efforts. There was an expectation of relative leniency on the part of the Shah's government, who had no choice but to let certain things slide in order to bolster the regime's image after oppressive measures were taken during and after the 1953 conflicts. The transition to modern practices was taking place rapidly in a top-down approach with some grassroots, creative approaches in different fields and development and renovation programmes pushing Iranians from a feudal, traditional society to a dependent capitalist one with a modern façade, and the political, class and populational structure of Iran changed in parallel. With the emergence of the middle class, society was exposed to drastic social changes and the competition between this class and the aristocratic groups was exacerbated. The number of intellectuals in society increased as a result of new educational policies and intensified the rivalry. Relying on the oppression of all opposition groups and perceived threats after the formation of SAVAK (Iran's secret police and security forces during the Shah's reign), the Shah was now confident that the bedrock of his government was strong. Thus, his main target was to keep the middle class and the intellectuals in line with the state, and so the state permitted a relative degree of freedom in cultural and artistic activities. The same freedoms were not extended to more overt forms of political activism by the SAVAK.

Despotism and oppression had stopped the natural growth of thought and artistic innovation in society. Nevertheless, the regime knew that it needed to have a presence in international artistic gatherings and to promote semi-modern policies, even if it was purely for the sake of appearances. Thus, it had no choice but to make modern liberal gestures in order to ingratiate leading scholars and artists. It maintained full control whilst presenting an image of tolerance, liberalism and democracy. This semi-open political and cultural atmosphere led to serious changes in the fields of literature, art and cinema. It allowed for a certain degree of political and cultural reform. It was under these circumstances that literature and cinema took up the banner of political and social reflection and set out to reflect the problems of society in forms that presented new aesthetic experiences and ideas.

The change in approach in literature, namely poetry, fiction and also drama, had come slightly earlier than any sign of change in the quality of cinematic products, but cinema entered this field eventually, as a natural extension of that movement. The attention of intellectuals to social and political issues and

Figure 4.2 Behrouz Vosoughi in *Tangsir* (1973), Amir Naderi's epic and realistic adaptation from Sadegh Chubak's novel.

their tendency to reflect social imbalances and conflicts between tradition and modernity, gradually led to the formation of a new style in literature and cinema. This style was rooted in their outlook towards the society around them. Thus, portraying the living conditions of people presented a form of realism that made a stand against the existing system. We can search for examples of this realistic tendency in literature in the works of writers such as Jalal Al-e-Ahmad, Ebrahim Golestan, Mahmoud Dowlatabadi, Ahmad Mahmoud and Gholamhossein Sa'edi and poets such as Nima Youshij, Forough Farrokhzad and Ahmad Shamlou.

Concurrent to the growth of *Filmfarsi* in the 1960s and its relationship with the common people, the imperative for an elevated cinema was brought about by the middle class and their cultural agents. In this era, criticism against *Filmfarsi* and its aesthetic elements was pervasive in the film magazines and among film critics. The New Wave of Iranian cinema was born in such a political and cultural context with many internal and external factors contributing to its formation.

One of the important factors in the creation of the New Wave in Iran was the establishment of *Kanoon-e Melli-e Film-e Iran* (the National Iranian Film Centre) in the 1950s. Set up in 1949 by Farrokh Ghaffari, the influence of this film club was critical to the accessibility and promotion of film culture in Iran. It was at this centre that Iranian filmmakers had a chance to watch the most important films of the history of cinema, which had never been released in Iran, and became familiar with different genres, trends, styles and cinematic movements of the day.

> Kamran Shirdal, a young member of the New Wave movement who came to the scene later in the 1970s describes how Farrokh Ghaffari's film club and similar film clubs of the 1950s influenced the development of the New Wave filmmakers of his generation: 'cinema clubs were very effective and acquainted us with the world of cinema and its masterpieces. When I was young, I escaped from school to attend the screenings of the film club that was run by Farrokh Ghaffari'.
>
> (Talebinejad 1993, p 171)

As I have detailed in previous chapters, film criticism also played a key role in the formation of Iran's New Wave. Indeed, in the 1960s and 1970s the famous intellectual and literary figures of the time such as Jalal-e Al-e Ahmad and Reza Barahani engaged in film criticism and would commonly employ cinematic references in their writings on literature. Al-e Ahmad's reviews of Alain Resnais's *Hiroshima Mon Amour* (1959), Ingmar Bergman's *Through a Glass Darkly* (1961), Andrzej Wajda's *Ashes and Diamonds* (1958), Fritz Lang's

M (1931) and Roman Karmen's documentary films were published in *Arash* and other literary magazines of the time.

In the 1960s, there was a great passion for studying and analysing films among Iranian filmmakers. Imports of foreign cinematic publications including *Films and Filming, Movie Mirror, Film Review, Screen Stars, Monthly Film Bulletin, American Cinematographer, Positif, Cineaste* and *Sight and Sound* spurred this desire and furthered understanding.

According to Kamran Shirdel:

> In the 1960s, English and French film journals were distributed in Iran, and we read the reviews of the films in these publications. *Cahiers du Cinéma* was not included but there were many popular film magazines available that we found interesting and quenched our thirst for knowing more about cinema. At the age of 15, I reviewed Vittorio De Sica's *The Last Station* (1953) in a film magazine and I criticized De Sica for his switching from neorealism to romantic comedies in Italian cinema.
>
> (Talebinejad 1993, pp. 171–78)

But among all the internal and external factors that contributed to the formation of the New Wave, modern Persian literature was the most definitive, as the movement grounded itself in the modern Persian literature of the 1960s and 1970s. Thus, we witnessed the effective collaboration and co-thinking which led to the creation of some outstanding *Mowj-e No* films such as *Gav* (The Cow, 1969), *Tranquility in the Presence of Others* (1969/73) and *Prince Ehtejab* (1974).

According to Saeed Talajooy, 'the Iranian New Wave was the child of Iranian drama and literature; its most celebrated works were produced by filmmakers who worked with novelists/dramatists or themselves had literary/dramatic backgrounds' (Talajooy 2019, p. 8).

From the 1920s onwards, but particularly from the mid 1950s, modern Iranian writers, whose styles and structures were in dialogue with those of American and European writers, introduced and developed new forms of narratives, characterization and plot development which would be radically different from the classical tradition of story writing in Iran. Whereas most of the Iranian writers were under the influence of Soviet writers and social realism and writers such as Maxim Gorky or Mikhaïl Cholokhov, there were also a few writers such as Ebrahim Golestan, Gholamhossein Sa'edi, Houshang Golshiri, Bahram Sadeghi and Bahman Forsi who preferred to write in styles similar to Hemingway, Faulkner, Proust, Kafka, Beckett and Camus. Modern writers, such as Golestan, Sa'edi and Chubak, looked carefully at society and the challenges of a transitional period and tried to reflect them in their novels and short stories. Thus, modernism as set forth by these writers was the paradigm by which the new generation of writers and New Wave filmmakers in Iran were determined to transform the nature of these cultural fruits. Among them, Ebrahim Golestan was a prominent exemplar of this tendency in both literature and cinema. Golestan, a prominent story writer and translator, before making *Brick and Mirror* (1965), instead of adapting his own stories, went to another writer, Sadegh Chubak, and bought the rights of his novel *Tangsir* and his short story *Vaghti Darya Toofani Shod* (When the Sea Became Stormy) although he later entrusted the rights for *Tangsir* to Amir Naderi for a screen adaptation, and the production of *Darya* (The Sea, 1962) based on *When the Sea Became Stormy* was left unfinished due to production difficulties and actor conflicts. Golestan's collection of stories, documentaries and his two long feature films *Khesht va Ayeneh* (Brick and Mirror, 1965) and *Asrar-e Ganj-e Darre-ye Jenni* (The Secrets of the Treasure of the Jinn Valley, 1974) proferred a kind of realism in form and content and helped break the boundaries created by traditional moralistic literature and their new, vulgar offshoots in pulp fiction and *Filmfarsi*.

The concept of modern and intellectual cinema had been used in the ongoing battle between popular and art cinema in Iran as described in the earlier chapters. The relationship between cinema and literature became stronger in the 1960s and arguably most of the outstanding New Wave films of that time were based on Persian novels, short stories and dramatic plays. The intellectual atmosphere of the 1960s was overloaded with literature and art. As Masoud Kimiai, one of the pioneers of the New Wave movement, describes: 'literature in the country opened up sooner than cinema. The political language of Golestan, Hedayat, Nima, Shamlou and Akhavan set our path' (Talebinejad 1993, pp. 82–9).

It was only after the formation of the New Wave cinema in Iran that serious adaptations were made on the basis of remarkable Iranian novels and short stories including *Gav* (The Cow, 1969), *Tangsir* (1973), *Shohar-e Ahu Khanoom* (Ahu Khanoom's Husband, 1968), *Shab-e Quzi* (The Night of the Hunchback, 1965), *Dash Akol* (1971), *Shazdeh Ehtejab* (Prince Ehtejab, 1974), *Aramesh dar Hozour-e Digaran* (Tranquility in the Presence of Others, 1969/73), *Malakout* (Divine One, 1976), *Sayeh-ha-ye Boland-e Baad* (The Long Shadows of the Wind, 1979) and *Dayereh-ye Mina* (The Cycle, 1975–8), all made by the New Wave filmmakers.

Figure 4.3 *Shohar-e Ahu Khanoom* (Ahu Khanoom's Husband, 1968), one of the first serious attempts in literary adaptation in Iranian cinema, directed by Davoud Mollapour.

Sa'edi's and Golshiri's contributions to cinema were also significant. They collaborated with New Wave filmmakers such as Mehrjui, Taghvai and Farmanara in scriptwriting and created an opportunity to see the cinema/literature relationship as a prism through which one could understand the dynamics of the critical discourse and the cultural debates taking place at the time regarding the future of both Iranian cinema and literature as modern phenomena. It happened at a time when the project of modernization by the Shah's government was in full swing, there was an intensive interest in cinema among ordinary filmgoers and intellectuals and new life was being injected into Iranian literature.

5

The external influences

One of the arguments in this book is that the films made by Iranian New Wave filmmakers are distinctive examples of Deleuzian time-image cinema. By employing Deleuzian film theory, I try to position my research within its wider context. The French philosopher and film theorist, Gilles Deleuze, suggests that we can identify two main contrasting forms of cinema. In the first volume of his book *Cinema*, he deals with various movement images of classical cinema: perception-image, affect image and action-image. The second volume of his book 'deals with the forms of the direct image of modern cinema' (Hugh Tomlinson and Robert Galeta's introduction to Deleuze 2005, p. xvi). For Deleuze, 'the movement-image is a form of spatialized cinema: time determined and measured by movement. In the time-image, which finds its archetype in the European modernist or art film, characters find themselves in situations where they are unable to act and react in a direct, immediate way, leading to what Deleuze calls a breakdown in the sensor-motor system' (Totaro 1999).

Deleuze considers the Second World War as a break between movement-image and time-image because the post-war period in Europe greatly increased those situations that we no longer know how to react to, in spaces that we no longer know how to describe. This is reflected in neorealist films such as *Europe '51* (1952), *Stromboli* (1950), *Germany, Year Zero* (1948) and *Bicycle Thieves* (1948) (Deleuze 2005, p. xi).

According to Deleuze, neorealism is a transition stage between these two kinds of images. The war has shaken the 'action-image', which was the main characteristic of American cinema. According to Deleuze, 'it was the crisis of both the action-image and the American Dream' (Deleuze 1986, p. 210), a crisis 'which only had their full effect after the war, some of which were social, economic, political, moral and others more internal to art, to literature and to the cinema in particular' (Deleuze 1986, p. 206). Deleuze recognizes five characteristics of the new image that appeared after the Second World War: 'the dispersive situation, the deliberately weak links, the voyage form, the consciousness of clichés and the condemnation of the plot'. In Deleuze's account, 'it was Italian neorealism which forged these five characteristics' (Deleuze 1986, pp. 210–12). Deleuze argues that the French New Wave cannot be defined unless we try to see that it has retraced the path of Italian neorealism for its own purposes – even if it means going in other directions as well (Deleuze 2005, p. 9). Deleuze's argument is relevant in the modern and intellectual trajectory of New Wave cinema in Iran.

The footprint of Italian neorealism

Italian neorealism was a cinematic movement that began as a response to the political and economic situation in Italy after the Second World War. The main characteristics of neorealism are perspectives of the poor and the working class, filming outdoors on location in poor neighbourhoods and the countryside, and using local people as well as professional actors. Neorealist films address critical issues such as poverty, oppression, injustice and desperation in post-war Italian society. They demonstrate a powerful sense of the ordeal of ordinary people suppressed by their political and social conditions that are out of their control.

The term *neorealism* was coined in 1943 by the Italian film critic and scriptwriter Antonio Pietrangeli in his review of Luchino Visconti's *Ossessione* (1942) (Cardullo 2011, p. 22). There has been uncertainty surrounding the exact timeline and which films constitute the neorealist movement, but its defining characteristics of being set on location in the streets and fields where its protagonists lived and worked and the use of non-professional actors playing weakened and uncertain characters are clear. These neorealistic elements can be found in the films of Roberto Rossellini, Luchino Visconti, Pietro Germi, Giuseppe De Santis and Vittorio De Sica in films such as *Rome, Open City* (1945), *Shoeshine* (1946), *Paisan* (1946), *Bicycle Thieves* (1948) and *The Earth Trembles* (1948). These films were a backlash against not only mainstream Italian cinema dominated by 'White Telephones' (*Telefoni Bianchi*) melodramas but also the socio-economic situation of post-war Italy.

Cesare Zavattini, an Italian scriptwriter and neorealist theoretician who collaborated with Vittorio De Sica on some important neorealist films such as *Bicycle Thieves* (1948), tried to specify the main characteristics of neorealism in his manifesto 'Some Ideas on the Cinema' published in 1952. According to Zavattini, in neorealism 'the camera has a hunger for reality and the invention of plots to make reality palatable or spectacular is a flight from the historical richness as well as the political importance of actual, everyday life' (Cardullo 2011, p. 22).

The intention of neorealist films was to display real life, similar to documentary films. They refused to use adornments or film in a studio environment. In fact, neorealism was the first cinematic movement that liberated filmmaking from the artificial confines of the Italian and the Hollywood-inspired studio system. What makes neorealism a significant movement in the history of cinema is the way in which it aims to observe and record the reality of daily life within a work of cinematic fiction.

As Gilles Deleuze states in the second volume of *Cinema*, 'neorealism invented a new type of image, which Bazin suggested calling fact-image' (Deleuze 2005, p. 1). Deleuze justifies utilization of the 'sequence shot' by neorealist filmmakers such as Rossellini and De Sica instead of the use of montage when he says: 'instead of representing an already deciphered real, neorealism aimed at an always ambiguous, to be deciphered real, this is why the sequence shot tended to replace the montage of representations' (Deleuze 2005, p. 1). Therefore the 'sequence shot' or long take is considered as an essential stylistic approach in capturing the reality in neorealism. André Bazin even 'considered this not just one aesthetic option among others but in fact the very essence of modern cinematic realism' (Cardullo 2011, p. 9).

According to Pierre Sorlin, in neorealist films, 'unemployment, misery and loneliness are the crises of post-war Italy' (1991, p. 113). In *Bicycle Thieves* (1948), 'unemployed Antonio Ricci is offered a job as a bill-stickcr which requires the use of a bicycle. The very day he begins working, his bike is stolen and he searches for it hopelessly throughout Rome' (Sorlin 1991, p. 113).

As a result of losing his bike, Ricci's life falls into despair. In his article on neorealism, the French film critic André Bazin explains how unemployment brought misery to the working classes:

> The fear of misery because of unemployment plays the role of a fateful menace in the lives of the people. Living means trying to escape from this predicament.

> Working and, through work, keeping one's basic human dignity, the right to minimal happiness and love – these are the sole concerns of the protagonists of Renato Castellani's *Two Cents' Worth of Hope* (1951), just as they are of the protagonists of *The Road to Hope* or *Bicycle Thieves*.
>
> (Cardullo 2011, p. 22)

Ricci's failure and humiliation in front of his son at the end of the film is a tragic ending that was a common feature of many neorealist films. According to Sorlin, in 1946, for 'those living in the poorest areas, there was no hope'. In De Sica's *Umberto D*, the main character 'wants to die in the house where he has lived for decades, but the centre is being modernised and there is no more room for those who do not have enough money' (Sorlin 1991, p. 119).

Although neorealism was fairly short-lived, it had a profound effect on Italian and world cinema including Iranian cinema particularly during the second half of the twentieth century. André Bazin would say of the Italian neorealist movement that it 'had a profound impact on filmmakers in countries that once lacked a strong national cinema of their own', citing India and Satyajit Ray's *Apu* trilogy as examples (Cardullo 2011, p. 28). Had Bazin, who died in 1958, become aware of the early Iranian filmmakers' attempts to capture reality in the way the neorealist filmmakers did in their films, he would probably have also counted Iran amongst the nations upon which neorealism had an overt influence. Neorealism's influence on Iranian filmmakers such as Golestan, Ghaffari, Naderi, Shirdel and Mehrjui is undeniable. In their works, stylistic elements of neorealism such as long takes, handheld camera movements, wide focus and natural lighting can be found alongside neorealism's thematic concerns with social and political problems.

Louis Bayman believes that 'neorealism was not a conscious movement, and no convention occurred to determine its constitution except imperfectly and in retrospect' (Bayman 2011, p. 57). It can similarly be asserted that the films of many Iranian filmmakers including Golestan, Ghafarri and Rahnema follow conventions which later came to be a defining part of the Iranian New Wave. The New Wave movement emerged from a fusion of modern narrative, poetic images and documentary-style filming – elements that can be found in Italian neorealist films of the 1940s. According to Ahmad Mir Ehsan, Iranian intellectual cinema was based on the 'aesthetic and ideological world of the Italian neorealism, blended with the existentialism of French New Wave' (Mir Ehsan 2000, p. 85).

The neorealistic aspects of Iran *Mowj-e No* are linked with Italian neorealism, particularly if one applies Gilles Deleuze's concepts of 'time-image' and 'movement-image' to this filmic tradition. This is evident in the films of Farrokh Ghaffari, Ebrahim Golestan, Sohrab Shahid-Saless, Amir Naderi and many Iranian New Wave filmmakers which are a distinct departure from traditional cinema and instead place a deliberate focus on the 'time-image'.

In Iran, the New Wave movement had to start from a zero point. According to Deleuze, Italian neorealism challenged the tradition of established American cinema and it was the unique condition of Italian society that made neorealism possible. It was also the particular economic, political and cultural situation of Iran that caused the emergence of New Wave cinema. Like *Bicycle Thieves*, the narrative of Golestan's *Brick and Mirror* follows the protagonist over the course of a 24-hour period, in which a taxi driver finds a baby in the back seat of his car, desperately tries to get rid of him/her, and argues with his girlfriend as she wants to keep the baby. Though one night has been compressed into the running time of a film, this realistic passage of time is also present in the narrative/sub-narrative structure of Ghaffari's *The Night of the Hunchback* where we follow the proceedings of a group of people who try to conceal what they believe to be a corpse.

Farrokh Ghaffari's first two films were exemplary of the Italian neorealist cinematic tradition, in their overall themes and in the utilization of real locations and non-actors. Ghaffari skilfully manages to combine traditional and folk Iranian literature in his films. His inclination towards neorealism on the one hand and the comedy genre on the other, and finding the means to effectively combine these two, was something that few Iranian filmmakers were able to achieve, thus distinguishing him from his peers.

Ghaffari's neorealist approach is most wholly preserved and apparent in *The Night of the Hunchback* (1964), which takes place in modern Tehran in the early 1960s and is based on an ancient tale from *Hezar-u-Yek Shab* (One Thousand and One Nights/Arabian Nights), known as 'The Hunchback's Tale'. However much of the characterization is changed and the premise reworked, for instance in the original story the King demands retribution for the people who caused the death of the hunchback, but there is no such character in Ghaffari's story and the criminal element is indifferent to the plight of the hunchback. In this film, he makes use of farcical comedy to take a critical view of the corrupt bourgeoisie and criminal classes who plunder the cultural heritage and wealth of the nation and smuggle them abroad for their own gain at the expense of the masses.

However, in his final film *Zanburak* (The Running Canon, 1975), Ghaffari tells a more fantastical historic adventure tale which nevertheless retains a strong connection to contemporary Iranian society with the use of contemporary language and a road/ensemble film style reminiscent of the European picaresque genre. This film revolves around the adventures of the main character (Picaro) who goes on self-contained adventures, relying on his mischievous wit to overcome the many obstacles that he encounters.

Whilst Ghaffari's original cut of his first film *Jonoub-e Shahr* (South of the City, 1958) has been destroyed, even in the highly vitiated copy of *South of the City* – released without a director's credit, as a compromise between Ghaffari and the Shah's censors under the name *Reghabat dar Shahr* (Rivalry in the City) – one can track down Ghaffari's tendency towards neorealism and his critical and outwardly social cinema.

Ebrahim Golestan's *Brick and Mirror* mainly drew its influence from the well of neorealism. As Tom Gunning states, *Brick and Mirror* fulfils a desire that the Italian neorealist filmmaker Cesare Zavattini expressed in the 1950s, to film a single day in the life of a man in whose life nothing happens. According to Gunning, '*Brick and Mirror* opens onto a world, the world of the modern city and a passage of time, a single day and its daily round of darkness turning to light and then back again' (Gunning 2007).

In the opening sequence of *Brick and Mirror*, the narrative is interjected by an ominous monologue from a woman who is not a character in the roster of the

Figure 5.1 Taji Ahmadi in Ebrahim Golestan's *Brick and Mirror* (1963).

main narrative. She informs the audience of the political situation of Iran that is the subtext of the story. Although the dialogue does not look cohesive in the classic style, it is nevertheless based on realism and resonates the dread and dark atmosphere in a naturalistic manner. According to Deleuze, Italian neorealism is a film movement that embodies the break between the movement-image and the time-image. Deleuze argued that the external circumstances for the creation of this movement had occurred due to post-war conditions in Italy. After the Second World War, circumstances internal to cinema made it ready to respond to these external conditions, particularly in post-fascist Italy. By Deleuze's account, it was Rossellini 'who in the situation at the end of the war discovered a dispersive and lacunary reality' in *Rome, Open City* and 'above all in Paisà' and 'it is the post-war economic crisis, on the other hand, which inspires De Sica to make *Bicycle Thieves*' (Deleuze 1986, p. 226).

Deleuze's account of neorealism can be applied to the study of the impact of external circumstances, including the socio-political and cultural contexts, on developing the formalist aesthetic of Iranian New Wave cinema. In fact, as Mir Ehsan argues, 'the world of Iranian New Wave cinema seems to have been based on the aesthetic and ideological world of the Italian neorealism, and the existentialist world of the French New Wave' (Mir Ehsan 2000, p. 85).

This argument is also raised in Mohammad Ali Issari's *Cinema in Iran*, in which he discusses the impact of French and Italian cinema on the works of Rahnema and Ghaffari (two of the major forerunners of the Iranian New Wave movement). Issari explains that Rahnema's aim was to lay the foundation of a 'free cinema' movement in Iran, one that is liberated from classical filmmaking structures and conventions – much as the *Nouvelle Vague* did in France fuelled by the *Cahiers du Cinéma* magazine group (Issari 1989). He argues that 'Ghaffari's first feature film *Jonub-e Shahr*/South of the City (1958) closely emulated Vittorio De Sica's *Umberto D*' (Issari 1989, p. 191).

In his reading of Golestan's *Brick and Mirror*, Tom Gunning tries to compare the neorealistic elements of the film and De Sica's *Bicycle Thieves*:

> The essence of neorealist filmmaking (and I think *Brick and Mirror* relates to the broad conception of this movement) lies in using the story to explore a world rather than using the world simply as a backdrop for a story. Zavattini's greatest script, for De Sica's film *Bicycle Thieves*, rather than chronicling nothing happening, uses an essential storytelling device, the search for a lost object. But that film uses the search mainly as a means to navigate the city, to allow us to

follow the man and his son as they search through its various neighbourhoods. The man's loss of his bicycle remains a life and death issue for him, it is never trivial.

(Gunning 2007)

In Gunning's opinion *Brick and Mirror* tells almost the opposite story, but in a similar way. According to him, instead of a lost object, this story deals with something found, not an object, but a child. Apart from the fact that neorealism can be traced back to the New Wave films of 1960s and 1970s Iran, some of these filmmakers, including Nusrat Karimi and Kamran Shirdel who studied cinema in Europe, were directly influenced by neorealism during their studies abroad. On their return to Iran, they tried to make neorealist style films. Kamran Shirdel, a graduate of the Rome Film School in the early 1960s, returned to Iran after graduation and started to make films with a social and realist approach. Shirdel's *An Shab ke Baroon Omad* (The Night It Rained, 1967) is considered one of the most important documentaries in the history of Iranian cinema. The film, which is about the derailing of a train in northern Iran, depicts the event with a sarcastic tone, while putting together various contradicting official and informal narratives of the incident.

Shirdel also made *On the Morning of the Fourth Day* (Sobh-e Rooz-e Chaharrom, 1972) which was influenced by French New Wave cinema and was a homage to Jean-Luc Godard's *À bout de soufflé* (Breathless, 1960). Shirdel explains the impact of studying at the Rome Film School under the supervision of the great Italian filmmakers such as Fellini and Pasolini, in the following terms:

> The rich Italian cinematic culture had a great impact on me and my friends. Although I entered Italy during the fall of neorealism, its influence was still alive, and a very dynamic film trend had begun to emerge from within it. And at the same time a similar cinematic stream was on the way in Iran. When I returned to Iran in the 1960s, I began to make documentary films, and when my short documentary film *The Night It Rained* won the best documentary film award at the Tehran International Film Festival in 1974, film critics evaluated it as a neorealist film. Neorealism showed Iranian filmmakers how reality can be captured and documented, and how to challenge filmic style and the conventions of cinema.

(Talebinejad 1993, p. 153)

In his early short films, Abbas Kiarostami was clearly deeply influenced by Italian neorealism. In one of his masterclasses, he talked about the influence of the movement on his introduction to filmmaking: 'After getting acquainted with Italian cinema, I remember thinking that my neighbor could be the hero of such films. In some places, Iranian culture is similar to Italian culture, which may be the reason why neorealism is so influential in Iran ... It has been on me' (Cronin 2017, p. 187). Some of the most important features of Kiarostami's style in his short films, such as working with children and non-actors, using long takes, simple mises-en-scène based on static shots or very slow camera movements, open endings and paying attention to offscreen space and sound, became the emblematic features of his later films.

The global impact of the French *Nouvelle Vague*

The term *Nouvelle Vague*, meaning New Wave, was coined by Françoise Giroud in 1958 in the weekly *L'Express* to refer to a new socially active youth class (Powrie and Reader 2002, pp. 20–3) but it soon became synonymous with the avant-garde in general (Monaco 1976, p. 9), eventually taking on the same meaning in a cinematic context.

By Susan Hayward's account:

> The term very quickly became associated with current trends in cinema because of the appeal of the youthful actor Gerard Philipe and, more especially the tremendous success of twenty-eight year old Roger Vadim's *Et Dieu Crea La Femme* [And God Created Woman] (1956)...
>
> [It] refers to films made, on the whole, by a new generation of French filmmakers which were low-budget and, most importantly, went against the prevailing trends in 1950s cinema of literary adaptations, costume dramas and massive co-productions – a cinema which had been labelled by the *Cahiers du cinéma* group as *le cinéma de papa*.
>
> (Hayward 2000, p. 145)

More than one factor played into the formation of the New Wave in France, the first of its kind to be identified as such. One commonly cited galvanization was the admittance of Hollywood films and formerly banned French films such as Jean Renoir's *The Rules of the Game* (*La Règle du Jeu*, 1939) in French cinemas after the Second World War; another was access to technological advances, such as the lightweight camera which could be operated without a tripod.

Likewise, it would be unfair to characterize the French New Wave as one completely unified movement. Instead, it would make more sense to view it as a mobilization of dozens of filmmakers, most of whom were involved in film criticism and associated with *Cahiers du Cinéma*, the iconic and influential film magazine that popularized the *auteur theory* (*La politique des auteurs* in François Truffaut's words) in the 1950s, and who were inspired by the momentum of one another to realize their respective cinematic visions. They all possessed different intellectual and philosophical tendencies and artistic tastes, yet all stood unified in their diametric opposition to the prevailing and dominant form of filmmaking in France and the tradition of 'quality films' that they referred to as *le cinéma de papa* (Daddy's cinema), which they believed was on course towards its own funeral (Truffaut 1987, pp. 211–19).

Alexandre Astruc can be considered to have taken the first key step in developing this revolutionary theory with his *caméra-stylo* or 'camera-pen' theory. According to Astruc, film directors should employ their cameras as writers would use their pens, or a painter uses their brush (Astruc 1968, pp. 17–23).

It was this idea which was deployed and developed upon by François Truffaut and his associates at *Cahiers du Cinéma*, who were key in creating the declarative essay, laying out the groundwork for what to do differently in order to elevate French filmmaking from what they considered a sort of pedestrian stasis. The new filmmakers placed a high importance on the impetus of the directors; they believed the director elevated filmmaking, being able to capture authentic human emotions, filming what was considered to be 'unfilmable', which led to the creation of the principles underlying their *auteur theory*.

According to these filmmakers, French cinema in the 1950s was stifled by adherence to cinematic conventions through its over-reliance on adaptations of literary works and sticking to the rules and processes governed by the studios. Unwilling or afraid to break taboos, it adhered closely to formulaic techniques which complacent film critics and bourgeois cinemagoers praised and wrongly regarded as subversive (Truffaut 1987, pp. 211–19).

Truffaut and others believed that the domestic cinematic output was no longer able to meet the creative urges and demands for cinematic innovation by the new generation, and its current structure had to be changed in some way. Thus the French New Wave filmmakers got together to discuss what could be done in response to this, to set a guide path which could be followed by a – sometimes loose, sometimes highly collaborative – collective. They were united in their understanding of the auteur 'whose personality or personal creative vision could be read, thematically and stylistically, across their body of work' (Kuhn and Westwell 2012, p. 26).

In a broad sense, two main trends can be distinguished in French New Wave cinema:

> The first trend belonged to the filmmakers affiliated with *Cahiers du Cinéma* film magazine. The radicalism of these filmmakers was shaped during the time that they were involved in this magazine that placed such high importance on the form of cinema, perhaps more so than the very content of the films. Emilie Bickerton describes *Cahiers du Cinéma* in very succinct terms as 'a film journal that had marked a break with the prevailing regimes of taste in the artistic culture of the post-war'.
>
> (Bickerton 2009, p. ix)

The magazine was co-founded in 1951 by André Bazin, the veteran French film critic and theorist and the spiritual father of New Wave cinema. As Emilie Bickerton writes, '*Cahiers* proposed a very different notion of cinema and turned consensus opinion on its head' (2009, p. ix). But this was less precipitous than was suggested; their influences were cyclical in nature and the *Cahiers du Cinéma*'s writers/critics advocated the classic American films and regarded their directors to be auteurs worthy of consideration and homage. Bazin even visited Hitchcock on the set of *To Catch a Thief* (1955) and devoted an entire issue of the magazine to the director.

James Monaco lists five filmmakers/critics, namely Truffaut, Godard, Chabrol, Rohmer and Rivette, who wrote for *Cahiers du Cinéma* in the 1950s and argued for a new theory of film (Monaco 1976, p. vii). Thus, the aesthetics of the New Wave cinema, in terms of film criticism was situated in the critical response of a number of creative intellectuals to the French cinema of the 1940s – 'a cinema of classical virtues, literary scripts, smooth photography and elegant décor' (Cook 1996, p. 81).

In her outstanding commentary on the French New Wave, Dorota Ostrowska emphasizes the artistic nature of the movement. She states:

> The 1950 was a time when a new way of looking at films, in particular American films which populated the screens of French cinemas after the war, was advanced. It secured a new cultural place for cinema as an art, and led to the creation of a host of new films and filmmakers, known as *La Nouvelle Vague*, the French New Wave.
>
> (Ostrowska 2008, p. 1)

Truffaut, Chabrol, Rohmer, Godard and Rivette looked to classic Hollywood cinema and, under the influence of the most competent golden age filmmakers such as Howard Hawks, John Ford and Alfred Hitchcock, as well as André Bazin's realist film theory, began creating very low-budget films on location and with minimal access to equipment. Their lack of resources meant they needed to be more resourceful and this, combined with their urge to break from protocol, led to improvized solutions. One example is the tracking shots in Godard's *À bout de souffle* (Breathless), which were filmed whilst the cinematographer Raoul Coutard was on a wheelchair being pushed along by the director!

These filmmakers broke away from the common 180-degree axis of camera movement, exchanged tripods for handheld cameras and broke the fourth wall and editing continuity in order to challenge conceptions about realism in cinema. The objective reality that these filmmakers tried to capture was in relation to real locations, natural lighting, improvized screenplays and the camera on the moving hand. In *Breathless*, the iconic introductory scene to Jean Seberg's character, which has Patrica and Michel (Jean-Paul Belmondo) walk the streets, talking, whilst the camera follows continuously through the streets of Paris, there is a very strong sense of authenticity to the location – what we see in the film is really where we are. It does not matter to Godard whether passersby acknowledge the camera or even communicate with the actors.

The second trend, concurrent to the efforts of the *Cahiers du Cinéma* collective, was the *Left Bank*, which was represented by filmmakers with a literary and documentary background such as Alain Resnais, Agnes Varda, Alain Robbe-Grillet and Chris Marker. They also had quite experimental cinematic tendencies, and their films had strong documentary and literary roots due to their background. They were inspired by the literary and enigmatic narrative of the *nouveau roman* movement and writers like Alain Robbe-Grillet and Marguerite Duras, who were themselves also involved with the 'Left Bank' cinematic movement. The *Left Bank* was rather conscious to diverge their aesthetic sensibilities, politics and cinematic approaches from both conventional cinema and the other wing of the *Nouvelle Vague*. They would introduce complex literary fictional aesthetics to their films such as the novel use of flashbacks, voice-over narration and ellipsis.

Among the *Cahiers du Cinéma* collective, they each had a style distinctly their own. Whilst Truffaut's cinema was more romantic and liberal, Godard's cinema was focused on the radical and law-breaking, and he sought to part with all accepted narrative structures and formal rules and patterns.

Jean-Luc Godard was a technical rebel who presented his own style of objective reality in films such as *Breathless* and *Pierrot le Fou* (1965). Most prominently, Godard challenged the conventional structure of film with bold editing choices and stark jump cuts, utilizing long takes and wide focus as means of creating a more emotive and visceral cinema.

Of the *Left Bank*'s proponents was Alain Resnais, already a well-regarded documentary and short filmmaker. His feature-length films like *Hiroshima Mon Amour* (1959) and *Last Year at Marienbad* (1961) can be described as enigmatic, almost transfixing experiences which lack a traditional narrative structure, and were highly unconventional and stylized to the point of appearing otherworldly, even compared to the other New Wave films being made. A key distinction was the importance Resnais placed on collaborating with other writers, as opposed to writing his own screenplays.

Alain Robbe-Grillet, who wrote the script for Resnais's *Last Year at Marienbad*, himself later turned to filmmaking and explored a meta approach, which was a coalescence of his literary style and filmmaking, with erotically charged dramas such as *L'immortelle* (1963) and *Trans-Europ Express* (1966).

These two groups, and other directors who perhaps fell outside of these two categories (Louis Malle, for example) were still close to each other and shared ideas about cinema. The talent that these filmmakers displayed and their audacity for bringing new ideas and perspectives had a snowball effect. These artists worked conjunctly, in conditions that were highly conducive to creative liberty, with relatively good access to financial backing and production methods. Whilst at times they could vary drastically in their cinematic expressions and underlying philosophy, and even may have had their fair share of squabbles, their alliance can be considered indisputable.

There were times when the writers of *Cahiers* and *Positif* magazines would be in fierce disagreement with one another and, at others, they may have been more collaborative – Fereydoun Hoveyda would at different times write for both of these magazines, for instance, while perhaps the more ardent contributors were less willing to do so. One could very easily draw parallels between this movement and the fine arts movement which had the same disruptive tendencies and some level of disagreement amongst their ranks, as put by Joe Queenan:

> The most amazing thing about the New Wave is how little the directors had in common – artistically, philosophically, politically. What united them was a shared determination to breathe life into the corpse of French postwar cinema.

In this they resembled the impressionists, who banded together in the 1860s and seemed to have taken an informal vow to blind themselves before they would paint yet another picture of Horatio at the bridge.

(Queenan 2009)

In Queenan's view, 'Godard made movies with his brain; Truffaut made movies with his heart' (Queenan 2009). It could be argued that their only notable uniformity was in their spurring reaction towards these past elements. According to Dorota Ostrowska, although the *Nouvelle Vague* was rather short-lived – the height of its success lasted only for about three years between 1959 and 1962 – the impact it had was tremendous (Ostrowska 2008, p. 1).

According to Michel Marie and Richard Neupert, 'the years 1959–60 were characterized by the appearance of a number of new directors, spread around the globe, who broke with the aesthetic norms of their times. Their disruptions often paralleled those undertaken by the New Wave, without necessarily having any direct influence' (Marie and Neupert 2002, p. 134). Many of these international directors were seeking an innovatory status within their national cinema and thus may have been reluctant to admit to being directly influenced by this one movement and its directors in particular.

However the international influence of French *Nouvelle Vague* was a near-certain inevitability and was acknowledged by many film scholars and film historians in a variety of settings. To quote Marie and Neupert again, 'This was all a consequence of the international reception of French films of the New Wave that had begun in 1960' (Marie and Neupert 2002, p. 134). Other scholars such as Roy Armes, David Bordwell and Kristin Thompson, who examined French *Nouvelle Vague* from a formalist perspective, indicated the emergence of new trends amongst the filmmakers of different countries simultaneously during the 1950s and 1960s, a development that can also be observed in the rise of what would eventually come to be known as *Mowj-e No* (the New Wave) in Iran. According to them:

> The late 1950s and early 1960s saw the rise of a new generation of filmmakers around the world. In country after country there emerged directors born before World War II but having grown to adulthood in the post-war era of reconstruction and rising prosperity. Japan, Canada, England, Italy, Spain, Brazil, and the United States all had their 'New Wave' or 'Young Cinema' groups – some trained in film schools, mainly allied with specialised film magazines, most in

revolt against the established elders of the industry. The most widely influential of these groups appearing in France.

(Bordwell and Thompson 1994, p. 479)

It was a drastic and sensational transformation of not only French cinema but consequently that of other national cinemas around the world. The widespread distribution and enthusiastic reception that these *Nouvelle Vague* artists received motivated discussion about the nature of cinema and evoked young filmmakers in other countries to challenge their mainstream cinema and the conventions prevalent in their domestic filmic output. It was after the French New Wave and under its influence and legacy that New Wave cinematic movements were propagated in countries such as Brazil, Japan, Germany, Eastern European countries and Iran, taking shape and following different agendas. The subjects, narrative structure, technical approaches and the urge to somehow infuse a sense of reality can also be found in the films of these international artists.

I struggled to find very many direct, or even indirect, allusions to early Iranian cinema placed within this context of being derived from the French, so one could falsely and hastily conclude that perhaps it was somehow a diminished or less acutely observable phenomena in Iran. But even with scant mentions outside of Hamid Naficy's and Roy Armes's seminal books covering the topic in later years, I argue that our understanding of what happened in Iranian cinema from the late 1950s onwards is intrinsically and oftentimes quite tangibly linked to the French *Nouvelle Vague*.

Although such movements truly emerged in other countries in unique and fascinating ways, almost none of them achieved the scope, scale and impact of the French *Nouvelle Vague*. In relative terms it was a short-lived movement, yet one that had a profound impact on the world stage. It was an aesthetic revolution that changed film history and commonly serves as one of the first and foremost topics of learning when it comes to understanding film at many academic institutions, with good reason.

The French *Nouvelle Vague* and the Iranian *Mowj-e No*

For Gilles Deleuze, French *Nouvelle Vague* cinema forms a new kind of intellectual cinema, 'a cinema of the brain' (Deleuze 2005). This, of course, confirms the general agreement that *Nouvelle Vague* put into practice, the idea of cinema as art, which was first developed by the critics and writers of the famous French film magazine, *Les Cahiers du Cinéma*. Roy Armes in his study of French cinema highlights the background of the French New Wave filmmakers as film critics and argues that, 'young critics under the guidance of André Bazin were laying the foundation of a new approach, particularly in *Cahiers du Cinéma*' (Armes 1970, p. 7).

Similarly in Iran, the first indication of the trend was found in the Iranian film journals and publications of the 1950s. In fact, most of the first generation and the forerunners of New Wave cinema were involved in film criticism and writing about cinema before becoming involved in filmmaking. Filmmakers such as Ebrahim Golestan, Farrokh Ghaffari, Hajir Dariush, Fereydoun Rahnema, Ahmad Faroughi Kadjar (Qajar) and Houshang Kavoosi were heavily involved in film criticism and used any opportunity to publish their ideas on art films or quality films in general. These filmmakers/critics harshly criticized the dominant form of Iranian cinema and posed a challenge to the establishment. Soon, however, these critics realized that producing written criticism did not provide enough impetus to change the quality of the films, so some were propelled to move from theory to practice and create their own. Another factor was the significant increase in the number of film magazines in the 1950s, as well as the screening of the French *Nouvelle Vague* films, which created a unique atmosphere for the introduction of the French New Wave and its filmmakers.

Iranian filmmakers were influenced largely by the films screened in *Kanoon-e Melli Film-e Iran* (the National Iranian Film Centre), founded by Farrokh Ghaffari in 1949. It was like a film club in which films by Godard, Truffaut, Chabrol, Bergman and other European modernist filmmakers were shown, often for the first time, to Iranian audiences. It fostered a new-found intellectual enthusiasm for higher calibre and intellectually challenging titles on which Iranian artists could set their aspirations to creating domestically.

In his article, *Zibayee Shenasi-e 100 Sal Sinemay-e Iran* (The Aesthetics of 100 Years of Iranian Cinema, 2000), Ahmad Mir Ehsan investigates the relationship between the French and Iranian New Wave cinema and argues that a great number of stylistic and aesthetic features exemplified in the works of Iranian New Wave filmmakers, such as their narrative, form and editing, have been influenced by French New Wave filmmakers.

The fact that filmmakers and critics such as Rahnema and Ghaffari were publishing new aesthetic views in French film magazines and journals during their residence in France greatly supports Mir Ehsan's view. I would also like to suggest that many cinematic innovations observed in the films of pioneer New Wave filmmakers were the result of aesthetic influences by Godard and Resnais, especially innovations in editing, breaking time and avoidance of classical narrative, which can be identified in the films of Golestan and Rahnema.

According to Deleuze, in French *Nouvelle Vague* films, when the circumstances no longer extend into action, films give rise to pure optical and sound situations. Something has become too strong in the image, something which cannot be reduced to what happens or 'what is perceived or felt by the characters' (Deleuze 1986, p. 207).

As Deleuze suggests:

> It is here that the voyage-form [*la forme-balade*], is freed from the spatio-temporal coordinates which were left over from the old Social Realism and begins to have value for itself or as the expression of a new society, of a new pure present... In these [films] we see the birth of a race of charming, moving characters who are hardly concerned by the events that happen to them... and experience and act out obscure events which are as poorly linked as the portion of the any-space-whatever which they traverse.
>
> (Deleuze 1986, p. 227)

It is in films made by Ghaffari, Golestan and Rahnema during the 1960s that this disengagement with the space first takes hold, eventually becoming a prominent occurrence in future Iranian films. A comparison of the early films by the *Mowj-e No* filmmakers produces little, if any, common micro elements or trends. Unlike the French New Wave, Iran's New Wave did not pursue any specific aesthetic statements. The common element is more apparent in the political statements found in these pieces, which had hardly ever been observed in prior Iranian films. Nasser Taghvai, a New Wave filmmaker with a literary background, disparages the significant and direct influence of the French New Wave:

> Our films were not in any way similar to each other. The only common factor that can be found in them is our views about society. We were all looking for a cinema we desired for. When Kimiai's *Qaysar* was shown, suddenly a wave of thoughtful people entered Iranian cinema such as Hatami, Beyzaie, Naderi and Shahid-Salles.
>
> (Talebinejad 1993, p. 133)

But upon closer investigation of the relationship between French and Iranian New Wave cinema, we find that many stylistic and aesthetic features exemplified within the works of Iranian New Wave filmmakers clearly display the influence of French New Wave filmmakers. These include episodic narrative, shooting on location, breaking the rules of continuity editing and use of free editing style, jump cuts and tracking shots, as well as employing a documentary style. Dariush Mehrjui, a New Wave film director, acknowledges the influence of Italian, French and American cinema:

> I believe that I've been influenced by the works of the great European and American filmmakers, such as Orson Welles, Chaplin, Antonioni, Bergman, Fellini, and the French New Wave. For making *The Cow* (*Gav*, 1969), I had a lot of influence from neorealist films such as *Bicycle Thieves*, *Rome, Open City*, *Miracle in Milan*, and also the works of Bergman and Antonioni.
> (Talebinejad 1993, pp. 113–24)

Mehrjui's portrayal of impoverished village life, his use of real locations and his combination of actors and non-actors are some of the neorealistic features of *Gav* (The Cow, 1969). Like neorealist films, in *The Cow*, Mehrjui explores the conditions of the rural poor. Mash Hassan's (Ezzatolah Entezami) relationship with his cow is similar economically to that of Antonio Ricci (Lamberto Maggiorani) and his bicycle in *Bicycle Thieves* (1948). The cow is Hassan's only source of income, just as Ricci's bike is his whole life, without which he loses his job. But unlike *Bicycle Thieves*, this relationship in *The Cow* goes beyond the economic aspect and becomes psychoanalytic after Mash Hasan's metamorphosis.

Mehrjui also mentions the prominent influence of French New Wave on his films:

> Our films [the New Wave films] were spectacular shocks to Iran's cinema, and created a new tendency among the filmmakers. Just in the face of a crisis of identity with humorous feelings, *The Cow* created a new atmosphere and proved that another kind of cinema could be made. Maybe Beyzaie made *Downpour* (*Ragbar*, 1971) on the success of *The Cow* or even Sohrab Shahid-Saless also made his *Yek Etefagh-e Sadeh* (*A Simple Event*, 1974) later. We made our films and were not supposed to be stuck in the trap of the cinemagoers.
> (Talebinejad 1993, pp. 113–24)

The influence of the French New Wave on Mehrjui's work can be seen in the existential themes of his films which often stress the individual and the acceptance of the absurdity of human existence, his dangling characters stuck between tradition and modernity (*Mr. Naive*, 1970; *The Postman*, 1970), together with his use of illusory images and of long takes.

Like the French New Wave films, most of *Mowj-e No* films of the late 1960s and early 1970s, for instance *Qaysar*, *The Cow* or *Tranquility in the Presence of Others*, have tragic and bitter endings and are associated with the fatality of a pivotal character. In Masoud Kimiai's *Qaysar*, the central figure, Qaysar, is shot by the police after taking revenge on those who raped his sister and killed his brother. In *The Cow*, Mash Hassan, after the death of his cow, which is his only means of income and sustenance, goes mad and considers himself a cow, and eventually falls from the top of a valley and dies. In *Tranquility in the Presence of Others* the army colonel, suffering from mental and physical illness, dies in hospital. According to Mohammad Reza Aslani, another New Wave filmmaker with a literary background, these kinds of ending of the New Wave films represent the historical and political defeat of the Iranian society and are rooted in 'Eastern tragic dramas' – likely referring to performances such as *Ta'zieh*. In Aslani's view, the New Wave was trying to achieve an identity from various directions, and whether or not it was successful at that time does not matter (Talebinejad 1993, p. 198).

Fereydoun Hoveyda, the auteur theory and Iran's New Wave

La politique des auteurs (the auteur theory) originated in the French film criticism of the late 1940s and was later developed by François Truffaut and then by the American film critic Andrew Sarris. It was mainly derived from Alexandre Astruc's idea of *caméra-stylo* (camera-pen) which invoked a notion of the film director as an individual artist comparable to a painter or an author, wielding his production unit like a novelist using his fountain pen (Bickerton 2009, p. 10).

La politique des auteurs considered the film director as an auteur whose personality and individual sensibility and artistic vision must be regarded in studying their work. The phrase *La politique des auteurs* was coined by François Truffaut in his essay *Une certaine tendance du cinéma français* (A Certain Tendency in French Cinema) published in 1954. In Truffaut's view, an auteur director, like a novelist or playwright, has overall control on any aspects of the filmmaking process (Truffaut 1987, pp. 211–19).

According to *auteur theory*, every auteur filmmaker has his or her unique and distinctive film style and personal works that is considered their authorial signature (Kuhn and Westwell 2012, p. 26). According to Kuhn and Westwell, 'the impact of the auteur policy can hardly be overestimated. The initial debate and its take-up shaped film criticism, film culture, and the development of film studies and film theory in a range of cultural contexts' (2012, p. 26).

The theory was highly influential; not only did it influence the *Cahier du Cinema* writers and the *Nouvelle Vague* filmmakers but it also had an impact on Iranian film critics and the New Wave filmmakers. Fereydoun Hoveyda, the Iranian film critic and a founding member of the editorial board of *Cahiers du Cinéma* – who also developed *La politique des auteurs* in the 1950s (Lang 1993, p. 392) – spoke about Truffaut's understanding of *auteur theory* in an interview with Robert Lang in 1993. In response to the question to what extent he agreed with the *auteur theory*, he replied: 'many of us did not follow Truffaut to such extremist views. We only shared some of the points of the theory, namely the reaction against the impressionistic evaluation of films, which continues to be at the basis of most America reviews, overflowing with adjectives like, "superior", "touching", "brilliant", "amazing", "flat", "terrific", "deceiving", "vibrant", and so on' (Lang 1993, pp. 392–400).

Hoveyda was highly respected amongst the *Nouvelle Vague* filmmakers and also maintained close friendships with Iranian auteurs such as Golestan and Ghaffari when he was travelling between Tehran and Paris. According to Dan Geist, 'In 1952 he left the diplomatic corps but stayed in Paris to work for UNESCO's Department of Mass Communications, where he would spend nearly a decade and a half facilitating freedom of the press and media modernization in the developing world. It was during this period that Fereydoun Hoveyda became a core figure in the French-Iranian Film Connection' (Geist 2020).

Hoveyda served as one of the connecting bridges between these two movements and he would help with the distribution and introduction of Golestan's *Brick and Mirror* and perhaps other films in France to film critics such as Jean Duchet, yet he was not necessarily a great advocate for Iranian cinema in the West. It may be a partial exaggeration to say that he was very deeply involved with the Iranian film industry; he would be more than willing to perform certain tasks such as subtitling Golestan's *Brick and Mirror* in French. Fereydoun Hoveyda also co-wrote the script of a short film called *Bon Bast* (Cul-de-Sac, 1957) for Farrokh Ghaffari with the help of Claude Bonardo (according to my interviews with Golestan and Ghaffari).

Figure 5.2 Fereydoun Hoveyda in Éric Rohmer's *The Sign of Leo* (*Le signe du lion*, 1962).

As a filmmaker and writer, Ebrahim Golestan regarded the 'camera as a pen' even before he took the plunge into filmmaking. Like the French film critics at the *Cahier du Cinéma*, Golestan was looking at cinema through the literary prism of authorship. In his conversation with me, when I asked him why he stopped writing stories when he became involved in filmmaking, he answered: 'No I never stopped writing. For me filmmaking was a sort of writing, but this time I was writing with a camera instead of a pen' (Jahed 2005, p. 147). Golestan's idea about using the camera as a pen is the same as French film critic Alexandre Astruc's idea of *caméra-stylo* (camera-pen). In his essay 'Le Manifesto de la Camera-Stylo' (first published in 1948 in issue 48 of the Parisian literary journal *La Nef* and reprinted in Astruc's *The Birth of a New Avant-Garde: La Caméra-Stylo* in 1968), which was a key precursor in the study of cinematic authorship, Astruc equates writing with one's camera with writing with one's pen. In the essay, Astruc suggested that something qualitatively new was happening in cinema. According to him, film 'is quite simply becoming a means of expression, just as all the other arts have been before it, and in particular painting and the novel' (Astruc 1968, p. 17).

At the heart of Astruc's theory was the relation between the filmmaker and the writer. There is a strong auteurist claim in his essay when he writes: 'Direction is no longer a means of illustrating or presenting a scene, but a true act of writing.

The filmmaker/author writes with his camera as a writer writes with his pen' (Astruc 1968, p. 22). In his opinion there is no longer a 'scriptwriter' because 'the distinction between author and director loses all meaning'. Astruc's essay became the manifesto of the auteur theory of the French New Wave, which made the filmmaker, like the writer, an artist engaged in forging a personal style. As Ghislaine Geloin says, for filmmakers like François Truffaut, 'the camera was to become the pen of the twentieth century, and there would be no field that it could not master' (Aycock and Schoenecke 1988, p. 140). For André Bazin, the filmmaker was 'no longer the competitor of the painter and playwright, he is, at last, the equal of the novelist' (Bazin 1967, p. 142).

Whilst the *Nouvelle Vague* filmmakers ridiculed the 'quality tradition' closely linked to adaptations of literature that had become so entrenched within French cinema by the 1950s, and as a result chose to distance themselves from literary works, the Iranian New Wave filmmakers gravitated towards modern Iranian literature as source material. This attitude, in turn, mapped out a history of different and distinct relationships between literature and cinema in the two movements. According to Chislain Geloin,

> In France, film has always had an ambiguous relationship to literature, a relationship charged with a love-hate tension, as film continues to claim at the same time its affinities to and independence from freedom that the cineasts of the '60s – the auteur film in general – turned against the film adaptations of the fifties, for they found the philosophy implicit in making them unacceptable. This attitude was best exemplified by Godard's cinema which, time and again, proclaimed outrageously, no more stories of any kind.
>
> (Aycock and Schoenecke 1988, p. 204)

Unlike the *Nouvelle Vague* filmmakers who preferred to write directly for the screen, Iranian New Wave filmmakers were keen on experimenting with literary adaptations. Their films were the first successful attempts at adaptations to be found within Iranian cinema. There were, however, a number of authors turned filmmakers, such as Golestan and Beyzaie, who preferred to write directly for the screen. It was a time in which film and literature worked side by side, and it was possible for films to be judged on equal terms with literature. Both the New Wave filmmakers and the modernist writers were searching for more accurate ways of looking at Iranian society, and engaged with the writings and adaptations of works by Hemingway, Camus, Kafka, Faulkner and Chekhov.

In a roundtable discussion about New Wave Iranian cinema, Kamran Shirdel, who was much younger than other early forerunners of the New Wave such as Ghafarri and Golestan, explained how the translation of modern Western literature changed the intellectual climate in 1960s Iran:

> When I returned to Iran the New Wave movement was not yet formed in Iran, but the Persian poetry and fiction were at their peak. The intellectual movement in Iran grew in the light of new literary works in general, and literary translations, in particular. Many translations of foreign novels were done by translators such as Mohammad Ghazi, Parviz Dariush and others contributing to this intellectual movement. I have been greatly influenced by Western literature. You may not see this clearly in my films, but I know for example how far Kafka and his translations to Persian have shaped my mind and my soul. Of course, there were also Hemingway and Guy de Maupassant. That is why most Iranian intellectual filmmakers at that time were fascinated by modern Western literature.
>
> (Talebinejad 1993, pp. 171–78)

Houshang Golshiri, a modernist writer whose two stories were originally adapted by Bahman Farmanara, noted:

> Iranian cinema to some extent owes a debt to the stories of contemporary fiction writers, and most of the outstanding films of the pre-revolutionary cinema, were adapted from contemporary stories. Even some of their directors were originally story writers or playwrights, from Golestan to Taghvai, Zakaria Hashemi and Beyazie.
>
> (Golshiri 2009, p. 64)

Davoud Mollapour's *Shohar-e Ahu Khanoom* (Ahu Khanoom's Husband, 1968) was one of the first Iranian film adaptations of an important contemporary novel written by the realist novelist Ali Mohammad Afghani. Saeed Talajooy regards the film as one of the most important films of the 1960s along with Mehrjui's *Gav* (The Cow), both of which were sourced from the same literary and dramatic pool (Talajooy 2019, p. 8)

Ahu Khanoom's Husband was initially set to be made by Arby Ovanessian, one of the second-generation filmmakers of the New Wave, with Mollapour as the producer and cinematographer of the film. Ovanessian filmed a few scenes of the novel, but because of disagreements with Mollapour, he left the project and Mollapour himself directed the film as well as conducting the cinematography and production, with remarkable technical competence. *Ahu Khanoom's Husband* is based on a novel that reflects the conflict between traditional values and practices and modernity, showing the profound social and cultural divide of Iranian society in the 1960s. In Hassan Kamshad's description of the novel:

> The significance of the book, apart from its literary and artistic value, lies in the fact that it is a social history, belonging to a certain time and place, and containing a message. Whatever our criticism of Afghani as a writer, there is no doubt that his novel is one of the very few contributions to modern Iranian fiction that clearly herald a promising future for Persian letters – a future compatible with a great literary heritage.
>
> (Kamshad 1996, p. 134)

Figure 5.3 Mehri Vedadian in *Shohar-e Ahu Khanoom* (Ahu Khanoom's Husband, 1968) directed by Davoud Mollapour.

Ahu is a traditional-minded and passive woman, but Homa is the complete opposite, a modern woman who refuses to be subservient to her husband and who is proud of her rebellious spirit. Mollapour's film was a straight adaptation of Afghani's novel, and there is no particular novelty or subversion. The film was technically challenging, particularly with respect to editing and performance, yet the source novel was so strong in its characterizations and atmosphere that it helped to make up for the weaknesses of the film. With all its shortcomings, the film paved the way for adaptations of modern Persian literature by other filmmakers and proved that Persian novels and contemporary stories have much potential for cinematic adaptations. According to Kamran Shirdel, *Ahu Khanoom's Husband* established the foundations of an indigenously derived cinema:

> We should remember that in any place in the world with the first film, which has a new orientation, it is not possible to immediately change the basis of the cinematic conventions or change the taste of the spectator. When the Italian neorealist films, especially Rossellini's films came to the Italian market, they were scoffed at by the Italian audience, but they were discovered a year later in France.
>
> (Talebinejad 1993, pp. 171–78)

Nasser Taghvai has a reputation for having created high-quality film adaptations of modern literature, whether from a Persian story by Gholamhosein Sa'edi, or an American story by Hemingway. Taghvai was a short story writer before starting to make films. His collection of stories, *Tabestan-e Haman Saal* (Summer of the Same Year), was influenced by the literary works of Hemingway and Ebrahim Golestan, and take place in Abadan and the southern regions of Iran. The collection is closely linked to the southern locale of his films, such as *Nakhoda Khorshid* (Captain Khorshid, 1987), which was a loose adaptation of Hemingway's *To Have and Have Not*; *Rahayee* (Liberation, 1971); *Nefrin* (The Curse, 1973); and *Sadegh Kordeh* (1972). He worked for some time as an assistant at Golestan Film Studios under Golestan's supervision, but in a conversation with me, Golestan denied Taghvai's assertion about having assisted him in the production of *Brick and Mirror*.

Nevertheless, Taghvai has always mentioned in interviews that he was influenced by Golestan and his stories and films: '*Aramesh dar Hozour-e Digaran* (Tranquility in the Presence of Others, 1969/73), is not a documentary film but due to my collaborations with Ebrahim Golestan, it has a documentary feel.

The story of the film is just like a real story, although its storyline is more intense than *Brick and Mirror*' (Talebinejad 1993, pp. 133–36).

Tranquility in the Presence of Others, Taghvai's feature debut, was based on a short story from Gholamhossein Sa'edi's collection of short stories *Vaheme-haye Binam o Neshan* (Nameless Fears). Sa'edi was a distinguished Iranian writer and playwright who also contributed to writing the script for the film. One of the most politically charged New Wave films made before the 1979 revolution, the film engaged with the pitfalls of the Shah's modernization project, and the alienation felt by intellectuals under pressure to conform, as well as presenting a look at the typical mindset and lifestyle of middle-class Iranians. In developing the characters and designing the sets, relying on his own independence and tastes, Taghvai created a film which moved beyond the field of literature, a film that, by employing the visual essence and expression of cinema, manages to demonstrate with deep perception the darkness and bitterness within Iran's society of the 1960s. The film has been regarded as one of the first Iranian New Wave films that boldly sought to open up a new, introspective horizon

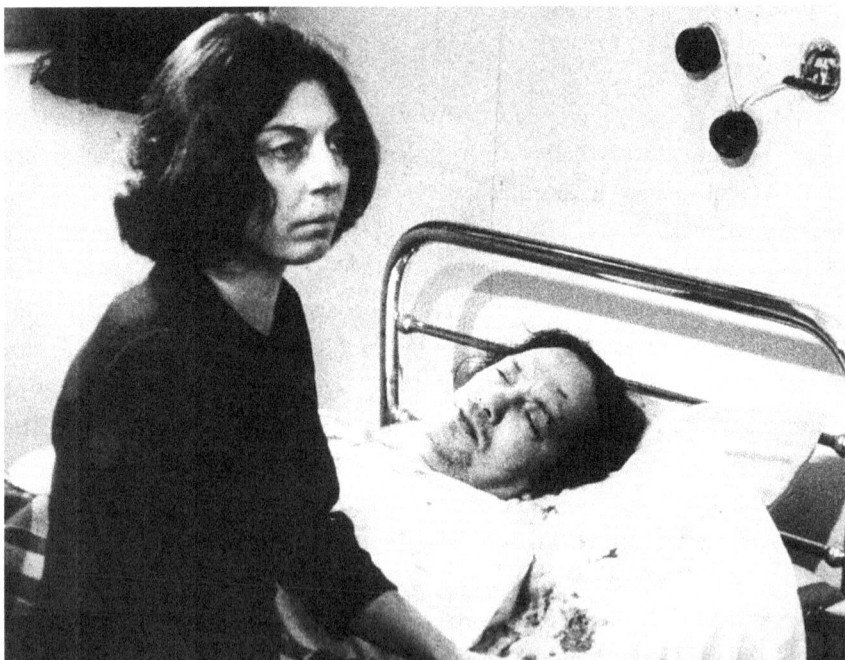

Figure 5.4 Akbar Meshkin in Nasser Taghvai's *Tranquility in the Presence of Others* (1969/73).

in Iranian cinema. It is a distinguished film in which the submerged and gradual psychosis of the middle-class and intellectual Iranians of the late 1960s is depicted. It shows the shattered dreams of people who, in their emotional vacuity and incurable malady of loneliness and fatigue, without prospects or satisfactory relationships, are looking for a haven in the darkness of the trees and the crowded nights of the big city.

Taghvai's *The Curse* was loosely based on the Finnish writer Mika Waltari's novel known as *Swamp*. The story is a tragic love triangle between a tormented, unsatisfied woman, her middle-aged, impotent husband and a young masculine sexy guy, which takes place on a deserted island in southern Iran. The film was not well received by film critics or general audiences. The film's symbolic and mysterious narrative, combined with Freudian themes of female lust and male impotence and the emphasis on the loneliness of the characters, made *The Curse* a distinctive film in Iranian New Wave cinema. Taghvai's use of the island as the main location of the film, its problematic and sexually charged characters, and his emphasis on the subject of death, were reminiscent of Bergman's films, especially in *Through a Glass Darkly* (1961).

Sa'edi, one of the most influential figures of modern literature in Iran, collaborated with Dariush Mehrjui on two films: *Gav* (The Cow, 1969) and *Dayerh-ye Mina* (The Cycle, 1975–8).

Sa'edi's stories were of interest to Iranian New Wave filmmakers due to their rich visual aspects, social realism, thoughtful tackling of philosophical themes and critical views of post-coup Iranian society. Sa'edi created mysterious and illusory spaces and provided terrifying images of rural existence in Iran. These literary features which included inexplicable occurrences with an emphasis on gradual deterioration brought Sa'edi's works closer to examples of Latin American magical realism and made them appealing to film directors. Sa'edi's collaboration with Dariush Mehrjui in *The Cow* and *The Cycle* is a unique case of collaboration between a good filmmaker and a well-known writer which produced extraordinary results. Mehrjui's familiarity with modern literature and cinema enabled him to write, with the help of Sa'edi, solid cinematic texts based on significant stories, while introducing the cinematic aspects of the original stories and characters. In his conversation with me, Mehrjui talked about his choice of Sa'edi's episodic novel *Azadaran-e Bayal* (The Mourners of Bayal) and his collaboration with Sa'edi:

I liked Sa'edi for his existential outlook and the mysterious and poetic aspects of his stories, especially *The Mourners of Bayal*, which was a very good work. Incidentally, it was Sa'edi that suggested that I watch a tele-play based on *The Mourners of Bayal* on television and see whether it would make for a good film. I saw it and felt that it was rich in content, but was very short for a feature film, more suitable for a thirty–forty minute short film. That is why I took some characters and incidents from the other stories in the novel and brought them together and put them into a new context that first begins with the village idiot. Then I introduced Kadkhoda and his son. It was cinema and was different from literature. Then, we have the story of Mash Hassan and his love for his cow and his madness and his transformation into a cow and at the end, his death in the hospital. None of these were in the episode on Mash Hasan or in the play based on it. These were the things that I combined to help shape the structure of the film.

(Jahed 2006)

The Cow was an existential realistic film with allegorical motifs and expressionistic images and was the result of the combination of Saedi's philosophical and critical thought and Mehrjui's poetic, modern cinematic

Figure 5.5 *Gav* (The Cow, 1969), an existential modern film made by Dariush Mehrjui.

vision. Mehrjui ingeniously utilizes the dynamic between the protagonist Mash Hassan and his cow, which in Saedi's story was a purely economic one, transcending it into a tale of psychological dependence and a haunting breakdown of a man's mental state.

We see not only the influence of Italian neorealism and French New Wave but also signs of German Expressionist cinema, such as the use of strong shadows, high contrast and low-key lighting and ambiguity within the scenes. *The Cow* was an existentialist study of a society suffering from alienation, loneliness and loss of identity, the main features of Sa'edi's stories and a theme which they shared with modern European literature, particularly works by Sartre, Camus and Kafka.

The making of *The Cow* was a turning point in Iranian cinema. Saedi's creative collaboration with Mehrjoui in scriptwriting made *The Cow* a proof of concept for the successful adaptation of literary sources in Iranian film. The international success of the film encouraged young filmmakers of the New Wave to look at modern Iranian stories as ready-made sources for cinematic adaptations. This approach became *de rigeur* for filmmakers such as Nasser Taghvai, Amir Naderi, Masoud Kimiai and Bahman Farmanara who all adapted modern Iranian literature and created remarkable films such as *Tranquility in the Presence of Others* (1969/73), *Prince Ehtejab* (1974), *Tangsir* (1974), *Dash Akol* (1971), *Khaak* (The Soil, 1973) and *Dayereh-ye Mina* (The Cycle, 1975–8).

New Wave adaptations of Persian stories continued in the 1970s with Kimiai's *The Soil*, his adaptation of Mahmoud Dowlatabadi's novel *Owsane-ye Baba Sobhan* (The Tale of Baba Sobhan, 1968); Sadegh Hedayat's *Dash Akol*; Amir Naderi's adaptation of Sadegh Chubak's *Tangsir* (1963); and Bahman Farmanara's adaptations of Houshang Golshiri's *Shazdeh Ehtejab* (*Prince Ehtejab*, 1970) and *Sayeh-Haye Boland-e Baad* (*The Tall Shadows of the Wind*, 1975).

The unavoidable consequences of such adaptations were made apparent with the controversy around Kimiai's adaptation of Mahmoud Dowlatabadi's *Owsane-ye Baba Sobhan* for his film *The Soil*. The changes that Kimiai had introduced to the story led to an exchange of very heated letters between Kimiai and Dowlatabadi, which were published in various widely read journals at the time. This discourse exemplified the divide between a filmmaker and a writer's understanding of what makes for a good adaptation of a literary work. Kimiai explained to me that it was his right as a film director to alter the story: 'I had the right to act freely' (Jahed 2006). In response, Dowlatabadi explained to me

Figure 5.6 The original poster of Masoud Kimiai's *Khaak* (The Soil, 1973) based on Mahmoud Dowlatabadi's *Owsane-ye Baba Sobhan*.

the cause of his dissatisfaction with Kimiai's adaptation: 'Unfortunately, Kimiai ruined my story. He made lots of changes which I did not like, and still do not like. It was all naked violence' (Jahed 2006).

Sadegh Chubak's *Tangsir* was an epic novel which had the potential to be a remarkable cinematic adaptation due to its powerful characters and dramatic elements. In addition, the atmosphere of the story, which takes place in the south of Iran, and its justice-seeking and anti-colonialist themes were particularly attractive for a southern Iranian filmmaker like Amir Naderi who was very keen on topics of self-determination, anti-oppression and justice seeking, with fearless anti-heroes who rebelled against the status quo. Naderi remained faithful to the novel's general storyline, characters and main events, and his changes and omissions as a whole were minimal in terms of the narrative. Chubak's novel is narrated from the point of view of the protagonist, Shir Mohammad, while in the film we follow the events from an omniscient point of view. The ending of the film is also different from the book. In the book, Shir Mohammad becomes involved with the gunmen and, after disarming them, he gets lost in the sea with his family; however, in the film, he escapes from the gunmen after killing Abul-e Gondeh Rajab and vanishes alone in the darkness of the night. The story of *Tangsir* takes place in the south of Iran in an anti-British atmosphere and has an anti-colonial theme, but Naderi has reduced the main conflict of the novel to the individual revolt of an oppressed man against the oppression of a few greedy and brutal usurers.

Bahman Farmanara's *Prince Ehtejab*, which was based on Houshang Golshiri's *Shazdeh Ehtejab* (1970), one of the most significant novellas of the time, proved to be one of the most important cinematic adaptations in Iranian cinema. Working with Golshiri, Farmanara penetrated the complex cerebral world and narrative structure of the novel and depicted the world of the decaying aristocracy of the Qajar dynasty. Farmanara explained how he collaborated with Golshiri in writing the script: 'When I met Golshiri, the first thing I told him was that we had to change many things for the film, and he agreed to do that because he loved cinema and he wanted his stories to be turned into films.' *Prince Ehtejab* was a successful adaptation due to the close cooperation between the writer and director, with a focus on maintaining the creative essence of the story whilst making the necessary alterations to realize it on-screen.

Khosrow Haritash's *Malakout* (Divine One, 1976), based on Bahram Sadeghi's novel of the same name, was a surreal and psychological crime thriller which was unique in drawing inspiration directly from German

Figure 5.7 Bahman Farmanara's *Shazdeh Ehtejab* (Prince Ehtejab, 1974) based on Houshang Golshiri's modern novel of the same name.

Expressionist films such as Robert Wiene's *The Cabinet of Dr. Caligari* (1920), a film which most likely never got a public release in Iran. *Malakout* (Divine One) is among the foremost modern Persian novels to be written after Sadegh Hedayat's seminal masterpiece *Boof-e Koor* (The Blind Owl). It is most famous for its extremely dark and grotesque themes and psychological, eerie atmosphere, making the German Expressionist style extremely suited for cinematic adaptation. Mr Mavadat, a mysterious aristocrat, is poisoned at his garden party and is taken by his friends to Doctor Hatam (a tyrannical Dr Caligari-esque figure). But the doctor is hiding many dark secrets in his basement which are revealed little by little.

The film was shown only once at the Tehran International Film Festival and was then met with the unfortunate fate that many of the bold, early *Mowj-e No* films were condemned to: having been banned shortly afterwards, it is claimed a copy of the film survives in the archives of the National Film House of Iran (*Filmkhaneh-ye Melli Iran*) but it has not yet surfaced for people to view. The novel was written in a fluid way and begins with the reincarnation of a demon in the body of Mr Mavadat; Haritash changed the possession event into a case of poisoning, removing the metaphysical aspects of the novel, most likely for the purposes of verisimilitude.

According to Abbas Baharlou, Haritash was not successful in transposing the eerie, mysterious and subjective atmosphere of Sadeghi's story into cinematic language (Jahed 2006).

Violence, critique of the status quo, alienation, the conflict between traditional practices and an ill-defined modernity, the conflict between the city and the village, class divisions and the absence of justice were the most important common themes between modern Persian literature and the Iranian New Wave films. The collaboration between the New Wave filmmakers and modern Iranian writers was fruitful and resulted in the production of some of the best Iranian New Wave films. Meanwhile, filmmakers such as Bahram Beyzaie and Ali Hatami, relying on their literary and theatrical experiences, created a cinema with a native identity based on Iranian history, culture and mythology.

Bahram Beyzaie, filmmaker, playwright, theatre director and screenwriter, began with *Ragbar* (Downpour, 1971), a relatively realistic fish-out-of-water story with romantic themes, taking place in a patriarchal society struggling with modernity and highly bound to traditional values. Beyzaie's *Kalagh* (The Crow, 1976) is a mysterious noir film in the style of Alfred Hitchcock and Henri-Georges Clouzot. Despite its modernism, Beyzaie's cinema is rooted in Iranian mythology, history and popular culture, as well as ritual and traditional performances such

Figure 5.8 Parvaneh Masoumi in Bahram Beyzaie's *Ragbar* (Downpour, 1971), a poetic love story taking place in a patriarchal traditional society struggling with modernity.

as *Taziyeh*, *Ru Howzi* and *Pardeh khani* (which literally means reading off the screen/curtain). The influence of Akira Kurosawa's epic cinema and Japanese traditional plays such as Kabuki can be seen in Beyzaie's ritual dramas such as *Gharibeh va Meh* (The Stranger and the Fog, 1974) and *Charike-ye Tara* (Ballad of Tara, 1979) as well as his plays and unproduced screenplays. Beyzaie was able to successfully combine ritualistic and epic styles with noir elements in his films.

Like Beyzaie, Ali Hatami was another auteur director heavily involved in the history of Iran during the Qajar period as well as Iran's traditional culture and folklore. Hatami's cinema is one of dramatic and romantic narratives which are derivative of Iranian miniature and traditional painting influences and extremely rich in terms of their detailed visuals, mise-en-scène and composition. His first film *Hassan Kachal* (Hassan the Bald, 1970), which is regarded as the first proper Iranian musical, is a unique story inspired by a well-known folk tale of a loveable but lazy man (played by Parviz Sayyad) who is forced to go on an adventure. It is steeped in the tropes of Iranain fantasy and was a great commercial success, although not many Iranian musicals were made afterwards. His second film *Towghi* (The Ring-necked Dove, 1970) followed in the footsteps of Kimiai's *Qaysar*: a tough young man (played by Behrouz Vossoughi, defined by his role in *Qaysar*) elopes with a young girl that his uncle had designs on, and it leads to bloody consequences. The theme of romantic rivalries and intrafamilial conflict is one that can be found in many of his films. Hatami's *Khastegar* (The Suitor, 1972) is a romantic comedy, again, starring Parviz Sayyad, who is desperately vying for the attention of an aristocratic girl with a never-ending stream of suitors; and was a box office success. In *Ghalandar* (1972), Hatami depicts the story of a forbidden and secretive love triangle which once again highlights the chauvinistic and honour-driven conflicts of urban toughs. Hatami's *Sattar-Khan* (1972) is a historical drama about a national figure of Iran's Constitutional Revolution which was a failure at the box office and was coldly received by the critics as well. Hatami's last pre-revolutionary film, *Sooteh Delaan* (The Lonely Hearts, 1977), is another tale of intrafamilial relationships and complicated love entanglements which captured the unique and, now for the most part lost, family dynamics of the past, and it was regarded as his best film by the critics.

Last but not least, Parviz Sayyad as a director, producer and actor had a hugely significant role in the development of the New Wave movement. Sayyad created the Samad (or Samad-Agha) character, the likeable, extremely simple but also deceptively savvy rural man who appeared in Sayyad's successful *Samad* film series during the 1970s and became an iconic comic figure in pre-revolutionary Iranian cinema. In 1977, Sayyad made his New Wave film *Bonbast* (Deadend)

Figure 5.9 Parviz Sayyad's *Bonbast* (Deadend, 1977), loosely based on a short story by Anton Chekhov.

loosely based on a short story by Anton Chekhov. It was a melodramatic film with a political tone which was immediately banned before the revolution. After the revolution it was screened for a very short period of time and then banned forever.

Deadend is about a young girl (played by Mary Apick) who lives with her mother in a small house located in a dead-end alley in Tehran. She daydreams about love and her ideal man before falling in love with a handsome, mysterious man who is always following her and waiting in her alleyway, staring up at her window. The man is a government secret agent (SAVAK) looking to arrest her brother for his political anti-Shah activities but unaware of this, she assumes that he is merely infatuated with her.

As an actor and producer Sayyad worked on many films including Ebrahim Golestan's *Asrar-e Ganj-e Darre-ye Jenni* (The Secrets of the Treasure of the Jinn Valley, 1974), Farrokh Ghaffari's *Zanburak* (1975), Sohrab Shahid-*Saless's Dar Ghorbat* (Far From Home, 1975), Ali Hatami's *Hassan Kachal* (Hassan the Bald, 1970), *Khastegar* (The Suitor, 1972) and *Sattar-Khan* (1972). He also produced Shahid-Saless's *Tabiat-e Bijaan* (Still Life, 1974) and acted in Nasser Taghvai's TV series *Daei Jan Napoleon* (My Uncle Napoleon, 1973).

To conclude, influenced thematically and stylistically by Italian neorealism and the French New Wave, and borrowing from the rich literary tradition of 1960s Iran, the New Wave of Iranian cinema succeeded in reflecting on social, cultural and political problems of Iranian society in a period of rapid modernization.

6

The forerunners of the New Wave cinema in Iran

As explained in Chapter 3, the young generation of Iranian intellectual filmmakers were opposed to *Filmfarsi* and considered it contemptuous of its intended audience and an affront to the potential expressive powers of the medium. These filmmakers, despite their differences in cinematic outlook and underlying ideologies, were united in their desire to create an alternative modernist cinema to *Filmfarsi*. In this chapter I examine the contribution of Ebrahim Golestan, Farrokh Ghaffari and Fereydoun Rahnema, three pioneering figures of this alternative filmmaking, whose main commonality was their exposure to modern Western art.

Ebrahim Golestan and writing with a camera

Ebrahim Golestan was a truly seminal figure of the Iranian New Wave. While he generally refuses to be pigeonholed, he is best recognized as a veteran Iranian filmmaker, writer and ex-political activist. Though his cinematic career was not prolific, spanning over two decades with only two feature-length films, *Khesht Va Ayeneh* (Brick and Mirror, 1965) and *Asrar-e Ganj-e Dare-ye Genie* (The Secrets of the Treasure of the Jinn Valley, 1974), and a few documentaries, he holds a unique rank in the history of Iranian cinema.

The significant impact and widespread influence he had on Iranian filmmakers and writers, and his contribution to the New Wave in Iran, are undeniable. As an intellectual who was influenced by Western culture, whilst firmly rooted within the realms of Iranian wisdom and cultural heritage, he has always tried to go his own way and maintain his independence. Remaining open to the gains of commercial success, as well as state support and sponsorship under the Shah's regime, perhaps more so than his other contemporaries, he was shrewdly able to take advantage of more commercialized avenues to pursue his artistic endeavours in a viable manner.

Golestan is celebrated not only for his literary works (short stories and Persian translations of American literature) but for his outstanding documentary films including *Yek Atash* (A Fire, 1961), *Mowj, Marjan, Khara* (Wave, Coral and Stone, 1962) and *Tappeh-haye Marlik* (The Hills of Marlik, 1965). Among them *A Fire* introduces Golestan's poetic approach to documentary filmmaking and his innovative style in editing, using narration and sound effects. It is a short documentary film about one of the greatest oil fires in the history of Iran which took seventy days to be extinguished. *A Fire* was the first Iranian film ever bestowed with an international award, winning a bronze medal at the 1961 Venice Film Festival.

Born Ebrahim Taghavi, in Shiraz in 1922, his father was the publisher of a local newspaper named *Golestan*, which his father would use to change the family name. He was a student of law at the University of Tehran but left his studies unfinished and began to write short stories in 1949, publishing his first collection of stories *Azar Maah-e Akhar-e Payeez* (November, the End of Fall) in the same year. He was an active member of Iran's hard-left Hezb-e Tudeh (Tudeh Party of Iran/the Masses Party), a legally sanctioned communist party that was active in Iran until the American and British engineered coup in 1953. He was initially in charge of the foreign section of *Rahbar*, the official publication of the Tudeh Party, later becoming editor-in-chief. He discontinued political activism and distanced himself from the Tudeh Party around 1946, engaging exclusively in literary and artistic endeavours. As a translator, he was one of the first to introduce the works of Ernest Hemingway, William Faulkner, Ivan Turgenev and Bernard Shaw and many other famous writers to the Farsi-speaking public. Although he strenuously denies it, there is significant influence from Ernest Hemingway in his story writing and accordingly he managed to establish a style of writing never before present in Iranian fiction. Golestan's short prose, multifaceted characterization and realistic approach would also seep into his films.

His early films consist of short industrial documentaries commissioned by the Iran Oil Company and similar entities, including *A Fire*, which shows the efforts of workers to extinguish an oil-well fire in the south of Iran. It is an expository documentary with a compelling poetic tone and an overarching subtext. The film was made as part of Golestan's first series of

Figure 6.1 Ebrahim Golestan – photograph by Parviz Jahed.

documentaries, called *Cheshmandaz* (Perspective), which he made between 1957 and 1962, with the help of Alan Pendry, Forough Farrokhzad, Soleyman Minassian, Herand Minassian, Mahmoud Hangwall and Shahrokh Golestan amongst many others. The *Cheshmandaz* series served as pieces of reportage for current events mainly in connection to the oil industry and the effects of industrialization on the lives of rural people in Iran during the late 1950s and early 1960s.

As an intellectual, Golestan held a prominent position among his peers and was noted for his originality and strong contributions to both literature and cinema. A differentiating aspect between him and other writers and filmmakers of his time was his blunt acerbic tone and the individualistic approach to his work; many were also keen to cast aspersions on him because of his collaboration with the Shah and the British Oil Consortium. In the words of fellow intellectual Jalal Al-e-Ahmad, a close friend of Golestan who fell out with him over such perceived transgressions and imperialistic complicity, he says:

> I was friends with Golestan since our breaking apart from the Tudeh party in 1945... he was intelligent, a good writer and photographer, he'd write stories and do translations that were sometimes good other times extremely good. But it's unfortunate that he wasn't properly educated, to say he was a Nakhandeh

Mullah (self-proclaimed/underinformed sage) [...] When we broke away from the Tudeh party, he didn't come with us but went on his own, and wrote his own statement of intent to break away. He did this because he was a narcissist and didn't want his name to be part of any group [...] He went to the town of Abadan to do his own thing by himself there, and he 'went mad' in isolation which was the phrase he likes to say about others. I saw this madness in him and mentioned it in my critique of his stories *Shekar-e Sayeh* (Shadow-Hunting, 1955) and *Kashti Shekasteh-ha* (Broken Ships, a translation compilation of the works of Ernest Hemingway, William Faulkner, Stephen Crane, Stephen Vincent Benét, Anton Chekhov). When this review was published Golestan got upset and I saw that he has lost the ability to hear criticisms about himself.

(Al-e-Ahmad 1964, p. 21)

He cites another reason for their falling out which is interesting since it shows another critical view from a fellow intellectual:

This was the case until Golestan became an employee of the Oil Consortium. Yes, this is how an intellectual is bought. I asked Bahram Beyzaie to write a critique of his documentary *Mowj, Marjan, Khara* (Wave, Coral and Stone, 1962) for publication in *Ketab-e Mah*, and in it Beyzaie referred to Golestan as a tool of propaganda for the Oil Companies.

(Al-e-Ahmad 1964, p. 22)

The establishment of Golestan Film Company (*Studio Golestan*) can be considered a turning point in the history of Iran's documentary filmmaking. When Iran's oil industry became nationalized, Golestan was making newsreels for the American NBC and CBC networks. At the same time, he pursued his cooperation with the National Iranian Oil Company (NIOC). It was during these times that the US-British-led coup d'état against Mohammad Mosaddeq (the democratically elected Prime Minister of Iran from 1951 to 1953) resulted in his being overthrown. Golestan was filming these events as they occurred using reversal film and sending them abroad by aeroplane (Jahed 2005, pp. 101–13).

Golestan was later transferred to the Iran Oil Consortium and managed the bureau of film and photography. In 1957 he went to the south of Iran to film oil excavation and composed a documentary from the footage he had taken. This was later entitled *Az Ghatreh ta Darya* (From a Drop to the Sea, 1957) and became his first serious documentary film. The film was received favourably by the officials of the Consortium and it was the beginning of his documentary filmmaking career and the first stage of the establishment of the Golestan Film

Company. In an interview with the author, he explained how the Golestan Film company was shaped:

> [The Anglo-Persian Oil Company] intended to establish a film department. I also wanted to leave Anglo-Persian Oil Company, so I resigned, but they asked me to make another film for them. I signed a contract with the Consortium independently to produce a documentary film about *Khark Island* and the oil pipeline from *Aghajari* to *Khark*. According to this contract, the Consortium undertook the task of providing us with equipment and accessories in instalments and would deduct these instalments from my income over three years. I then purchased a piece of land and built a place for the studio and gradually settled my accounts with the Consortium.
>
> (Jahed 2005, pp. 119–35)

The process of equipping the studio lasted until 1956, and after that it continued to make films about the oil industry. The Shell Oil Company, which had been engaged in commissioning reportage and advertising films in Iran, sent Alan Pendry, a British documentary filmmaker employed by Shell, to the country. And it was during this time that Golestan was able to make some of the best documentaries of that time.

Golestan's documentary films were the first Iranian films to receive international acclaim. *Khaneh Siah Ast* (The House is Black, 1962), a Golestan Film production made by Forough Farrokhzad, the most famous female Iranian poet and Golestan's partner, won the 1963 grand prize for documentary films at the Oberhausen Film Festival in West Germany. Golestan met Forough in 1958, when she was becoming famous for her feminist perspectives and powerful poems. The two started a close, romantic relationship which continued until her passing in a car accident in 1967.

During her seven years of collaboration with Golestan Film Studio, Forough contributed as an editor to the production of Golestan's significant documentaries such as the six-part series *Cheshmandaz* (Perspective) for the National Iranian Oil Company including *Yek Atash* (A Fire), *Aab va Garma* (Water and Heat) and *Gardesh-e Charkh* (Wheel Circulation) between 1957 and 1961.

Forough was able to surprise many with the flare that she demonstrated in editing Golestan's short films. Her cinematic ability culminated in her only documentary film, made with Golestan, *Khaneh Siah Ast*. In the autumn of 1962, Farrokhzad travelled to Tabriz to make a film about the life of the leper colony inside the *Baba Baghi* leprosarium for Golestan Film Studio. This

142   *The New Wave Cinema in Iran*

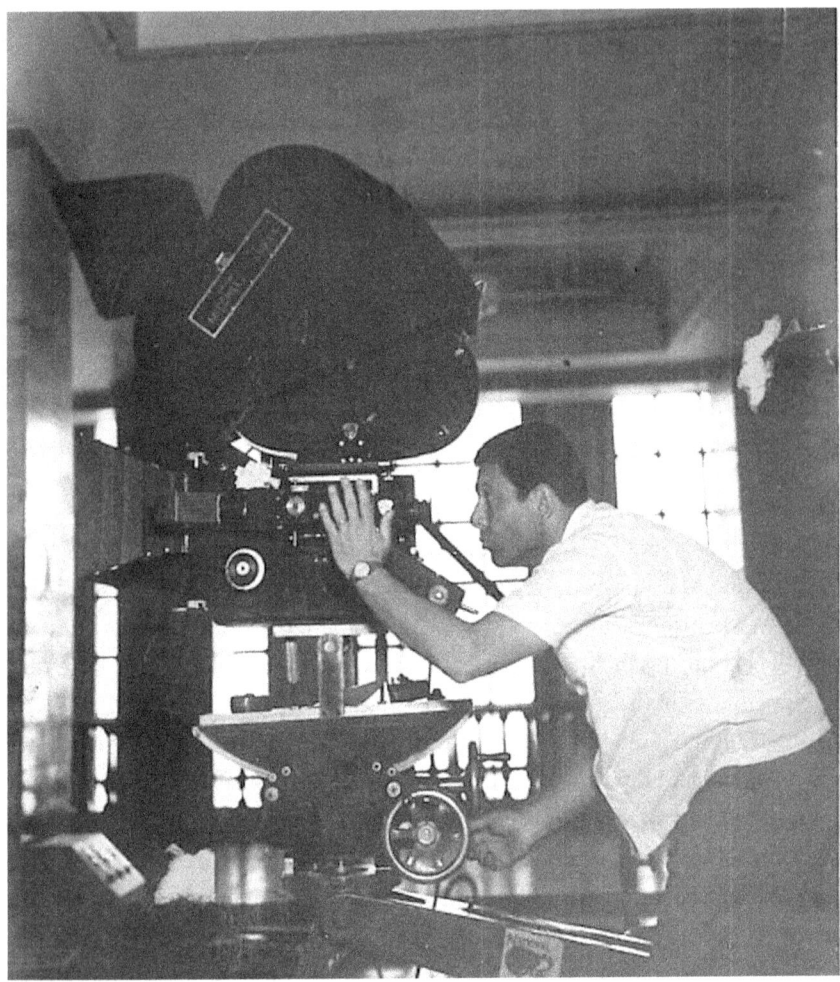

Figure 6.2 Ebrahim Golestan on the set of *Brick and Mirror* (1963).

stark, lyrical documentary was met with immense praise inside Iran and also in the West years after Farrokhzad's untimely demise. The film was an ode to the interplay and combination of contrasting feelings of despair and hope, boredom and joy, suffering and happiness, ugliness and beauty, nothingness and survival, death and life. The film demonstrates Farrokhzad's command of the Old Testament and the unsettled and desperate social conditions of her time. Whilst the subject itself was extremely engrossing, she managed to display a unique compassion for people who were ostracized from their homes and to present intricate scenes of daily life, overlaid with Forough's own poetic narration.

The ancient disease of leprosy serves as metaphor for the socio-political situation of the era in which Forough's film was made. Forough highlights the dichotomy of light and darkness, and the proverbial black house heavily alludes to the filmmaker's interpretation of the dark times in which they lived. During their twelve-day stay on the leper colony, Forough managed to gain the trust of the lepers, bringing Soleyman Minassian's camera as close as possible to them. Everyday moments and special events of the lepers' daily lives, such as weddings, applying make-up, breastfeeding, prayers and supplications, were staged for the camera with believability. Forough's cinematic look never sensationalized her subjects, but rather treated them with respect. Her camera shows the utmost sympathy for the people. She also adopted one of the young children from the colony.

As Saeed Talajooy remarks: 'Forough's poetic vision and Golestan's literary and filmmaking skills reshaped their creative output in ways that set the stage for a new momentum in Iranian cinema, which foreshadowed the documentary and feature tendencies of the Iranian New Wave in the following decades' (Talajooy 2019, pp. 7–8).

Golestan's documentaries featured a distinctly poetic style which helped to emphasize the message within them. This approach is a key component of nearly all New Wave films. Conveyed through the tempo and rhythm of these images,

Figure 6.3 Forough Farrokhzad on the set of *The House is Black* (1962).

the narrative was reinforced by flowing voice-over narration spoken by Golestan himself. This was in line with the general perception of Iranian film critics of the time about Golestan's documentaries, giving Golestan a unique position in the history of Iranian cinema as the founder of so-called 'real' documentary cinema in Iran. Featuring an epigrammatic voice-over in English, with Persian subtitles and shots of the fire and the efforts of the oil workers, *A Fire* is an intriguing film. The editing by Forough Farrokhzad which so acutely reflects her poetic vision and sensibilities is also stunning, elevating the film head and shoulders above a simple reportage about a disaster. As Golestan noted:

> We knew that our images represented a gigantic event and we did not want to rely on this characteristic or advantage. Many oil wells were burnt before and many films were made about those incidents but we wanted to create a different atmosphere and space…
>
> (Jahed 2005, p. 16)

Golestan's use of camera angles is distinctive; he focuses on the machinery and the industrial landscape and the human (the workers and the villagers). In addition to showing the fire and the subtext of the film is the continued effect of the fire on the lives of the nearby villagers and farmers; whilst there is no overt environmental message here, the film highlights how disruptive this modern industry is to traditional ways of life.

A Fire was highly praised by viewers and film critics inside and outside Iran, accruing much credit for Golestan's filmmaking talents and establishing a cinematic reputation that he would live up to in his future endeavours. In his review of the film, Bahram Beyzaie praised its poetic and epic aspects and considered Golestan's depiction of the fire as something more than a mere interruption in the process of oil extraction: 'this film was an epic of labour,a depiction of the frightening beauty of a rebellious fire, one that is both magnificent and frightening […] It shows the unsung heroes engaged in taming a fiery monster, muzzling the well's volcano, an epic display of hard work' (Beyzaie 1962).

Poetic narration is a significant characteristic of Golestan's documentary films. The powerful poetic voice-overs recited by Golestan himself imparted a historical and philosophical aspect to the films. In *Mowj, Marjan, Khara* (Wave, Coral and Stone, 1962), Golestan's highly poetic voice-over conveys his commentary on the oil industry and the modernization project in Iran. His literary background allows him to narrate with a poetic tone and expression. The sequence that depicts the island of Khark through Golestan's camera for the first time is an outstanding example of poetic narration in documentary film in Iran: 'And here is Khark, a coral sitting before the sun. The ancient witness of time's constant wave. A memory from an ancient era is congealed in the chest of its rocks' (from Golestan's *Wave, Coral and the Stone*).

In his documentary films about the oil industry, Golestan considers oil to be a natural resource crucial to the transformation of Iran from a backward country to a modern one, a treasure that can change the lifestyle of the Iranian people but can also damage and destroy nature and the rural landscape, causing disruption for the villagers who live in poverty in a wealthy land that is of no value to them. Golestan's *The Hills of Marlik* (1963) was another poetic documentary about the archaeological excavations in the Marlik area in Iran. The film features a poetic tone and philosophical expressions about life in Iran and the country's civilization and cultural heritage. In an interview, he stated that his intention was not to make a report on the archaeological findings in Marlik or to produce coverage of historical facts, but rather create an abstract expression. In his own words:

> Marlik isn't a lecture on archaeology. I wanted to make cinema [...] the cinema that I aim to create is different from a series of pictures used to illustrate a concept [...] of course, I want the spectator to understand my work, but if he doesn't it doesn't mean that the work is incomprehensive. If he doesn't comprehend it, we should help him to understand, not to change the work [...] Art derives from honesty. It is honesty which is important not complexity.
>
> (Golestan 1964)

Golestan made only two feature-length films, *Brick and Mirror* (1965) and *The Secrets of the Treasure of the Jinn Valley* (1974). The first of these, *Brick and Mirror*, is regarded as his masterpiece and his most striking film by many non-Iranian film critics. As explained in previous chapters, Golestan's feature films were not very well received by Iranian film critics, yet according to the assessment of well-regarded international film critics such as Jonathan Rosenbaum (Rosenbaum, 2021) and the French film critic Jean Douchet, *Brick and Mirror* was triumphant and effective in its artistic expression. As a result, they would think highly of Golestan in comparison to other Iranian contemporaries.

Brick and Mirror is a black-and-white film about the life of a Tehran taxi driver (Zakaria Hashemi) and his girlfriend. He finds a weeping infant in the back of his car just after giving a lift to a mysterious veiled woman (played by Forough Farrokhzad). His efforts to get rid of this unwanted baby is the starting point of his journey into the darkness of Tehran and its strange inhabitants. The film demonstrates a harmonious combination of social realism and expressionism. Golestan did not appreciate classifications of his films as a part of the 'New Wave' as he did not believe the movement could be categorized as such. But by the same token he believed there were others such as Zakaria Hashemi and Arby Ovanessian who were not given due credit for their filmmaking (Jahed 2005, pp. 45–57).

However, with this film, Golestan succeeded in presenting his thoughts and ideas in a polished cinematic form and defying industry conventions and tropes. In his own words: 'Why should we follow rules, especially externally imposed rules? Why shouldn't we impose our own rules?' (Jahed 2005, p. 195)

The interplay of cinema and literature is most discernible in this film, a reflection of its distinctive narrative style and storytelling. As a storywriter acquainted with modern narrative structures – whether in story writing or script writing, Golestan employed modern techniques.

As Ebrahim Golestan points out in an interview with the author:

> I wrote the stories *Lang* (Limp) and *Dar Kham-e Rah* (At the Bend of the Road) 5 years prior to the 1953 coup d'état… long before there was any quantifiable notion of a modern Iranian cinema. At that time there was 'only one poet in Iran' who could be considered 'modern' in their approach and that was Nima, who brought forward an astonishing poetic sensibility.
>
> […] with regards to myself, what you can see exists in my stories was also later found in my films, and the vision that I had for that cinema existed in my stories.
>
> (Jahed 2005, p. 54)

The episodic nature of *Brick and Mirror* and Golestan's use of discontinuity editing and spatial jump cuts lean heavily on the influence of Jean-Luc Godard's *Vivre sa vie* (My Life to Live, 1962) and *À bout de souffle* (Breathless, 1960). Like the French New Wave directors, Golestan rejected the traditional linear structure of storytelling and, instead, opted to apply his own aesthetic and narrative vision.

The structure of *Brick and Mirror* is divided into several parts. Apart from the main narrative, there are also sub-narratives within the film which contain

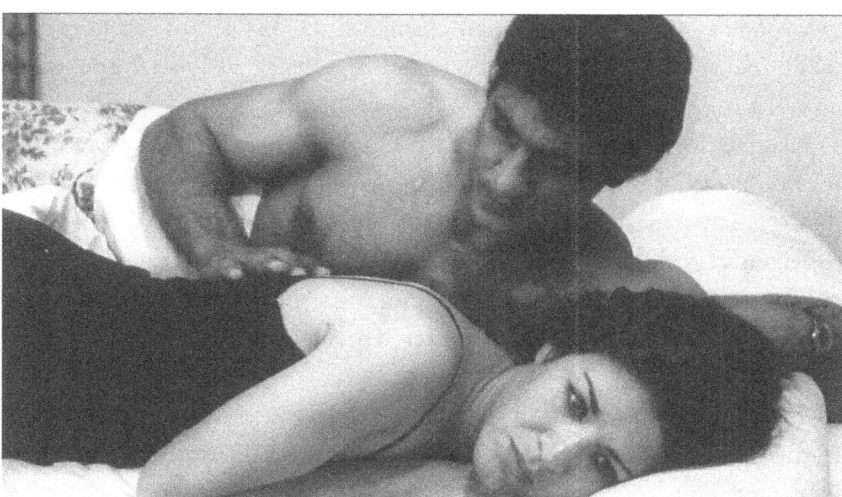

Figure 6.4 Zakaria Hashemi and Taji Ahmadi in *Brick and Mirror* (1965).

hitherto unseen and controversial subjects for Iranian cinema. By just grazing the socio-economic themes in the film, Golestan does not delve into the deeper psychology of the characters; instead he offers perfect snapshots of the space and time and the exterior atmosphere. In abandoning the classic forms of storytelling, Golestan departed from the traditional principles of Iranian popular cinema and expanded on the formerly simplistic approach towards the family melodrama, which was the core genre of Iranian cinema in that period and that continues to this day. In *Brick and Mirror*, Golestan took the same approach to reality that the neorealist filmmakers, such as Vittorio De Sica or Roberto Rossellini, had taken.

Alongside the main story which concerns a cab driver discovering a child in the backseat of his cab, there are subplots that play out in front of Hashem but concern other characters. Hashem goes to places such as the police station, the hospital, the judiciary and the orphanage, where he faces people of the town who each have their own stories, and we listen in on their stories as if from the perspective of Hashem himself. For example, there is a physician at the police station who has been the victim of a robbery and there is a woman in the hospital who is infertile and pretending to be pregnant by stuffing clothing under her dress. Hashem's situation at the police station is very similar to Antonio Ricci's in *Bicycle Thieves*. When Ricci loses his bicycle, he visits the police station to report the theft, but the police offer him no support. As Pierre Sorlin says of neorealist cinema: 'The police station and thefts are two common places of the Italian cinema of the 1940s. But the police are totally inefficient. Everyone in the city knows perfectly well that the police are powerless' (Sorlin 1991, p. 122).

Like the neorealists, Golestan took his camera to real places and recorded the lives of ordinary people. The realistic look of the film which emanated from the depiction of the details of people's everyday lives in the streets, together with Golestan's poetic slant, had a marked impact on the filmmaking style of the New Wave film movement in Iran. With a socially conscious eye the director presented a stark, bitter take on the everyday subsistence living of Tehranians in the 1950s.

The film was a metaphorical representation of the crisis-ridden, stagnant and fearful society of Iran after the 1953 military coup. It also served as a criticism of the country's intellectual atmosphere and particularly scorned the preoccupation of intellectuals of the period with abstract and pompous discourses they would hold in cafés, who paid little heed to what went on around them, with no feeling of a sense of responsibility or societal consciousness.

This, along with early ventures such as *South of the City* (1958) and *The Night of the Hunchback* (1965), both directed by Farrokh Ghaffari, were the first sparks that ignited *Mowj-e No*. All these ventures were funded by the director himself, despite being at this point a completely unproven business prospect. Whilst Golestan had his own studio, and found it easier than Ghaffari to secure the freedom to work outside of industry norms, this was still a highly risk-laden ordeal. If there was any sort of market incentive for making *Brick and Mirror*, it would lie in demonstrating the director's abilities to make a feature film in order to provide confidence for his future endeavours, rather than the expectations of any sort of direct returns at the box office.

The film's domestic release was highly self-aware, embracing its controversiality in its marketing. An advertisement for the film in *Kayhan* newspaper (Iran's biggest newspaper at the time) used the slogan 'A film that may upset you or even force you to leave the cinema, but it will make you think' (*Kayhan*, 25 January 1965). Even so, its divergence from the norm and its layered storytelling made comprehension of the film far too challenging for spectators accustomed to the narratives of *Filmfarsi* and its Indian/Egyptian counterparts.

Thus it did not find box office success or many accolades, and was instead disparaged by the film critics and cinematic writers of the time, who referred to it as intellectual gesturing. Shamim Bahar, a well-known film critic, would write scathingly of it:

Brick and Mirror is a bad film, with all the shortcomings and artistic pretences which can be seen in most of the debut films of an average filmmaker. It has not the power to do what it aims to do. It is full of long, extra, boring minutes and futile mistakes and exposition of the obvious. It is an experience, but it is an unsuccessful one.

(Bahar 1966)

Parviz Davaei, another well-known film critic of the time, also criticized the film for its lack of popular resonance and appeal and called it 'a waste of money, time and energy [...] Mr Golestan you cannot make films for the people' (Davaei 1965, p. 86).

Brick and Mirror was still a true watershed moment. Golestan avoided all the clichés and conventions of *Filmfarsi* and its familiar attractions such as sex, violence, dancing and singing. The only dancing and singing scene of the film holds no resemblance to the typical singing and dancing of a *Filmfarsi* production. The dancer is kept in long shot in the background, and Golestan's camera never brings her into the foreground. In this way Golestan de-emphasizes a stereotypical element of *Filmfarsi*. Golestan created a severance from the old principles of Iranian popular cinema that presented a simplistic approach to family melodrama. For example, the final sequence of *Brick and Mirror* shows the separated couple left alone in the street, more or less in the same situation as they were at the beginning of the film. This was a component derived from European art cinema, creatively employed by Golestan. The scene set inside the orphanage before the film concludes, with a long-take shot of the nursery's babies bouncing and crying, is outstanding and a stunning piece of social realism.

Figure 6.5 Taji Ahmadi in *Brick and Mirror* (1965).

The monochrome black-and-white cinematography of Soleyman Minassian, with its smooth yet complex camera movement and poetic use of lighting, conducive to the melancholic atmosphere of the film, helped establish *Brick and Mirror* as a masterpiece, which paved the way for the formation of the *Mowj-e No* in Iranian cinema. The dialogue and monologues contain subjective and philosophical concepts, which apart from their poetic essence, did not resemble the day-to-day conversations of ordinary people or those that are typically found in screenplays. Taji Ahmadi and Zakaria Hashemi's performances are sincere and vulnerable, and Solayman Minassian's masterful black-and-white widescreen cinematography renders a poetic and highly evocative aesthetic. The impact of the filmmakers on the next generation of Iranian filmmakers, such as Nasser Taghvai in *Aramesh dar Hozour-e Digaran* (Tranquility in the Presence of Others, 1969/73), Arby Ovanessian in *Cheshmeh* (The Spring, 1972), Hajir Dariush in *Bita* (1972) and Sohrab Shahid-Salless in *Tabiat-e Bijaan* (Still Life, 1974), is unmistakable.

Ten years after making his chef-d'oeuvre (*Brick and Mirror*), Golestan produced his second and final feature film, *The Secrets of the Treasure of the Jinn Valley* (released in 1974), a.k.a. *The Ghost Valley's Treasure Mysteries* by some English sources, an abject comedy and a notable early example of an Iranian political satire. The film is about a humble peasant who becomes rich and corrupt after discovering a cache of antique jewels in a cavern buried beneath his farmland. It is an allegorical film in the form of a screwball comedy, and with its utilization of a famous and popular Iranian-cinema cast, it boldly criticized the attempts made to modernize society by the Shah. The leading role, a rural farmer, comes upon an essentially unlimited treasure whilst working on his farm. Having never had much, he does not know how to spend this vast wealth wisely. He wastes it on possessions both alien to his old way of life and expressive of a new-found vulgarity and corruption. To the story, Golestan applies a thick coat of allegorical and symbolic meaning with brushstrokes that are highly critical of the Shah's regime, its contrived modernization policies and the swarming political corruption at a time when Iran's economy was booming from the oil industry. Golestan made the film in the fall and winter of 1971 but it was banned after two nights of screenings. Golestan's criticism was so sharp that it led to the confiscation of the film and his arrest.

According to Golestan, the censorship authorities were cognizant of the film's subversive message and harsh criticism of the Shah and his ministers (Jahed 2005, p. 66). The ban placed on the film by the censors did not allow the film to take its natural course of release and thus the level of its potential impact cannot be fairly determined. The ban was lifted in 1974 with the meditation of Mehrdad Pahlbod, the Minister of Culture and Arts, and the film was publicly screened in Tehran for two weeks only and created a sensation; soon afterwards it was interdicted again by the Shah's secret police (SAVAK), as they were concerned about the political impact of the film on the audience. The film was never again publicly screened before or after the Islamic Revolution. This was the second film of Golestan's to be banned by Iran's Ministry of Culture and Arts for its political content. (In 1965 he was commissioned by the Central Bank of Iran to make a documentary film about the Imperial Crown Jewels, but despite its ostensibly factual nature, the film was banned for its harsh criticism of the legacy of monarchist rule in Iran.)

In my interview with Golestan, he acknowledged the allegorical nature of *The Secrets of the Treasure of the Jinn Valley* and told me that he created the characters and events based on real people in Iran's political scene in the late 1960s. It was easy for the audience of the time to establish these links (Jahed 2005, pp. 203–06). The treasure in the film naturally represents oil, whilst all of the characters – the peasant, the teacher, the jeweller, the gendarme, the coffeehouse owner and the head of the village (*kadkhoda*) – serve as caricatures of Iran's political and societal strata, particularly the characters of the peasant and the teacher who represent the Shah and his long-term Prime Minister Amir Abbas Hovayda. There are also visual and thematic elements in the film that symbolically address the actual occurrences from the late 1960s such as the preposterous, phallic tower constructed on the farmer's orders which is an allusion to the Shahyad monument that was under construction in Tehran at the time. The seismic explosion that demolishes the ludicrous tower is a premonition of the revolution that took place a few years later in 1979 and destroyed the Shah's dream of progress and his 'Great Civilization'.

Like the Shah, the farmer wants to attain a modern lifestyle, but he has no notion of real modernization and merely favours the superficial aspects of it. For example, he buys elaborate chandeliers despite there being no electricity in his village. In the end, the farmer pays a hefty price for his ignorance and misguided aspirations. He is the victim of greed and ignorance on one hand and of deceit and the misguided plans of his henchmen on the other. Golestan cast some of the most popular actors of Iranian cinema and theatre, such as Parviz Sayyad and Mary Apick, for the film but he defamiliarized these actors, portraying them differently than they were typecast.

Parviz Sayyad, who plays the farmer, is a comedian famous for his character *Samad Agha*, a naïve but street-smart country boy who became a prominent comedic icon in Iranian cinema during the 1970s. Despite Sayyad's comic role in the film, this is not the type of casting one might expect, and his style of acting in the film is completely different to the familiar clichés of the *Samad Agha* character he had portrayed in films made before and after *The Secrets of the Treasure of the Jinn Valley*.

Furthermore, Golestan's satirical approach was a drastic departure from his previous gritty and realistic tone found in *Brick and Mirror* (1965). Whereas his previous film was stylized and featured careful aesthetics, this one was a bit clumsy and rough around the edges. Golestan reproduced familiar tropes of Iranian cinema and culture in the film and did not display multi-dimensional characters or different layers of society, as he did with his first feature film. If we were to disregard its metaphorical qualities and political agenda, it is hard to believe that it was made by the director of *Brick and Mirror*.

In 1974, after the film was banned, Golestan published a novel with the same title that was based on the characters and events of the film. Soon afterwards Golestan, who was now disillusioned with working in Iran, decided to go

Figure 6.6 Parviz Sayyad in Ebrahim Golestan's *The Secrets of the Treasure of the Jinn Valley* (1974).

into self-imposed exile. He shut down his studio and emigrated to the United Kingdom in 1975. Despite remaining partially active within the critical sphere, he has not produced a film since his self-imposed exile.

The last fictional piece to be released by him, the novel *Khoroos* (The Rooster), was first published in the United States in 1995 and in Iran in 2006 – only to be banned quickly thereafter. His films and books have also remained illegal in Iran but have been accessible to interested people as bootlegs, thanks to Iran's culturally unique and intellectually driven black market. During his period in exile Golestan rarely conducted interviews, whether with his fans or journalists. His reclusiveness and reluctance to meet journalists and researchers naturally led to rumours and hearsay, and he was thought of as an elusive and mysterious figure. When I conducted a lengthy interview with him and published it with his permission in 2005, the floodgates opened, and he has become more widely celebrated as a key cultural figure who is more than happy to share opinions about topics ranging from current events to discussion of former colleagues and acquaintances. All this being said, his contributions to the history of the New Wave have not yet been fully recognized and examined to the extent he deserves.

The legacy of Farrokh Ghaffari

Farrokh Ghaffari was a unique figure in the history of Iranian cinema, a veteran filmmaker, film historian and film critic. He founded Iran's National Film Archive and is regarded as one of the great exponents of the culture that progressed into New Wave cinema. He is familiar not only to Iranian cinephiles but also to the French film society for his film criticism, writing for *Positif* film magazine, and for his collaboration with Henri Langlois as an assistant at La Cinémathèque Française in Paris for many years.

Ghaffari's legacy and place in the history of Iranian cinema is of significant consequence and unfairly overlooked. Almost all of his own filmmaking endeavours were deprived of their true impact due to debilitating censorship by the authorities during the rule of the Shah, and neglect by Iranian film critics. Jalal Moghaddam, who wrote the script for *Jonoob-e Shahr* (South of the City, 1958) and *Shab-e Quzi* (The Night of the Hunchback, 1965) for Ghaffari, described him as 'A martyr of Iranian Cinema' (Moghaddam 1968). Distinctly inspired by Italian neorealism and the French *Nouvelle Vague*, Ghaffari made a few films, including *South of the*

City, *The Night of the Hunchback* and *Zanburak* (The Running Canon, 1975). The first can be regarded as the earliest example of modern cinema in Iran, and the others helped pave the way for the creation of meaningful and artistic cinema in Iran and served as the building blocks of the Iranian New Wave movement.

Ghaffari's legacy as one of the founders of modern cinema in Iran has been less acknowledged than Golestan's. A highly influential early figure, Ghaffari's role in the development of the film industry and film culture was in more than just his filmography. The son of an Iranian diplomat, Ghaffari attended school in Belgium and graduated in literature at the University of Grenoble in France. At that time, he became infatuated with cinema and started to write about films for local magazines and newspapers. Ghaffari's writings about films were published in various French film magazines and newspapers such as *Positif, Jean Define, Variete* and *Le Monde*. When Ghaffari was in Paris, as a cinephile and a regular attendee of La Cinémathèque Française, he became fascinated by film culture and the history of cinema and contemplated founding a film club in Iran upon his return.

Returning to Iran in 1949, he became involved with writing about cinema under the pen names M. Mobarak and Azargon (a possible contributing factor to his relatively low profile) for Iranian film and cultural journals such as *Setareh Solh, Saddaf, Ashena, Film va Zendegi* and *Setareh Cinema*. In 1950, Ghaffari published his first book, *Cinema va Mardom* (Cinema and the People), which was a collection of his writings about cinema in Iran. The influence of the French leftist film critics and historians such as Georges Sadoul is evident in this book and his other writings.

In my conversations with Ghaffari, he spoke about his relationship with Sadoul. 'My friendship with Georges Sadoul formed after World War II. I knew that he wrote about cinema before the war but I came to know him afterwards. He had some very unique ideas about cinema' (Jahed 2014, p. 88). On his return to Iran, the cinematic output of the country almost entirely consisted of superficial, low-quality *Filmfarsi* productions derivative of Egyptian or Indian popular cinema, with singing and dance numbers. He came to the conclusion that those who were involved in *Filmfarsi* production suffered from a lack of film knowledge and were completely unaware of the art form of cinema in Europe and all around the world.

In order to improve the state of filmic understanding and culture in Iran, he decided to provide a service akin to La Cinémathèque Française, and created the first Iranian film club in 1949 entitled *Kanoon-e Melli-e Film-e Iran* (The National Iranian Film Centre). In his article *San'at-e Cinema dar*

Figure 6.7 Farrokh Ghaffari - photograph by Parviz Jahed.

Iran (Cinema Industry in Iran) he showed concern for the situation of the Iranian film industry:

> In our country, with a population of 12 million there are about 60 cinema theatres. This number is really disappointing [...] there should be many cinema theatres built in Iran. The country has the capacity for 500 cinemas. These theatres will serve as a place for airing the artistic and cultural thoughts of people.
>
> (Ghaffari 1950, p. 11)

After a few months, the National Iranian Film Centre held the first British film season, a festival of sorts, organized with the assistance of other *Mowj-e No* filmmakers Ebrahim Golestan and Fereydoun Rahnema. In a bulletin published for this event, Ghaffari explained the aims and objectives of the National Iranian Film Centre:

> The current commercial cinema that is the unwanted child of real cinema, has become a dangerous tool in the hands of merchants that are after their own benefit, who have no goal but to stimulate and stupefy the non-human passions and feelings of spectators. It is a great pity that films exported to Iran are mostly likewise. They are films that intellectuals considered dangerous and harmful to Iranian audiences. These kinds of films are against their interests and *Kanoon-e Melli-e Film* is intended to show the real cinema to Iranian spectators and intellectuals who are fed up with these types of imports. The commercial cinema imported to Iran is not compatible with the needs and interests of Iranians, and it is the responsibility of intellectuals to fight against these vulgar and misleading films. *Kanoon-e Melli-e Film* hopes to take steps in the way of propagating and defending the real art of cinema, with the help of Iranian intellectuals, and pave the way for the creation of an artistic cinema in Iran.
>
> (Omid 1995, pp. 948–49)

From the very beginning, Ghaffari tried to develop Iranian film culture within its own practical limitations. In the British film season, he screened films made by Michael Powell, Emeric Pressburger, Carol Reed and some British documentary films. The aim of the programme was to introduce the different genres and styles of British cinema to Iranian audiences. He would later do a similar thing with a French season. The bulletin of this event clearly stated Ghaffari's intention to develop artistic approaches towards cinema. At that time, due to his Marxist leanings and his political engagement with Iran's *Hezb-e Tudeh* (The Masses Party), his articles were only published in political and leftist journals such as *Kabootare Solh* (Peace Dove) and *Setareh Solh* (Peace Star). In my interview with him he talked about his activities during this period:

> After 1950, leftist intellectuals supported us. They asked me to write film reviews in Tudeh Party's publications. I brought over whatever I had learnt in France. My references were Georges Sadoul and André Bazin. From the very beginning, I decided to write about Iranian cinema too [...] I was never a communist party member in France or in Iran. When I came to Iran, I gave my writings to a friend

and that friend published my work in a political newspaper, but I was not aware at the time that the newspaper was a Tudeh Party publication. And the person, who was publishing it, suggested that I use a nom de plume for security reasons, and I chose *Mobarak*, as that is a synonym for *Farrokh*.

(Jahed 2014, p. 46)

Having a controversial political view towards cinema and film criticism, Ghaffari began to challenge the predominant approach to film criticism in Iran. He wrote of his critical outlook:

A film critic should find fault with works of art, based on a particular social philosophy. Impartiality while judging and not getting any results from this judgment is a futile act. As we know, impartiality is a meaningless word. In artistic issues one must follow a special political and social philosophy and based on this philosophy the entire reactionary and anti-humanistic aspects of art should be oppressed. We should take the hand of the artist and put it in the hand of the people once more.

(Ghaffari 1951, p. 50)

Later, however, he became disillusioned with such hard-line leftist views and was severely critical of Georges Sadoul for his pro-Soviet approach to film criticism in the face of uncovered atrocities:

I had retained my left wing creed until after 1953 when Stalin died, the next year at the 20th Congress of the Communist Party Khrushchev stood behind a podium and exposed what a murderer Stalin was, and when I learnt that Stalin had spilt more blood than Hitler had in all his years in power, I cut myself off from all of it [...] when I found out that my mentor Georges Sadoul showed great support for the Soviet Union and for their substandard films, I made an ideological departure from Sadoul very early on, and I adopted a different approach towards understanding the history of cinema from Sadoul's ideological approach relating to the Soviet Union.

(Jahed 2014, p. 47)

In his writings about Iranian popular films, Ghaffari attacked the deficient plots, the stereotypical characters and the superficial aspects of Iranian commercial cinema and intended to liberate it from its conventions. His cinematic views and film criticism broadened the awareness of film culture and knowledge among Iranian filmmakers and ordinary cinemagoers. He was upset by the vulgarity and lack of effort in *Filmfarsi* and prescribed the formation of an Iranian national cinema (*Cinama-ye Melli*). According to Ghaffari, Esmail Koushan, the head of Pars Film studios, was originally keen to fund a feature film made by a European educated director such as Ghaffari. But when he provided Ghaffari with a four-page 'screenplay', Ghaffari realized he was not interested in letting him take free rein over the production process, and understood that he could not rely on the existing studio system in order to create a film that would meet his artistic ambitions (Jahed 2014, p. 56).

In his review of Esmail Koushan's *Sharmsar* (Ashamed, 1950), a very popular Iranian film of the time, he criticized the tropes and weak elements of the film:

> We see hundreds of conventions used in low-grade foreign romances that are made for a group of sleeping bourgeois or teenage girls who love Hollywood stars. All the characters are shallow, monotonous and arbitrary. A good guy is good and remains so till the end of the film. The city is a gutter of corruption and of course, the noble villager is initially a good guy who returns to the right path after thousands of mistakes.
>
> (Ghaffari 1951, p. 46)

Ghaffari was using the disparaging term *band-e tonbani* (literally translation 'waistband') to describe the weak aspects of *Filmfarsi*. In his view the failure to address the real societal problems was a key sticking point of *Filmfarsi*. In his review of Koushan's *Sharmsar* (Ashamed, 1950), he also pointed out that:

> The script of the film is nonsense and groundless and has nothing to do with the real lives of Iranian peasants and villagers. The thousands and thousands of arid and drought-stricken villages of our country and the oppressed life of peasants and the brutality of government officials and the oppressive masters and landlords have not been shown in *Sharmsar*!
>
> (Ghaffari 1951, p. 46)

The National Iranian Film Centre was active until July of 1951, when Ghaffari went back to Paris and worked as an assistant to Henri Langlois at La Cinémathèque Française. Fereydoun Rahnema (1930–75), a prominent Iranian filmmaker and poet, expressed his lament at the closure of the National Iranian Film Centre in his article published in *Sokhan* literary magazine: 'The first Iranian film club was closed down due to the emigration of its organizer Mr Ghaffari to Paris. At the time the club opened, lovers of true and noble cinema were few, but the situation has changed now' (Omid 1995, p. 955). The National Iranian Film Centre was reopened in 1959 when Ghaffari returned from France to Iran for the second time.

Ghaffari spoke of his collaboration with Langlois and how it informed the creation of Iran's National Film Centre:

> In 1949, I came to Iran and founded *Kanoon-e Melli-e Film*, by the suggestion of Henri Langlois. But, after 20 weeks of weekly shows, unfortunately it closed down after my return to Europe. In 1951, at Langlois's demand I accepted the position of executive manager at the International Federation of Film Archives (FIAF). I kept the position for five years from 1952 to 1956. I learned a lot from Langlois during this time. He was full of love, enthusiasm and excitement towards cinema and had exceptional taste in choosing films.
>
> (Jahed 2014, p. 45)

Upon its reopening, the National Iranian Film Centre became a favourite gathering place of Iranian cinephiles and people who were interested in modern and arthouse films. There, with the help of Ebrahim Golestan, Ghaffari managed to screen some masterpieces of European and American cinema, including those of Ingmar Bergman and Orson Welles, and of modern French cinema. Ghaffari was among the first to collect documents about the history of Iranian cinema. He published his notes on the archiving of these documents in 1950 in Iran with the aid of the Commission of Historical Research, and some parts of it were given to the International Federation of Film Archives (FIAF) and the United Nations Educational, Scientific and Cultural Organization (UNESCO). He intended to publish his research as a book, but did not succeed and only some chapters were published in issues of *Elm o Honar* (Science and Art) magazine in September 1951 and another chapter in volume 5 of *Film va Zendegi* (Film and Life) under the editorship of Fereydoun Rahnema.

The National Iranian Film Centre was officially relaunched in November 1959 with the screening of Robert Flaherty's documentary *Louisiana Story*. The promotion of film culture among Iranian audiences by showing artistic and cultural films and masterpieces of world cinema was the main objective of the centre. The club was renamed *Film-Khane-ye Melli-ye Iran* (the National Film House of Iran) in 1973 and was run by the Ministry of Culture and Arts until the Islamic Revolution. It is now a charity affiliated with the Ministry of Culture and Islamic Guidance. The role of the National Iranian Film Centre in the introduction of young Iranian filmmakers to different film genres, movements,

Figure 6.8 Farrokh Ghaffari as the art director of the Shiraz Festival of Arts.

styles and trends of world cinema is indisputable. Many of the filmmakers of the New Wave of Iranian cinema, including Bahram Beyzaie, Fereydoun Rahnema, Dariush Mehrjui, Nasser Taghahi, Mohammad Reza Aslani, Kamran Shirdel and Bahman Farmanara were members of the Film Centre, through which they were, often for the first time, exposed to the important film movements of the world such as Italian neorealism and the French New Wave. Hence the establishment of the National Iranian Film Centre by Ghaffari should be considered as one of the most important factors in the formation of New Wave cinema in Iran.

But running the National Film Archive and writing about cinema were not Ghaffari's only activities. He was also involved in making documentary films for different organizations such as the National Iranian Oil Company and the Ministry of Culture and Arts. His first documentary film was an educational piece about the prevention of tuberculosis, called *B.C.G.*, which he made for the Pasteur Institute in 1950 but left unfinished when he returned to Paris. During his stay in France, he made a short film called *Bon Bast* (Cul-de-Sac, 1957) with the help of Claude Bonardo and Fereydoun Hoveyda (the Iranian diplomat and also a member of the editorial board of *Cahiers du Cinéma*) in Paris.

Ghaffari makes the bitter socio-political conditions of the country, particularly the conditions of the underclass, the focal point and subject of his films. At a time when intellectuals held unanimous indifference, if not outward contempt, towards the mainstream cinema in Iran, Ghaffari's intention was to create a sort of balance between the trend in Iranian cinema to produce for a mass audience and a more artistic, challenging cinema that was closer to the European arthouse style of filmmaking. Being completely self-funded, he created his first two films by borrowing money from his family and selling part of his mother's estate (Jahed 2014, p. 56).

Upon his return to Iran, he opened his film studio *Iran Nama* in 1957 and made his debut feature film *Jonoub-e Shahr* (South of the City, 1958), a film that few have seen in its original state because it was screened only three nights in Tehran and was banned afterwards. Copies were destroyed by the board of censorship for its critical look at the impoverished parts of Tehran and the distressing economic situation of Iran's lower classes. It is the story of a young woman who has to work as a waitress in a café in the southern part of Tehran after the death of her husband. There are two hoodlums in the cafe who are competing with each other over the possession of the woman. It was the first Iranian film that looked with a neorealistic tone at the life of the bottom rung of society in the numerous deprived areas of Tehran. Several years later, a heavily censored and renamed version of the film entitled *Reghabat dar Shahr* (Rivalry in the City) was released in 1962.

In my interview with Ghaffari, he explained how he was inspired to add a stronger touch of realism to the original copy of the film and subsequently had to challenge the censorship department of the Ministry of Culture and Arts for its public screening:

> At that time I had just come to Iran, Jalal Moghaddam (film-maker and scriptwriter) wrote a script for me based on the life of lower-class people. Then together we went to the lower quarters of Tehran to find some locations for the film, and we saw the real lives of people that have never been captured in Iranian

cinema. I felt that there are differences between the way characters spoke in the script and the real people that I saw in the street. So we changed the script and created realistic people instead of superficial characters. The main character of the film was a cowardly macho man who had delusions of being a champion. We also added a hoodlum and a prostitute.

(Jahed 2014, p. 69)

In his opinion, a good national cinema was one based on Iranian culture and literature, that can show the life of the people in a realistic manner and maintain its appeal to ordinary people at the same time and communicate with them: 'Steps need to be taken to fill the huge gap between the commercial films and art films' (Ghaffari 1970, p. 156). As Ghaffari observes:

A film is either good or bad. A good commercial film is called a good film and a good intellectual film is called a good film too and vice versa. Though some are only after the selling of their film and some others don't think of the market at all. I think Fereydoun Rahnema's *Siavash dar Takht-e Jamshid* /Siavash in Persepolis (1965), Ebrahim Golestan's *Khesht va Ayeneh*/ Brick and Mirror (1965) and my films, *Jonoub-e Shahr*/ South of the City (1958) and *Shab-e Quzi*/ The Night of the Hunchback (1965) were the first stepping stones in building of Iranian modern cinema. This new movement was not only seen among a few intellectual filmmakers, it was also seen among the so-called commercial filmmakers.

(Ghaffari 1970, p. 156)

But Ghaffari would continue to be critical of *Filmfarsi* and its pandering to the lowest and basest of public taste. In his argument about the responsibility of Iranian filmmakers, he stated:

Any knowledgeable filmgoer can understand how the Iranian film-makers are just copying the most vulgar and worthless cultural products to make their so-called populist films. I would say it is OK for filmmakers to make films to match the interests of people in order to make money, but they also have a responsibility to promote the level of general understanding and knowledge of the audience, otherwise we have no choice but to get closer to the tastes of the ignorant. Unfortunately, not only in Iran, but all across the world, people want the simple and worthless things. We should fight against this love for all things facile and superficiality in Iranian cinema.

(Ghaffari 1970, p. 161)

Ghaffari's *South of the City* made attempts to blend artistic and commercial cinema, but it did not strike the right balance and the mass audience it hoped to enlighten did not come to see it in great numbers. It was also met by negative criticism from well-known Iranian film critics of the time such as Houshang Kavoosi. Kavoosi, a veteran film critic and filmmaker, had his film *Hefdah Rooz be E'daam* (17 Days to Execution, 1956) lambasted by Ghaffari for its supposed vapidness, and he perhaps saw an opportunity to retaliate in kind by publishing a negative review of Ghaffari's film: 'This film [*South of the City*] consists of a few scattered and ordinary scenes, and the only thing that has connected them together is the tape splicer of the editing, not cinematic thought' (Kavoosi 1958).

After the low box office turnout and poor critical reception of his second film, the comedy *Arus Kodum-e?* (Which One is the Bride? 1959), Ghaffari made his third film *The Night of the Hunchback* in 1965, which was a modern satirical adaptation of one of the stories from *Hezar O Yek Shab* (A Thousand and One Nights/Arabian Nights). The original story is set during the time of Caliph Harun al-Rashid, but Ghaffari brought forward the setting to modern Tehran in another gritty portrayal of 1960s society. It was a black comedy about smugglers who try to hide the body of a dead hunchback who is left on their doorstep.

In *Night of the Hunchback* Ghaffari allegorically deals with the notion of 'fear' within Iranian society after the 1953 coup d'état against Mohammad Mosaddeq in the form of an attractive and joyful Iranian satire:

> I wanted to somehow talk about the concept of fear not only in Iran, but within the Eastern mentality in my film, a fear of unknown origins. That is why I chose this particular story from One Thousand and One Nights (Arabian Nights) and worked on it for three years with Jalal Moghaddam. Iranian audiences did not like the film because I heard that people do not like to see the corpse being dragged from one place to another, but it was the main element that led to the success of this film abroad. In my original draft, the hunchback would come alive in the end and for some reason, we were forced to forgo his resuscitation. So, the difference between *Jonoub-e Shahr* (South of the City, 1958) and *Shab-e Quzi* (The Night of the Hunchback, 1965) was that the first was related to the language and culture of ordinary people and the latter had a more personal aspect and gauged specific issues.
>
> (Jahed 2014, p. 109)

A challenging and controversial film with a socio-realistic approach and an innovative narrative structure was totally new and shocking to the sensibilities of the day; it was therefore unlikely to be welcomed by the ordinary people of society that the film was trying to address, particularly when the taste of the public audience had been shaped by the simplicity of narrative and naïve themes of *Filmfarsi* productions.

As Ghaffari indicates above, *The Night of the Hunchback* was well received by international viewers after being presented at international film festivals such as the Cannes Film Festival, Karlovy Vary Film Festival and Lyon Film Festival. But on domestic viewings it received mostly negative criticism, although a few film critics such as Hajir Dariush admired the film and declared that from it 'a real Iranian cinema has been born' (Dariush 1964). With a darkly joyous, discordant and mocking atmosphere, *The Night of the Hunchback* addressed some critical issues within Iranian society. In his review of the film, Hajir Dariush put forward the idea that:

> *Shab-e Quzi* is addressing the current problems of society and intellectually criticises the different classes of people. But, the ingenuity of the filmmaker is to the extent that when in the last scene the police officer says: 'The death of the hunchback unveiled many issues' it makes you contemplate and you do not have the peace of mind you had before seeing the film. But if you are not intelligent enough you cannot correctly find the reason for your discomfort. Something has been said, a fundamental statement about you and people like you, belonging to this time and this place. But a curtain of ambiguity has deliberately covered this utterance. In short, it is a film that will not mesmerise the stupid.
>
> (Dariush 1964)

Ghaffari himself recognized the modern style of these films as the cause of its failure in a commercial setting and in communicating with Iranian audiences:

> When I finished *Shab-e Quzi*, Fereydoun Rahnema made *Siavaush in Persepolis* and Ebrahim Golestan made *Brick and Mirror*. My film was shown in six cinemas in Tehran but was not welcomed by spectators. Golestan was forced to rent a cinema, but his film was not noticed either. I believe the outlook and style of these films were too modern for the people who were used to the Egyptian and Indian junk films.
>
> (Jahed 2014, p. 64)

Starting with the performance of a popular theatre troupe, *The Night of the Hunchback* follows the sudden death of a comedian (the titular hunchback) in a farcical accident. The hunchback falls victim to a practical joke played by his foolish friends that goes awry. Subsequently his cadaver becomes the driving

Figure 6.9 Mohammad Ali Keshavarz in Farrokh Ghaffari's *The Night of the Hunchback* (1965).

force of the dark comedy as it gets passed around from person to person. The corpse works just like a Hitchcockian McGuffin, like the body of Harry in *The Trouble with Harry* (Alfred Hitchcock, 1955) and similarly reveals the corruption, hypocrisy and fear within a society living under the dominance of an almost unconscious horror and despotism. The corpse of the hunchback falls on the heads of a group of unscrupulous people involved in a felony, disturbing their composure and bringing out their true selves in panic-stricken and hasty self-preservation efforts.

The characters can be categorized into four groups: the naïve and the simple-minded (such as the members of the troupe), smugglers and gangsters (the landlady and the owner of the barbershop), the drunken and oblivious, and the authorities that want to control society (the police force). The comedic tone of the film is influenced by the French comedies of the 1950s, especially the films of Jacques Tati, but Ghaffari gives it an Iranian flavour by relying on Persian traditional performing arts. Ghaffari takes a critical and satirical approach towards upper-class Iranians in this film. Coming from an aristocratic family himself, Ghaffari was well aware of the cultural preferences and behaviours of wealthy Iranians and was, therefore, able to effectively convey these by juxtaposing rock and roll and Western forms of revelry with traditional attitudes. Ghaffari's profound knowledge of Iran's traditional and ritual performing arts, such as *Ta'zieh* and *Siah Bazi* theatre, enabled him to creatively use some of these attractive theatrical elements in his film. The whole story occurs within one night, one of the *One Thousand and One Nights* happening in modern Tehran in the 1960s. Thanks to the narrative structure of *One Thousand and One Nights* and the appealing theatrical features of Iranian traditional comedy plays, Ghaffari successfully manages to create a balance between the grotesque, the mysterious, and a realistically critical and modern approach towards Iran's society in the film.

The casting of some top stage actors of the time, for instance Pari Saberi, Mohammad Ali Keshavarz and Khosrow Sahami, demonstrates Ghaffari's leaning towards the idiosyncratic and the elite. The film was shown in some international film festivals, such as the 1965 Cannes and Locarno Film Festival and was welcomed by Western film critics and historians like Georges Sadoul. Despite some of its technical and narrative shortcomings, *The Night of the Hunchback* has a unique place in the history of Iranian cinema and is regarded as an intellectual film which developed the language and culture of cinema in Iran, and paved the way for the formation of the Iranian New Wave.

Farrokh Ghaffari's efforts were different in intention from the approaches of Fereydoun Rahnema and Ebrahim Golestan. He tended towards popular cinema, but the results were similar:

> Our filmmakers were in touch with what was happening around the world. They know that modern cinema has existed in the world for 15 years. They got to

know of the movements in Brazil, England, Japan, France and Ingmar Bergman's film tendencies in Sweden and America. And in turn, they tried to create a movement in Iranian cinema [...] People with capital should come and give a chance to these new and different film-makers, a chance with a limited budget. If producers are encouraged like this, a big step will be taken. Now I am talking to new up and coming intellectuals who want to make a pure and absolute cinema: come and take a look at other countries. See that others have taken the same path and reached somewhere. Like Buñuel, who was forced to make his living through cinema from 1940 to 1949.

(Ghaffari 1970)

Ghaffari's fourth and last film, *Zanburak* (1975), was a comedy inspired by Iranian folktales. The story occurs in the eighteenth century in central Iran and is about a soldier who gets lost in the middle of a war and is stranded from his squad, following the disastrous defeat of the army. He is in charge of a *zanburak*, a small running cannon mounted on a camel, which was an actual form of artillery used in Iran from the Safavid Dynasty period to the end of the nineteenth century. The narrative structure of the film was inspired by the structure and style of medieval chivalric and picaresque novels such as *Don Quixote* and Pasolini's *The Decameron*

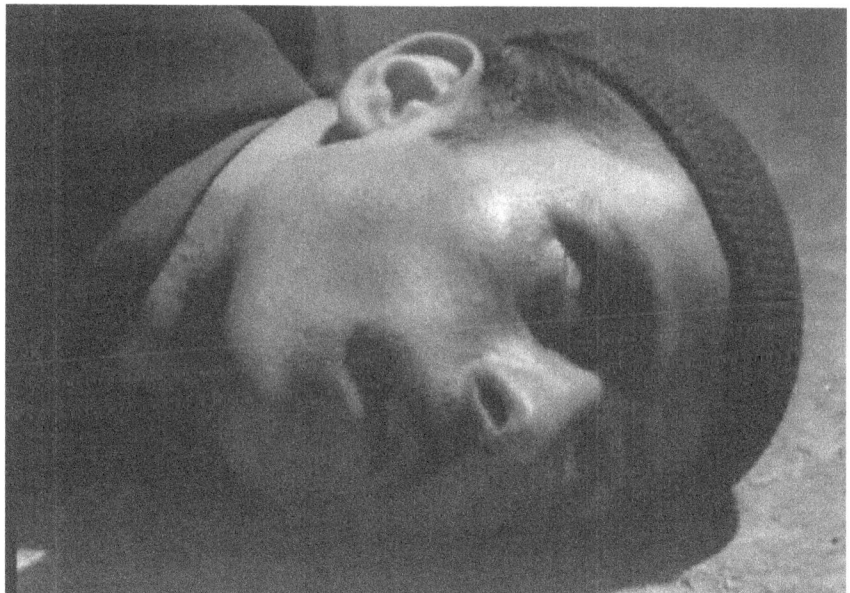

Figure 6.10 The corpse works just like a Hitchcockian McGuffin in *The Night of the Hunchback* (1965).

(1971) and *The Canterbury Tales* (1972). Following the style of the European and the Persian picaresque stories, the film consists of disconnected stories taking place in different settings with little exploration of the life of its main character.

Similar to the picaresque novels, the main character in *Zanburak* is a picaro who embarks on a lengthy, adventurous journey. Ghaffari incorporated elements of Persian classical literature in a very interesting way, indicating his great mastery of Iranian culture and literature. He takes the structure from the picaresque genre in literature and cinema to depict a classic Persian story in a modern way, which he had also used a decade earlier in his masterpiece *Shab-e Quzi*. *Zanburak* is a unique film in the history of Iranian cinema in terms of narrative, and evinces a brilliant visual style influenced by Persian miniature art.

Apart from filmmaking and writing about films, Ghaffari served in an administrative role at Iranian state TV before the victory of the Islamic Revolution in 1979. In 1966, Ghaffari was appointed the Cultural Deputy to Reza Ghotbi, the Head of National Iranian Radio and Television (NIRT). Being in this position allowed Ghaffari to implement some of his innovative ideas in producing artistic films. As Ali Issari points out, 'in 1969 NIRT established Telfilm, an affiliated company, to produce feature films as a commercial venture as well as for later release on television' (Issari 1989, p. 215). According to Issari, a number of young and foreign trained filmmakers who had criticized the local film industry for its materialistic attitude took advantage of this offer and made several films in collaboration with Telfilm (Issari 1989, p. 215).

Ghaffari thus made it possible for some young New Wave filmmakers such as Kimiavi, Taghvai, Hajir Dariush, Farmanara and Sohrab Shahid-Saless to realize their artistic visions with the funds provided by Telfilm. Ghaffari then became the main organizer of *Jashn O Honar-e Shiraz* (the Shiraz Arts Festival), an annual cultural and art event that was founded on the suggestion of Farah Pahlavi, the former Queen of Iran, in 1967, and ran for eleven years until 1977. It was a festival of traditional and modern theatre, music, dance and an extraordinary meeting place for artists from East and West. (For further information about Ghaffari's engagement with the Shiraz Arts Festival, please refer to my interview with Farrokh Ghaffari in *Az Cinémathèque Paris ta Kanoon-e Film-e Tehran* [Jahed 2014].)

Ghaffari was also interested in the craft of acting. He played one of the main characters in his film *The Night of the Hunchback* and also as William Knox D'Arcy, an English oil explorer and one of the principal founders of the oil and petrochemical industry in Iran in 1901, in Parviz Kimiavi's surrealist postcolonial satire *O.K. Mister* (1979). It is the fictional story of a historical character who arrives in a remote village in Iran with the intention of exploiting the natural resources of the land.

Following the Islamic Revolution, Ghaffari left Iran to live in Paris. Having been denounced by the state for his affiliation with the former regime by the Iranian government, he was never able to return and spent the rest of his life in exile. Where I met and interviewed him on two occasions, both were highly illuminating and a great opportunity to receive a first-hand understanding of his motivations and immense passion for developing Iran's national cinema. He died on 17 December 2006 from heart and kidney complications.

Fereydoun Rahnema and his self-reflexive cinema

Fereydoun Rahnema (1930–75) made only three films – a short documentary and two feature-length films – in his short life. He also published five poetry books in French and dozens of articles about cinema and literature. As a modern poet, filmmaker, film critic, and a serious advocator of modern and avant-garde movements in the field of literature, cinema and theatre, he had an indelible influence on the creation and development of modern poetry and cinema in Iran in the 1950s and 1960s. His three films avidly explore certain core ideas, namely the loss of identity amongst Iranians and the incompatibility between modern Iran and its historical and mythological past – themes that also are found in future New Wave films, though rarely as overtly.

Rahnema finished his high school education in France and graduated from the faculty of literature and film studies of Paris University. In his thesis, titled *Realism of Film*, Rahnema carefully illuminates his theoretical views on the concept of reality and realism in cinema, the nature of film and its relation to poetry, painting, music, architecture and theatre. In the introduction to his work he states:

> This thesis is a totally personal theory about cinema and art. Those who have seen my two films, have undoubtedly witnessed the application of this theory in my films... Here, I tried to show the different capabilities of film, most of which have come from other arts. That is why I will compare the art of film with all other fields of art.
>
> (Rahnema 1972, pp. 3–15)

When Rahnema returned to Iran in 1957, he started to write about film and literature sporadically for different film and literary magazines such as *Sokhan* (Discourse), *Talash* (Endeavor), *Sadaf* (The Shell), *Negin* (Jewel), *Cinemaye Azad Bulletin* and *Film va Zendegi* (Film and Life), for which he was the editor-in-chief for a short period of time. His first film reviews of popular Iranian films, for instance *Payan-e Ranjha* (End of Suffering, 1955), *Chahar-rah-e Havades* (The Crossroads of Accidents, 1955) and *Mahtab-e Khoonin* (The Blood Moon, 1955), were published in *Sokhan* literary magazine. Rahnema also wrote for *Film va Zendegi* journal for a short time in the 1960s.

In addition to his academic endeavours relating to cinema, Rahnema was heavily involved in poetry. His first collection of poems entitled *Poemes Anciens* (Ancient Poems) was published by Du Bress printing house in Paris in 1954 and featured an introduction by Paul Éluard, the surrealist French poet. In 1968, his second collection of poems called *Chants de Délivrance* (The Song of Freedom) was also published in Paris. The impact of his poems on many young and innovative poets of 1950s and 1960s Iran was unquestionable. Concurrent with the rise of contemporary Nima Youshij's followers as the major voices in modern poetry, known as *Sher-e No* (new poetry), Rahnema returned to Iran and began to assert an influence, both as a colleague and as a mentor, on the poets of his own generation, including Ahmad Shamlou, Yadollah Royaee, Farokh Tamimi and Mohammad Reza Aslani.

Figure 6.11 Fereydoun Rahnema, one of the forerunners of the New Wave cinema in Iran.

Ahmad Shamlou, arguably the most renowned modernist Iranian poet, refers to Rahnema's influence in the introduction of his book *Hamchoun Kocheh-ee Bi-enteha* (Like a Never Ending Alley):

> It was at this time that Fereydoun Rahnema came back from Paris after many years and brought with him a deep acquaintance with poetry from both East and West, a pile of books and records. Getting to know Fereydoun, who knew French modern poetry well, was precisely the great event which needed to occur in my life. It was with his unending help that we got our hands on books, poetry and music. We were scattered talents, not going anywhere, not having a book to read and having no chance to have anything. He opened all the closed doors to us. Fereydoun's house was the refuge of hope and our school… from a general acquaintance with the science of music and painting, to discovering pure poetry… With Fereydoun, we felt as though we were important individuals.
>
> (Shamlou 1995, p. 17)

With his literary and artistic background, Rahnema was a proponent of the romantic movement and sought to bring this perspective to Iran's cinema. In criticizing extant Iran's film industry, he would write: 'The producers of *Filmfarsi* are at times so busy counting their benefits and propagating their cinematic cells… it has to be said that they have nothing to do with art… The art and literature of this country have turned into a commercial business' (Rahnema 1975).

For Rahnema most of Iranian cinema, with the exception of some initial efforts by Abdolhossein Sepanta and Majid Mohseni, had no connection with authentic Iranian culture and the everyday lives of people. In his review of Samuel Khachikian's *Chahar Rah-e Havades* (The Crossroad of Events, 1955), he wrote:

> What turns this bourgeois drama into an Iranian porridge (an amalgam) are a few guns in these adventures plus some poolside shots and Iranian musical instruments […] The only part in this film that bears any Iranian aspect is the scene that shows Shah Reza Street and a bus. When I saw this scene, I wanted to break into applause, as it was the first time in an Iranian film such a scene from our everyday life had been filmed.
>
> (Rahnema 1955)

In criticizing Iranian popular films of the time, he notes this lack of depth and originality stems from grounding our conventions in imitations of other national cinemas:

Despite the fact that we have many valuable stories from our past, we still imitate American and Egyptian films. We employ the dancer from some cabaret to flaunt her beautiful body to the hapless viewer [...] Script writers and producers should know that no one can count on the ignorance and stupidity of people indefinitely.

(Rahnema 1955)

He was also displeased with the state of film criticism, and later, as a retort to film critics who condemned his films, he said: 'I wonder how someone who has no knowledge about cinema, can distinguish between a valuable film and a bad film at all?' (Rahnema 1969, pp. 18–22).

That is why Rahnema sought to create adaptations of Persian classic literature like Ferdowsi's *Shahnameh* utilizing a new approach: 'Some people criticised my conception of *the Shahnameh* and the story of Sudabeh and Siavash. I do not say my take is exactly like *Shahnameh*, no one can have such a claim, but what you see in my film is not that far from Ferdowsi's concept' (Rahnema 1969, pp. 18–22).

The *Shahnameh* could be viewed as a series of myths which sought to fill in the gaps in the true history of the Persian Empire lost to time; it has become an integral part of Persian culture and has helped preserve myths and legends in an almost archival capacity. In most of his articles and interviews, Rahnema talked about the necessity of creating '*Cinema-ye Digar*' (other cinema) with such lofty goals in mind. In an interview, he defined what he meant by this:

There was a time when terms like '*Cinema-ye Pishgam*' (Pioneer Cinema), Avant-garde, 'progressive cinema', 'young cinema' or 'new cinema' were popular. We still hear of them here and there. But, those who have used the term '*Cinema-ye Digar*' (other cinema) think that the point is not in reminding others whether a work is new or old, forwarding or reclining. The reason for using this term is mostly that this cinema differs from the current concept of cinema in Iran.

(Rahnema 1969, pp. 18–22)

This definition, when viewed in tandem with Rahnema's films, seems to suggest Rahnema was pursuing a timeless quality in cinema and aiming to create art that could stand on its own merits without the need to be compared against the films it was rebelling against. Unlike film critics who proposed various new fronts against *Filmfarsi*, he had a more unifying suggestion:

The answer to the real lovers of cinema is: No first, second, third or fourth front. Only the cinema front, the true cinema. By this I do not mean the progressive works like the films of Fischinger, or McLaren, or even experimental works of New York School. I just mean easy understandable films, which are valuable, like the films of John Ford, also comedy cinema like the films by Harry Langdon or Chaplin's primary films or Frank Capra or even Jacques Tati. I am telling this so that they know in my opinion a 'true cinema' is not necessarily a cinema that has no income. But it surely is a cinema that wants to search and find and has only one goal and that is cinema. Its goal is not only filling the pockets of this or that or begging for the emotions of the majority of people. None of these! Cinema and only this. [...] One cannot say that there has not been any preparedness for developing this thought. Fortunately, we can now mention films which have been made in that direction.

(Rahnema 1969, pp. 18–22)

From Rahnema's perspective, the efforts of people like Farrokh Ghaffari and Parviz Davaei to reform and improve *Filmfarsi* were to a large extent futile. Rahnema's only concern was improving the language of cinema. He was in search of a cinematic language that had an unbreakable bond with documentary cinema, poetry and literature:

As you see in *Siavash in Persepolis*, I stay away from the conventional forms of film language. A cinema that is made easily but is far away from the expression I am after. [...] The cinema that I like is one that looks for a higher goal. Some have every right to laugh at this cinema here or at any other place of the world, or even ridicule it. It is because they have other expectations from cinema. But, today, this type of cinema goes its own way very easily. Those who ridiculed it yesterday are now so curious about it. Anyway, we should not pay much heed to them, as their presence is natural. [...] I know you will say that they are dangerous and form gangs and so on, and I accept that but you should not give them the privilege of struggling. The producers of *Filmfarsi* pay no heed to the characteristics of the art of cinema. They forget that cinema is a collection of other arts. Cinema has characteristics that cannot be ignored. One of them is its documentary aspect. Any valuable film, before anything else, evokes the experience of documentary films. De Sica's *Bicycle Thieves* (1948), is in fact a documentary film. We have many examples of this type. It suffices to think of the works of people like Robert Flaherty, Joris Ivens, Rene Clement and the Italian director Roberto Rossellini. Most of these great directors started their important cinema work with the use of documentaries.

(Rahnema 1968)

The crux of Rahnema's work was centred on exploring the Iranian sense of self, reflecting on the history and mythology of the nation and its relation to current society. In 1967 he founded the Research Centre within the National Iranian Television, which later became a great source of funding for some Iranian New Wave filmmakers such as Nasser Taghvai, Parviz Kimiavi, Mohammad Reza Aslani and Rahnema himself. He was the producer of a TV programme called *Iran Zamin* which was a series of documentary films on Iran's different regions and cultures made by filmmakers such as Hajir Dariush, Jalal Moghaddam, Nasser Taghvai, Manouchehr Tayab, Parviz Kimiavi and Mohammad Reza Aslani, utilizing an ethnographical approach. His intention in making these documentaries was to record the important aspects of Iranian culture, which were in oblivion, a tendency towards authentic elements in a culture that can be found in his own cinematic works too. Rahnema believed in the young generation of filmmakers and his support of their cinematic efforts led to the evolution of an avant-garde movement called *Cinema-ye Azad-e Iran* (Iran's Free Cinema).

In 1960 Rahnema made his first documentary film, *Takht-e Jamshid* (Persepolis), with private funding; it was broadcast on Channel 13 of GBS Television in New York. In this film, Rahnema looks through the ruins of Persepolis with a poetic vision, searching for reality and examining the historical roots and identity of Iranian people. Rahnema lived most of his life in France. According to Hamid Naficy, for people like Rahnema, 'the return to the contemporary homeland seems insufficient, requiring nostalgia for another, earlier time and place to assuage the longing for home' (Naficy 2011, p. 94). That's why, in Naficy's view, Rahnema's debut documentary film *Takht-e Jamshid* (Persepolis, 1960) is suffused with nostalgic longing for the homeland and for the past (Naficy 2011, p. 94).

Rahnema possessed a greater depth of understanding in the realm of filmmaking than his compatriots did, having had direct, first-hand exposure to the neorealist and New Wave films and the movement whilst he was studying in France. As a result of the complexity and sophistication of his approach, Rahnema stood out amongst his compatriots who were striving for a modern Iranian cinema. There was little hope of him being understood by the Iranian intellectuals. Even his fellow *Mowj-e No* filmmaker Ebrahim Golestan was less than impressed, comparing his films to incomprehensible *telesm* (magical spells) which only scratched at the surface and failed to bring deeper meaning or bear any influence on future New Wave filmmaking (Jahed 2005, p. 58).

Figure 6.12 *Siavash in Persepolis* (1965), a documentary film directed by Fereydoun Rahnema.

Golestan conceded that *Cinema-ye Azad* (The Free Cinema), which was founded by Rahnema in 1968, was highly influential, but he ridiculed his films as unwatchable. What was interpreted by some as stuttering or incoherency, was actually a highly metatextual and conscious exploration of a completely fresh cinematic language. Rahnema firmly believed that the mythical world was a part of our ideology. That, through knowing our yesterday, we can recognize our today and even our future (Shoa'ee 1976, p. 93). His historical conscious and metatextual approach earned *Siavash Dar Takht-e Jamshid* (Siavash in Persepolis, 1965) the Jean Epstein Award for the development of film language at the 1966 Locarno Film Festival (Avery 1991, p. 798).

In *Siavash in Persepolis*, there are five characters looking through history and navigating dark mental and physical passages in search of some grounding in reality. Rahnema made this film with the funding of Iran's National Television. It was a modern adaptation of the *Shahnameh* which bore no resemblance to other previously made films about the mythical stories of *Shahnameh*, such as Mehdi Rais Firouz's *Rostam o Sohrab* (Rostam and Sohrab, 1957) or Manouchehr Zamani's *Bijan o Manijeh* (Bijan and Manijeh, 1958) which were more straightforward epics centred on heroism and romance. The beginning of the story ostensibly is about the hero and his trials during the wars between Iran

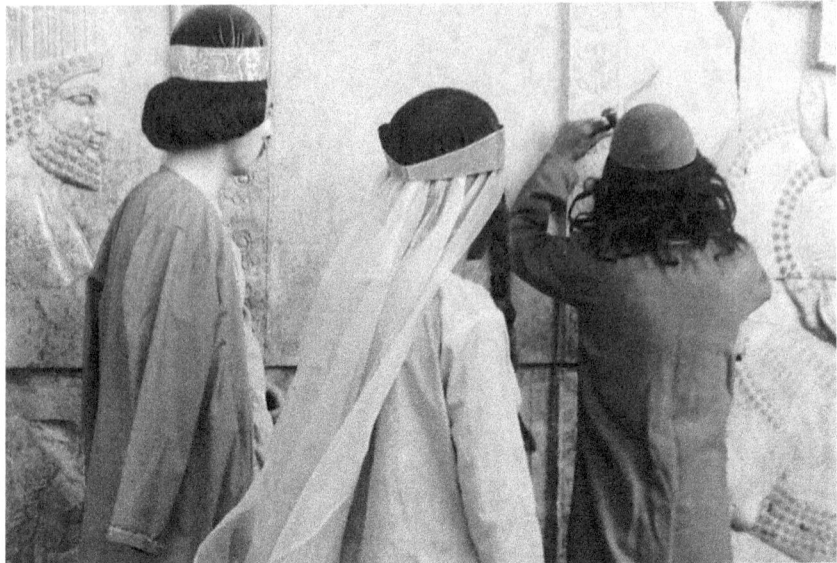

Figure 6.13 *Siavash in Persepolis* (1965), a modern adaptation of Siavash's story from Ferdowsi's *Shahnameh*.

and Turan. Rahnema literally brings forth the *Shahnameh*, a piece of literature that spans the history and mythology of Iran to the modern day. Set in the actual ruins of Persepolis, he intercuts with highly metatextual 'behind-the-scenes footage' of the director providing notes to the actors in the 'production' and clips of interviews with tourists asking them about the historic and mythic figures of the *Shahnameh*. Upon being confronted with such a new cinematic experience, the spectator is moved to see something different from his previous visual and narrative experiences; in the auteur's own words, 'the problem with the spectators who do not communicate with my films, is that they do not know their culture well enough, and they are not to blame for they have not been given the opportunity' (Shoa'ee 1976, p. 94). Rahnema was not looking for the epic aspects of *Shahnameh* and the story of Siavash; instead he was following the mystical and philosophical aspects of Iranian myths and providing a new cinematic form in narrative and literary adaptation. He defamiliarizes the heroes of Shahnameh. In his film, Siavash, Afrasiab, Rostam and Garsivaz are no longer the inaccessible and mythic heroes of *Shahnameh*, but ordinary people who are walking around the ruins of Persepolis and expressing their feelings and thoughts about their past and present situation. From the perspective of Rahnema, Siavash is a symbol of human oppression in a society full of lies and deception.

Iranians' lost sense of identity, and the cyclical relationship between the modern man and their connection to a historical and mythological past are brought to the forefront in this film. Rahnema does this in a striking fashion by literally bringing the past to life and placing these historical/mythical characters in the present time. In a scene in which the characters are talking about the war between Iran and Turan (a mythologically significant historic event), a young boy brings them a copy of the modern *Kayhan* newspaper which is announcing the possibility of an outbreak of a third world war.

Siavash in Persepolis was shown at La Cinémathèque Française in 1965 and was well received by the French film critics including Henri Langlois, the French film archivist and the co-founder of La Cinémathèque, but it made no headway in Iran. It was screened at the *Cinema Blvd* in Tehran for only four days. It was later submitted to the Locarno Film Festival in 1966 and awarded the Jean Epstein Prize for promoting cinematic language (Avery 1991, p. 798).

Pesar-e Iran az Madaresh Bi Ettela' Ast (Iran's Son Has No News of His Mother, 1974) was Fereydoun Rahnema's last film before his death. The film addresses Rahnema's preoccupations with Iranians' loss of national identity, the inconsistency of national history, and the relationship between today's modern Iranians and their past history and mythology that also he explored in his previous films *Persepolis* and *Siavash in Persepolis*.

In *Iran's Son Has No News of His Mother*, the protagonist (and director) is searching throughout history to find his identity in spaces that he is either a part of or alienated from, including once again, Persepolis. In response to why he had made Persepolis the subject of focus in his filmography, Rahnema replied: 'The reason that I focused on Persepolis was that its environment and ruins gave me the chance to declare my thoughts on life and art... what were these ruins? How true are the things we see today? What is the reality?' (Shoa'ee 1976, p. 76).

Rahnema attempts to engage with the unease that the modern Iranian experiences in coming to terms with their identity: 'As we may strive to be modern, and a part of the 20th century, and the industrial revolution, we are yet living with our mythical foundations' (Shoa'ee 1976, p. 4). As well as garnering praise from the likes of French-Iranian thinker Youssef Ishaghpour and the French film archivist and cinephile Henri Langlois (Shoa'ee 1976, p. 91), this served as the starting point for the specific principles of the New Wave cinema movement.

Rahnema repeatedly compared cinema to poetry. He would try to pursue the structure of poetry and its intended effects in his films: 'the poet is always in search of the meaning of existence: just as the filmmaker is a hunter of time and

Figure 6.14 *Iran's Son Has No News of His Mother* (1974), an alienated character searching for his identity by confronting the past.

existence. But he is not content with merely observing the calls upon all to see and at the same time, the poet speaks through imagery: just as the filmmaker does. Germaine Dulac was the pioneer of this thinking' (Shoa'ee 1976, p. 64).

He had an experimental approach towards cinema: 'We should not be afraid of experience. Life is a result of inexpressive and expressive experiences. It takes time to get a perfect way of expression in cinema and we should give people this time' (Shoa'ee 1976, p. 102). Nasib Nasibi, an avant-garde cinema practitioner of Iran and one of the founders of Iran's Free Cinema, in his conversation with Fereydoun Rahnema in 1971, admires him for his supportive attitude towards young and talented filmmakers:

> … You've always been supportive of young filmmakers. Not only of cinema people; but also poets, artists and theatre actors… When we were talking about *another* cinema and *experimental* cinema, the idea was to construct a huge wall between us and the cinema we liked and when we attempted doing so, you created the love and zeal of this cinema in us with your film *Siavash in Persepolis*.
>
> (Rahnema 1971, p. 72)

Rahnema's films were, as was the norm for all early New Wave films, maligned by the majority of Iranian film critics who criticized it as snobbish and incomprehensible. Speaking with Ahmad Faroughi Kadjar (Qajar), in response to the question 'What if the screening of your films in Iran is not financially successful?' Rahnema rationalized: 'It is exactly like you are asking me what will be the result of a passionate love affair? Without love and enthusiasm this film will never gain a colour to itself. All its aspects were difficult, from arranging the work to raising money, finding suitable cast and technical equipment' (Shoa'ee 1976, p. 91).

For Rahnema, mythology and history are contingent on one another. In fact, he never separates the two or distinguishes between them. In both *Siavash in Persepolis* and *Iran's Son Has No News of His Mother*, Rahnema used the metafiction structure of a 'film within a film' in a way that allows for a modern interaction, or conversation, with history. In *Siavash in Persepolis* a young director and his crew are making a film in the ruins of Persepolis about Siyavash, a Persian mythical figure in Ferdowsi's epic, the *Shahnameh*.

Siavash is a symbol of innocence and heroic martyrdom within Persian literature, someone who falls victim to the plots, deceptions and iniquity of the dishonourable people surrounding him. Being the son of Kay Kāvus, Shah of Iran, he was on the way to becoming a great and noble royal successor. He faced treason at the hands of his evil stepmother, Sudabeh (whose advances he rejected), and his father's ill-judged plan to kill the prisoners that Siavash captures. Thus he leaves Iran for rival Turan where he is wrongly executed by the order of the Turanian king, Afrasiab.

In *Iran's Son Has No News of His Mother* the young playwright who echoes Rahnema himself is fond of Iran's history and tries to depict, in a play, the war between the Parthians and the Greeks in an era when Iran battled with the West. In this meta play the Greeks can be seen to stand for Western imperialism and its influence whilst the Parthians are representatives of Iranians who are trying to come to terms with an unfamiliar force. The play suggests that the Parthians needed to know their foreign enemies in order to gain an accurate understanding of themselves. The playwright himself is presented as an alienated person who fails to comprehend the mentality of the group around him.

He is a legendary hero, a prince who, like Siavash, is a stranger to his own father and his nation. He feels alien in his own land and among his own people, and is closer to his enemies than to his own army, just like Siavash in the film *Siavash in Persepolis*. The Greek commander tells the Parthian commander: 'you are defending the people who see you as a stranger and obey us. You are defending an imaginary freedom'. The protagonist is worried about the Iranian loss of identity; he becomes rootless and cuts off all cultural connections with history and the past. The title of the film, *Iran's Son Has No News of His Mother*, is an allegory and is taken from a newspaper headline – a woman is looking for her child or the opposite, a child is looking for his mother (his motherland) Iran. Not knowing where the mother is, functions as a metaphor and shows how people are unaware of their identity and history.

The film was semi-autobiographical for the director who based it on his own personal experiences. He faced many problems in making the film and portraying his artistic and philosophical ideas. By showing the protagonist's difficulties in presenting the play, Rahnema explained parts of his own life and the atmosphere he worked in – encountering misunderstandings, jealousy and sabotage. His presence is actively felt through multiple scenes showing a hand writing his memories throughout the film and providing narration to the audience. This is, in fact, Rahnema hand writing his own memoir and the voice of the leading role of the film is dubbed by himself. Even the room, in which the main character of the film is located, is Rahnema's personal room. What he writes are short notes about the difficulties of screening the play, which are turned into haiku-like poems – the director's anecdotes: 'at times, life's invisible burden...'

The film's protagonist is an adventurous artist, his mind filled with questions that are not graspable by society at large. Despite all of the pressures, misunderstandings, harsh words and humiliation he suffers due to the behaviours of the people around him and interference and sabotage by fellow theatre players, he copes with all these shortcomings and never gives up, and in the end he succeeds. Similarly, despite the numerous difficulties and barriers he faced, Rahnema succeeded in making a different kind of film that was unusual at that time in Iran. However, his early and untimely death meant he was unable to witness the screening of his film for the first time in La Cinémathèque Française. This film could in fact be seen as Rahnema's last will and testament. Henri Langlois, director and co-founder of La Cinémathèque Française, described the film as a 'conversation between fact and fiction; a conversation between past and present, between history and the routine life of today' (Shoa'ee 1976, p. 91).

Rahnema was more of an archaeological thinker than a nationalist. His fondness for past culture and the nation's historic identity did not incline him towards chauvinist or absolute thinking, and he took a more critical approach to the past and history. In the film there is a quote from a Greek commander speaking to the Parthian commander: 'The rule in this land has been and is based on dictatorship and this is why this land is going to be destroyed; don't you ever forget it'. Though Rahnema was a patriotic Iranian, he never held any sort of hatred or grudge against the West and Western culture. He lived for years in Europe and spent a long time learning French, writing and publishing poems in the language. Westernized Iranians and their alienation towards their identity and to Iran's history was the major theme of many stories, plays and films made in Iran in the 1960s and 1970s, and this is strongly emphasized in Rahnema's films. The nativism in Rahnema's films and writings was a philosophical discourse common among the Iranian elites and intellectuals during the 1960s. It is an outlook that does not exist in today's world and in the routine lives of modern Iranians, and the filmmaker is remembering this with a sense of pity, regarding it as a loss of history.

In *Iran's Son Has No News of His Mother* we see the director writing: 'I see the oblivion scattered all over this land. Where is Iran? What is Iran?' Rahnema wants to bring the past to the present. He wants to remove the great distance between yesterday and today so that the people who are disconnected from their cultural and historical roots and identity and only think about and live in the present will remember their past. History and roots no longer have a place in the modern lives of superficially westernized Iranians and are only available to them in museum exhibits or theatrical performances.

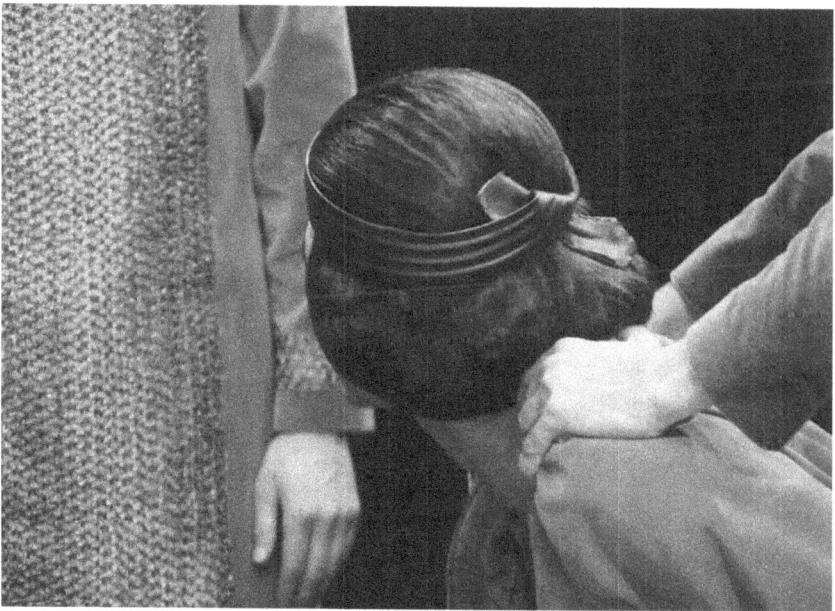

Figure 6.15 *Iran's Son Has No News of His Mother* (1974), a self-reflexive film consistent with the style of essay films.

The focus on Western-style rock and roll music and dancing shows Rahnema's concern for the tastes of the new generation and their loss of identity. Though he had lived in the West for a long time, he had never thought of himself as westernized in the sense that Jalal Al-e-Ahmad used the term, and he lived for Iran and its culture until the last moments of his life. The problems that the main characters of both films encounter are rooted in their sense of alienation from such 'westernized' people. Their history and identity prevent them from understanding or making any connection with such thoughts and views. Rahnema's observing camera in Iran's Archaeology Museum reflects his constant search through the history of Iran to discover the Iranian national identity. In the museum the camera pauses in front of a statue of a Parthian commander whose hand is cut out of the frame but appears in the next scene. This hand is filmed throughout the film, writing and narrating the story. Rahnema is suggesting that there are other hands that can replace the hand of the Parthian hero to complete the unfinished job for him.

Iran's Son Has No News of His Mother is an essay film reminiscent of the cinematic style of Jean-Luc Godard and Chris Marker. Rahnema's preachy tone in the film may be seen as damaging its narrative structure, but it is consistent with the style of essay films. Making space in the narration to intercut to the past (for example, the scenes in which they rehearse for the play) was highly innovative at the time. Rahnema benefits from a variety of audio visual material to express himself in the film, including photographs, historical documents and artefacts. The film's main weak point is the exaggerated and somewhat poor performance of its actors. The actors' artificial tone in their dialogue delivery is a barrier that prevents the audience connecting with the film and suspending their disbelief.

Rahnema separates the two worlds of yesterday and today through the use of colour; however, he avoids the cliché of showing the past in black and white by presenting it in colour, while all the scenes related to the present are in black and white. Only the rehearsal scenes and the show's performance are in colour. Rahnema's awareness of the spirit of the society around him is successfully reflected in the film. That is to say, he is aware of the criticisms likely to be raised because of the film's narrative structure, language, dialogue, the method of acting, and the way he looks to the past throughout the film. In fact, the film is Rahnema's harsh criticism of the cultural and intellectual climate of Iran's society in the 1960s. For example, Reza Zhian, the actor playing the role of the Iranian commander, protests about the royal focus in the play and tells the director: 'You know what? This play is all about royalty; the royalty which has caused us so many problems.' He then leaves the scene in protest. In other scenes, the producer and the players rail against the elitist way the show is presented, and the idealized and aristocratic way that history is viewed. They want the director to quit and to change the content of the play, so that it would appear more hopeful to the ordinary people. The new writer and director believe that the aristocratic hero of the film should be changed. This scene is not only a criticism aimed at the norms of cinema and art in Iran, but also a critique on the tendencies towards leftism and populist views common among the Iranian intellectuals of that era. The director of the play says to the theatre group members who want him to quit: 'A coup d'état against the director with the purpose of making the play popular is a democracy, isn't it?' In another scene, the carpenter who is the protagonist's best friend asks him: 'Why don't you choose a play which is modern and has less cost?' He replies: 'What they do [the Parthians] is related to today. What did the Parthians ask for? They asked for a better country.'

The dialogue continues:

Carpenter: Yes, I agree, but does anyone listen? Nowadays, people are so busy with their lives that they don't listen to facts anymore.
Director: This was true of the people at that time too. But Parthians could make people understand it.
Carpenter: But they were aristocrats, weren't they?
Director: So what?
Carpenter: Well, it is different. They didn't understand the ordinary people.
Director: How do you know? How do you know who understands the people?

Rahnema presented this conversation in a fixed sequence without cutting it into a number of shots or applying camera movement. This style of filmmaking was previously used by Arby Ovanessian in *Cheshmeh* (The Spring, 1972) and shows how much Rahnema and his generation of filmmakers were influenced by French cinema, especially the works of Robert Bresson, which had a radical impact on Iranian cinema at the time. *Iran's Son Has No News of His Mother* was a unique example of Iranian experimental and New Wave cinema because of the rigour with which it synthesized techniques found in new European cinema with distinctly Iranian motifs.

After the screening of the film at La Cinémathèque Française, Henri Langlois praised him in the following terms:

Fereydoun Rahnema was exactly the symbol of knowledge and wisdom. He was not only an intellectual but also a rustic wise man who understood the earth...

Figure 6.16 *Iran's Son Has No News of His Mother* (1974), Fereydoun Rahnema's last film.

> He was a reclusive person not because of his nature, but because they had made him so... He was a noble Iranian and we may not be able to find many Iranians like him.
>
> (Shoa'ee 1976, p. 91)

In the era that anti-Westernism and nativism (in the shape of radical nationalist ideologies or radical politicized Islam) was the main cultural and political discourse amongst Iranian intellectuals, Rahnema's nativism, while referring to ancient historical identity, was neither anti-Western nor reactionary. It was more like a warning against a perceived historical ignorance and an invitation to reassess history from a modern, unorthodox perspective. Rahnema wanted to build a bridge between Iranian thought and Western modern thought, and the anachronistic nature of his film and the floating of time between past and present reflect the postmodernist aspect of his cinema.

With his cinematic innovations and formalistic approach, Rahnema played an important role in Iranian New Wave cinema and made a major contribution to the promotion of the language and culture of arthouse cinema in Iran. Today, perhaps his cinematic language seems rather dense and even confusing to those who are not submerged in that culture and state of discourse. Yet Rahnema's bravery in using unconventional film language and his deliberate avoidance of the dominant sterile methods of structuring a film was a profound leap forward, and a powerful testimony to the true capabilities of Iranian cinema.

7

New Wave successors and new film aesthetics

Many filmmakers who came on the scene later in the 1970s would build upon the ideas developed by pioneers such as Golestan, Ghaffari and Rahnema, having been provided with a proof of concept and an effective framework through which they could convey notions and allusions that would otherwise not evade censorship, production and budgetary restrictions had they been relying on more conventional filmmaking.

A key difference between the various *Mowj-e No* filmmakers is seen in their different formal strategies as put forward by François Truffaut as part of his *auteur theory* and the rest of the French New Wave. *Mowj-e No* was an auteur-centric movement, with individual filmmakers trying to introduce their own personal styles and concepts, just as identifiably theirs as Truffaut's, Godard's or Hitchcock's. They would all realize such intentions with low budgets and limited equipment, sacrificing the merits of mainstream production methods for a fresh and modern look at their surroundings, almost always shooting on location rather than in studios.

The main difference between the *Mowj-e No* filmmakers was their approach to reality and the way that reality was represented in their films. Based on this notion, two general trends can be discerned within the *Mowj-e No*. The first trend is related to filmmakers with a formalist approach to cinema, namely those who were mainly concerned with the aesthetic elements and had a conscious style in the delivery of narrative. The second trend is related to those filmmakers with a tendency towards social realism and political films, namely those who were concerned with socio-political issues and realism. Although films such as Mehrjui's *Gav* (The Cow) and *The Cycle* are based on realistic imagery, material conditions and actual events, the auteur would stylize these themes in their own way.

Formalistic approach

Representation of reality in films such as *South of the City*, *Brick and Mirror*, *The Night of the Hunchback*, *Qaysar* and *Tranquility in the Presence of Others* were more explicit without reliance on symbolism, whereas other films had a more allegorical and metaphorical language. However, certain films such as *The Cow*, *The Mongols*, *Postman*, *O.K. Mister*, *Siavash in Persepolis*, *Prince Ehtejab*, *The Chess of the Wind* and *The Stranger and the Fog* had expressionist, surrealist, fantasy, mythological-ritual and historical aspects in them, on the one hand, and were connected with social and political realities of Iranian society, on the other.

Filmmakers such as Arby Ovanessian, Abbas Kiarostami, Parviz Kimiavi and Sohrab Shahid-Saless, influenced by modern European cinema, formed their own aesthetic by artfully pairing diegetic simplicity with stylistic elements which served as a font of inspiration for many later directors. In their films, the camera is used as a method of commenting on the subjects, a means of emphasizing its essential rather than its objective nature.

Regarding the narrative structure, some of the *Mowj-e No* films have a classic and linear narrative structure, such as *Ahu Khanoom's Husband*, *Gav* and *Tangsir*, but others have a modern, episodic and unusual narrative structure such as *Brick and Mirror* (1965), *The Mongols* (1973) and *Siavash in Persepolis* (1965). Films of this latter category are connected via what Deleuze referred to as 'irrational cuts' – breaking the barriers of reality and the imaginary world that allows for the creation of the 'new image of thought' (Deleuze 2005, p. xvi). This was a central conceit of Deleuze's that was made apparent by the modern cinema of the post-war period by the likes of Orson Welles, Alain Renais and Marguerite Duras. According to Deleuze, the 'new image of thought' no longer relies on the world or subject but instead is connected through such irrational cuts between the non-linked sequences and confrontation taking place between outside and inside (Deleuze 2005, p. xvi).

This results in a more subjective quality rather than an objective one, as the filmmaker chooses to represent the internal crises of the characters. This is in contrast to the prior category of films such as *Qaysar* (1969) or *The Night of the Hunchback* (1965), where the strife of the characters in the narrative is set against external forces and society at large. This differentiation is apparent in the films' use of dialogue: they feature long monologues which help to reveal more about the mental state of the character rather than trying to propel the films' narrative. As an example, in Golestan's *Brick and Mirror*, Hashem the taxi driver encounters an old lady on the outskirts of town talking to herself; her words are incomprehensible, but help emphasize the ominous tone of the film and elaborate on the feeling of angst and suffocation felt by the protagonist: '... we sleep in the day and awake at night... they took the wheat, the barley, kept digging, building foundations, keep raising walls, wall above our heads...'.

Such psychological exposition, in particular the mental anguish, psychological unease, or general sense of insanity, which reflected the intellectual atmosphere of the time, was often explored in many *Mowj-e No* films including *Brick and Mirror*, *The Cow*, *Tranquility in the Presence of Others*, *The Cycle* and *The Stone Garden*.

Although Golestan's approach in *Brick and Mirror* is social realism, Michelangelo Antonioni's influence is evident in Golestan's use of jump cuts and discontinuities in editing, and his long takes with fluid camera movements following his wandering characters in the streets of Tehran at night. It has commonality in this sense with Antonioni's *La Notte*, *Red Desert* and *Eclipse* in terms of its episodic structure and free-flowing narrative style, its emphasis on dead time, its visual claustrophobia and 'trapping' of characters with long take shots and wide focus as well as its existentialist themes with lonely and alienated characters wandering in the city like a *flâneur* figure in Charles Baudelaire's nineteenth-century poems. The inability of the protagonist to find respite in his relationship and the wider environment also evokes the concept of the *flâneur*, a French term meaning 'stroller' referring to the casual wanderer amongst and observer of modern urban life. The *flâneur* for Baudelaire was a man who could 'reap aesthetic meaning from the spectacle of the teeming crowds – the visible public – of the metropolitan environment of the city of Paris' (Tester 1994, p. 2).

It was Walter Benjamin who borrowed the term from Baudelaire and turned this figure from a street wanderer to an observer of the damaging effects of modernity and capitalism and the object of scholarly interest in the twentieth century (Shaya 2004, pp. 41–77). This *flâneur* character trope/street wanderer serves as an effective means to communicate larger societal woes without the need to directly centre the motivation and actions of the character on such matters; this makes the social commentary more subtle and indirect whilst letting the audience feel the full force of it. As a result, it is a convention that can be found in many New Wave films. *Brick and Mirror* features many scenes dedicated to the wandering of Taji and Hashem through the streets of Tehran. In

Nasser Taghvai's *Tranquility in the Presence of Others* (1969/73), a retired and depressed army colonel walks down the street of the capital without any specific purpose other than to observe the goings on. The colonel's monologues are used to emphasize the sense of a disturbed and melancholic mindset: 'The worst hours of my life were spent sleeping, I never took comfort in my sleep, my hell is sleep, strange nightmares, in the dark they sit in front of me and gaze at me'. As this film was a direct adaptation of a short story written by Gholamhossein Sa'edi and the subjective quality is one of the key characteristics of Sa'edi's stories, Taghvai incorporated this element into the film.

The other point of differentiation between the New Wave films is the approach to utilization of time. There are films that use chronological sequences and narratives, whilst in another set of films the physical and rational continuity of time is broken. The images in these films are 'no longer linked by rational cuts and continuity', as with Deleuze's concept of time-image in modern cinema. As Deleuze says, what these films lose in explicit structure they relink using 'false continuity and irrational cuts' (Deleuze 2005, p. xii). In *Brick and Mirror* (1965) and Sohrab Shahid-Saless's *Tabiat-e Bijaan* (Still Life, 1974), whilst the passage of time is linear in both films, time is not deployed purely to drive forward the narrative, but is also used for conveyance of implicit meanings, including the emotional states of characters as well as themes such as exhaustion, existential dread, isolation and foreboding. Within *Brick and Mirror*, there is a scene set in an orphanage where Taji (the female lead) is looking for the child who was left abandoned at the hands of Hashem. Upon not being able to find her, the shot slowly tracks out and away from Taji, emphasizing her isolation, frustration and loneliness. This is not done merely to drive forward the plot but to reveal the internal strife and mindset of Taji at that moment. In Sohrab Shahid-Saless's *Tabiat-e Bijaan* (Still Life, 1974) there is an almost 7-minute-long, still shot of an old woman trying to thread a needle. This ostensibly bears no direct relevance to the overall plot and instead serves as a deliberate temporal interruption. We see the application of what Andrei Tarkovsky referred to as 'pressure of time in a shot', allowing for a length of shot dictated by a poetic/organic rhythm. As Adam Bingham remarks in his article on Shahid-Saless's cinema,

> he employs what at times feels like a conventional continuity decoupage (an analytical breakdown of space, establishing shots, shot/reverse shots, etc) that directly affects the relationship between spectator and text, and frustrates both a documentary aesthetic and an overt and obvious art cinematic methodology.

This conflation of styles and frustration of any single, dominant paradigm or framework lends a certain timeless quality to the film.

(Bingham, in Jahed 2017, p. 51)

Sohrab Shahid-Saless is undoubtedly one of the pivotal figures of the *Mowj-e No* movement and a highly formalist Iranian filmmaker. With his two feature films that he made in Iran, *Yek Etefagh-e Sadeh* (A Simple Event, 1973) and *Still Life* (1974), he established an outstanding film style in Iranian cinema that had not existed hitherto. *A Simple Event* won two awards at the 1974 Berlin Film Festival.

According to Adam Bingham, 'Shahid-Saless was a major influence on Abbas Kiarostami and other modern Iranian directors, and made at least one landmark film that extends the parameters of European art cinema, conflating both national and international paradigms into a picture that redefined the boundaries of Iranian national filmmaking at a critical juncture in its history and development' (Bingham in Jahed 2017, p. 49).

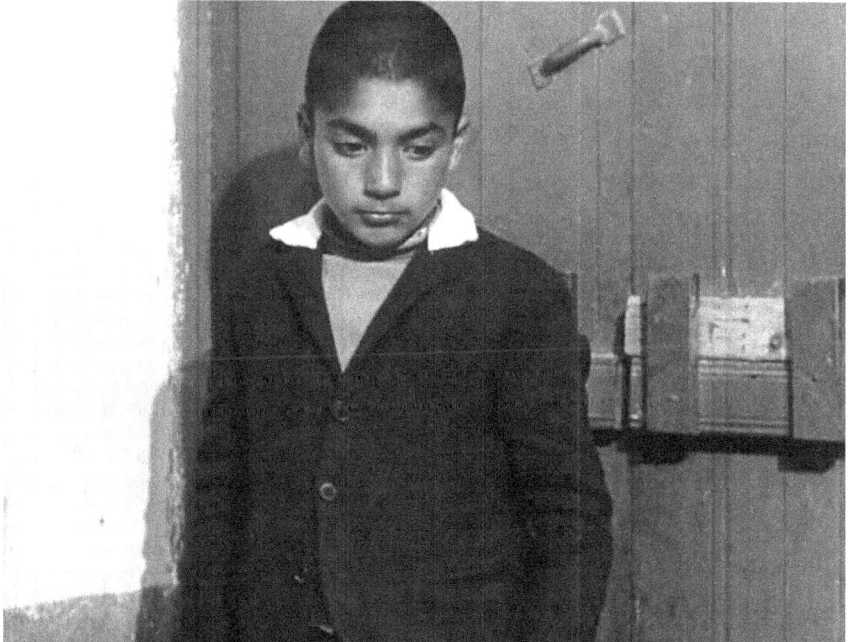

Figure 7.1 *A Simple Event* (1973), an outstanding New Wave film directed by Sohrab Shahid-Saless.

Shahid-Saless was a stylistic, minimalist filmmaker who attempted to establish a sense of continuity of space and time through long takes, static frames, tracking shots and emphasis on dead time instead of quick cuts and dramatic elements, paying regard to seemingly trivial events and extended pauses in action. He shows the boredom, despair and loneliness of the repetitive and monotonous lives of his characters through continuous and fixed long takes. Realism, slow rhythm, use of silence and pauses, emphasis on repetitive moments and motifs, avoiding sentimentalism and theatrical acting are characterizations that were highly influential on later filmmakers. European filmmakers such as Béla Tarr and Chantal Akerman would employ such techniques, but the extent to which they were exposed to Shahid-Saless's work at that time is unknown.

Shahid-Saless's unstoppable urge for creative expression was at odds with the restrictions of the Iranian government upon his freedoms and ability to realize his visions. He emigrated to Germany shortly after making *Still Life*, and he would create the remainder of his filmography in Germany, producing several films that are mainly set in German society and have little direct connection to Iran. One exception was his first film made in Germany, *Dar Ghorbat* (Far From Home, 1975) about a middle-aged immigrant (played by Parviz Sayyad, who also financed and produced the film) living an extremely isolated existence and unable to make a life for himself in the diaspora. The director's techniques had also changed to a large extent with these films – he would no longer use non-actors and would employ techniques such as a moving camera – although his main themes remained universal human ones, not limited to a specific environment and geography.

The poor orphaned child of *A Simple Event* or the elderly railway signalman of *Still Life*, although Iranian, are relatable to any audience and not just limited to Iranian society. The dull, universally identifiable struggles of the day-to-day lives of ordinary people can also be found in the films of Robert Bresson, Yasujiro Ozu, Chantal Akerman and Béla Tarr. The Turkish immigrant workers of Shahid-Saless's *Far From Home* or the prostitutes that are found in *Utopia* (1983) are not only to be found in Berlin, but also in the streets of London, New York and Tehran.

In his early films, Shahid-Saless achieved a kind of cinematic style which relies on his neorealist aesthetics and minimalist approach, a methodology that later became the hallmark of Abbas Kiarostami and some of his followers in Iran. The murky atmosphere of Shahid-Saless's films is more like the cold, depressing and gloomy atmospheres of Robert Bresson's or Béla Tarr's films without the spiritual and religious aspects of Bresson's cinema.

A Simple Event is a minimalist film with a very simple plot that follows the monotonous daily life of a little boy in a remote small town in the north of Iran. He has to deliver the fish that his grumpy and patriarchal father catches illegally to sell to the local shop while his mother is deathly ill at home. There is no music in the film and Shahid-Saless uses silence as an aesthetic element to emphasize the mundane aspects of their lives. The death of the boy's mother has no effect on him.

Shahid-Saless's films are full of silence and convey the psychological and emotional damage and loneliness of people not through conversation but through the silence that flows between his mute characters. The external and the internal rhythm in his films are in a precise balance. Time stretches and suspends in his films. Unlike Tarkovsky's films, in which the slowness of rhythm and the heaviness of the passage of time are used to convey a transcendental concept that seeks rhythm in search of something sublime, Shahid-Saless uses it to convey the monotonous and boring state of everyday life.

The simple narrative structure, using non-actors, filming on location and using long takes are some neorealist aspects of *A Simple Event*. By avoiding conventional rules of cinema such as chains of cause and effect,

Figure 7.2 In *Still Life* (1974) Shahid-Saless shows the boredom, despair and loneliness of the repetitive and monotonous lives of his characters through continuous and fixed long takes.

dramatic conflict, suspense, climax and dénouement, Shahid-Saless was able to introduce a new language of film into Iranian cinema. The film was made during the height of the forced modernization of society by the Shah's government, and was a swipe at the hype and flamboyant propaganda of the Shah's 'Great Civilization'.

The impressive visual aspects of Shahid-Saless's films rely mainly on the open and abandoned places and spaces of his films. The desolate and depressing remote island of Ashuradeh in *A Simple Event* or the cold, winter landscapes around the railway line in *Still Life* are highly abstract and melancholic spaces that are organically related to the boredom and the loneliness of his characters. It is in these spaces that the futile life of the boy in *A Simple Event* and his fisherman father or the retired signalman of *Still Life* takes shape. We also see such a relationship between the melancholic spaces in Berlin and the film characters in *Far From Home*. Shahid-Saless, like Michelangelo Antonioni in *Red Desert* (1964) or Nuri Bilge Ceylan's in *Uzak* (Distance, 2002), uses washed-out dirty green and blue colours to turn the modern urban space into a deserted place that alienates.

Shahid-Saless was fascinated by his favourite writer, Anton Chekhov, and his engagement with the everyday life of ordinary people. In interviews he would go out of his way to acknowledge Chekhov's influence on his work: 'I don't have a role model in cinema. My role model is Chekhov. If Chekhov were alive, he could easily bring his stories back to the film. I've got the rhythm of my films from Chekhov's stories. I'm also indebted to Chekhov in developing the theme of my films' (Amini Najafi 2010).

He was not shy about his intention to stand out from the ordinary and was more than willing to take creative risks without fear of failure. When asked about his style of filmmaking he said, 'People do not go to the North Pole and fall off icebergs; they go to offices, quarrel with their wives and eat cabbage soup' (Close-Up Film Centre 2017).

Shahid-Saless continued his filmmaking in Germany in exile. He made *The Willow Tree* based on a short story by Anton Chekhov in 1984. He also paid homage to this great Russian writer who had a profound influence on his cinematic vision by making a documentary film about him called *Chekhov, a Life* (1981).

Abbas Kiarostami is arguably the most famous Iranian filmmaker in the world. He has won many prestigious film awards, including the Palme d'Or at the Cannes Film Festival for his *Ta'm-e Guilass* (Taste of Cherry, 1997).

Kiarostami was one of the founders of *Kanoon-e Parvaresh-e Fekri-e Koodakan va Nojavanan*, better known as *Kanoon*/the Center for the Intellectual Development of Child and Adolescent (CIDCA), a cultural institution which, along with Telfilm an affiliated company of National Iranian Television (NIRT), had an important role in the development of arthouse cinema in Iran in the late 1960s. It was a film centre where many young Iranian filmmakers such as Beyzaie, Taghvai, Naderi, Kimiai, Shahid-Saless and Aslani made their first short films.

Although Kiarostami started making films before the revolution, making short films about children at *Kanoon* (CIDCA), it was not until after the revolution that he gained worldwide fame and achieved credentials for Iranian cinema with his films. Kiarostami has been active in Iranian cinema for more than four decades, and with his short and feature-length documentaries and fictions, and his poetic and minimalist approach, he has had a profound impact on Iranian and world cinema.

In Kiarostami's films, language and locations are not limited to ritual and cultural issues, and could be easily understood by worldwide audiences; in this respect his films are very similar to the cinema of Shahid-Saless. Kiarostami's filmmaking methods are related to, if not directly, Shahid-Saless's in many ways, namely usage of long takes, deploying non-actors, filming in remote areas, using silence and dead time and the contrast between stillness and moving images.

Alberto Elena would write about *Nan-o-Kocheh* (Bread and Alley, 1970), Kiarostami's first film he made at *Kanoon*,

> the film has no dialogue, like many others he made during his years at Kanoon, but Kiarostami expertly chooses silence or music to back particular sequences. Silence is used to great effect to underline the dead times, which are also the most important decision-making times for the protagonist, when he must discover for himself the solution (a recurring and important word in Kiarostami's short films) to his dilemma.
>
> (Elena 2005, p. 19)

Focusing on the worldview of children and their dilemmas and the ingenuity and strength they show in being able to solve problems and overcoming obstacles that stand in their way, their relationship with adults, their embarking upon a journey as a means to understand the world around them are all themes that Kiarostami perpetuates in his short films at *Kanoon*. Emphasis on off-screen

Figure 7.3 *Bread and Alley* (1970) introduces Kiarostami's minimalist style.

sound, capturing the rhythms and the tempo of real life with a microscopic view of life's details were some of the stylistic features of his film that are perpetuated in his later films. In fact, Kiarostami was the first director to turn his attention to children in Iranian cinema; previously the real life of children and especially those in underprivileged communities had been largely ignored, like the infant in Golestan's *Brick and Mirror* (1965) who society has abandoned. With Kiarostami's films in *Kanoon* the floodgates opened on the subject and it found its rightful place in Iranian cinema with a host of films made about children and the worlds of children, some of them being the most recognizable and iconic examples of arthouse films in Iran.

There is a similar scene to Kiarostami's *Bread and Alley* in Shahid-Saless's *A Simple Event* when the little boy has to deliver the fish his father caught illegally to the local shop, he confronts a guard and tries to escape but has to drop the fish. There is no dialogue or even music in the scene, and Shahid-Saless uses a long take to show the dangerous situation of the boy without resorting to stereotypical elements such as suspense or excitement and avoids using close-ups to stress the fear on his face.

In his analysis of Kiarostami's second feature-length film, *Gozaresh* (Report, 1977), Alberto Elena discovers a relationship between *Report* and the strict minimalism of Shahid-Saless's films (Elena 2005, p. 47). Lack of dramatic features, empty spaces, slight and subtle camera movements and long sprawling takes, repetitive motifs and scenes, and use of non-actors comprise the common elements. Kiarostami and Shahid-Saless started to make films at *Kanoon* at the same time, so this similarity could be totally accidental. Although Kiarostami always showed respect to Shahid-Saless and his work, he never mentioned any influence of Shahid-Saless on his films. Furthermore, while they were both formalist and minimalist they had different philosophies. Shahid-Saless was a pessimist filmmaker whereas Kiarostami was more optimistic about life and existence.

Kiarostami's *Gozaresh* is a family drama focused on a marital crisis of a middle-class couple in modern Tehran of the late 1970s, a self-portrait of Kiarostami's own family crisis. It was the only pre-revolutionary film that Kiarostami made outside of *Kanoon* with professional actors in the main roles. It is also one of Kiarostami's most pessimistic films; his other films always expressed hope even in bitter, grimy films such as *Ta'm-e Guilass* (Taste of Cherry, 1997). In *Report*, he chose melodrama to tackle some critical social issues such as corruption, financial problems of middle-class Iranians, bribery and the bureaucratic system. According to Elena, 'the demoralization of the whole country can be

Figure 7.4 Kiarostami's *Gozaresh* (Report, 1977), a family drama focused on a marital crisis of a middle-class couple in modern Tehran in the late 1970s.

clearly perceived in the *Report*, where we find no less than a society sinking inexorably into ruin, in exactly the same way as the Firuzkuis's marriage; its emotional and sexual breakdown provides a perfect illustration' (Elena 2005, p. 46).

Kiarostami always said that his approach to cinema was instinctive and spontaneous: 'I do not make films with any theory in my mind. I make films very instinctively' (Cronin 2017). Many film theorists including Jean-Luc Nancy and Laura Mulvey, however, acknowledged the postmodern aspect of his cinema. Uncertainty, open-ended stories with narrative gaps left open to audience interpretation are among the postmodernist features of Kiarostami's films. According to Mulvey, uncertainty is one of the postmodern aspects of Kiarostami's cinema. 'Uncertainty is built into Kiarostami's cinema' and is what differentiates him from Shahid-Saless and other Iranian New Wave filmmakers: 'While Kiarostami has played an important role in defining the aesthetic and formal characteristics of the Iranian New Wave cinema, his films reach out towards key questions about the nature of cinema as a medium' (Mulvey 2002, p. 260). In Mulvey's view it is the questioning of the nature of cinema that makes Kiarostami's films so impressive to Western cinephiles and film theorists.

While Shahid-Saless's and Kiarostami's New Wave films represent contemporary Iranian society and its internal tensions, filmmakers such as Beyzaie, Kimiavi and Rahnema engage in the challenges of modern Iranians with their past and historical identity. In the works of Rahnema, Kimiavi or Beyzaie we find the primary characters have been disturbed by past trauma and memories and are constantly moving back and forth between their present and their past. Beyzaie's *Kalagh* (The Crow, 1977) has a plot centring around an advert for a missing girl, who in fact turns out to be a photograph of the protagonist's own mother as a child. In Beyzaie's *Shayad Vaghti Digar* (Maybe Some Other Time, 1988) the protagonist has a tenuous connection to her identity and her past memories; we see flashbacks of her being abandoned as a child in the streets and hounded by a terrifying street dog.

Parviz Kimiavi, in his first feature film *Mogholha* (The Mongols, 1973), plays a film director who is making a film about the Mongols' invasion of Iran and explores the parallels between the history of the invasion and the expression of his own identity. *The Mongols* is a self-reflexive film dealing with the notion of anachronism and combines the past, present and future to show a filmmaker who is caught between different times in his dreams and his real life. The director, who has been struggling with his screenplay on the history of cinema,

Figure 7.5 Parviz Kimiavi's *Mogholha* (The Mongols, 1973), a modern self-reflexive film dealing with the notion of anachronism.

is sent on a mission to oversee the installation of a television relay station in a remote region of southeast Iran near the Afghanistan border. Meanwhile his wife is working on her thesis on the Mongol invasion of Iran. Like Godard's avant-garde films, Kimiavi juxtaposes the history of cinema and the history of the Mongol invasion with the struggle of the main character who is obsessed with his project.

One of the most overt examples of experimentation with time is found in Bahram Beyzaie's film *Charike-ye Tara* (Ballad of Tara, 1979), where a character exists within the film referred to as 'Historical Man'; his presence is logic defying as he has ostensibly come from a different realm and time than the other characters of the film, in the search for his ancestors' sword. He is operating on a different level than the other characters, simply appearing in scenes. His dialogue is out of place among them, with lines such as ' from my ancestry nothing has remained but this sword'. In one scene as Tara (the female character) and the Historical Man are near a historic castle where he fought a battle in the past, he says 'this was the place where my head cracked, and this is the rock upon which our hope was broken. We were deceived by fate'. In his speech the Historical Man is providing historical context and exposition for a narrative that is not directly apparent within the plot.

Alongside filmmakers like Beyzaie and Rahnema who were dealing with the issue of Iranian identity and Iran's historical past and made films with a utopian approach, filmmakers such as Mohammad Reza Aslani and Arby Ovanessian were more inclined towards Islamic and Christian mysticism and a kind of spiritual cinema with a formalistic approach. Their films were mainly influenced by filmmakers such as Robert Bresson and Carl Dreyer and could fit well within a categorization that Paul Schrader referred to as 'Transcendental Style' cinema. According to Schrader,

> Yasujiro Ozu in Japan, Robert Bresson in France, to a lesser degree Carl Dreyer in Denmark, and other directors in various countries have forged a remarkably common film form. This common form was not determined by the film-makers' personalities, culture, politics, economics, or morality. It is instead the result of two universal contingencies: the desire to express the Transcendent in art and the nature of the film medium. In the final result no other factors can give this style its universality.
>
> (Schrader 2018, p. 35)

For Schrader, films employing a transcendental style can be studied from a personal and cultural perspective, displaying a spiritual truth that is achieved by 'objectively setting objects and pictures side by side that cannot be obtained through a subjective personal or cultural approach to those objects… This form [beyond the personal and cultural differences between Ozu, Bresson and Dreyer] is remarkably unified' (Schrader 2018, p. 41).

Some of the elements that he attributes to the transcendental style, like austere camerawork, acting devoid of self-consciousness and editing that avoids editorial comment, are keenly present in Ovanessian's *Cheshmeh* (The Spring, 1972) and in Mohammad Reza Aslani's recently rediscovered film *Shatranj-e Baad* (The Chess of the Wind, 1976).

Like Golestan and Kamran Shirdel, Mohammad Reza Aslani, a modern poet in the first instance, began his filmmaking career as a documentary filmmaker. He worked with Fereydoun Rahnema as a member of his *Iran Zamin* TV documentary series and made *Jaam-e Hassanlou* (Hassanlou Cup, 1968), an experimental documentary film that was highly controversial at the time. Like Shirdel, Aslani's contribution to the movement was two scripts that he co-wrote and just one film that he was able to make before the Islamic Revolution. This was *Shatranj-e Baad* (The Chess of the Wind), a gothic thriller that was never given a chance to be screened in Iran publicly except for a damaged copy of the film that was shown at Tehran International Film Festival in 1976 (that is, until recently, when a restored print of the long-lost film was discovered in an antique shop in 2014 and restored in 2020 by Martin Scorsese's the Film Foundation's World Cinema Project). It is a period drama that takes place near the end of the Qajar era and tells the story of a disabled noble woman living in a gothic-style mansion inherited from her mother whilst warding off the attempts by her stepfather and his nephews to take over the inheritance.

The influence of European arthouse cinema is evident in the film. Aslani acknowledges the influence of Carl Dreyer, Luchino Visconti and Robert Bresson on his film style, but he is also inspired by European painters such as Vermeer as well as Iranian miniatures for the compositions found in the film. The film was unusual for Iran, especially of that time period, due to its sapphic erotic elements and for merely being a female-centred story.

Arby Ovanessian's *Cheshmeh* (The Spring) could be considered an outlier film even by the standards of pre-revolutionary New Wave Iranian cinema. An allegorical film loosely based on the *Spring of Heghnar*, a novel by Megreditch Armen, an Armenian novelist, the film premiered at the first Tehran

Figure 7.6 Mohammad Reza Aslani's recently rediscovered film *Shatranj-e Baad* (The Chess of the Wind, 1976), a gothic thriller that was never given a chance to be screened in Iran publicly.

International Film Festival and at the Venice Film Festival but was not well received by Iranian audiences and film critics at the time despite its stunning visual and narrative structure. Some critics felt personally offended by a perceived slight on Islamic sensibilities and values by Ovanessian, a Christian filmmaker, covering topics such as infidelity with unwonted candour.

The events of the film occur in an unnamed, remote Armenian village. A young woman with an elderly husband begins an affair with a young lover. Their secret is revealed and the woman resorts to commiting suicide. It is a sign of faith and an eternal love which is reflected in the characters of a woman and her two lovers. By mixing the present with the past and reality with imagination, Ovanessian succeeds in transferring the poetic qualities of the novel into film. It addresses spiritual themes and is built around a dualistic viewpoint, with dichotomies of life and death; good and evil; light and darkness; love and hatred; innocence and peccadillo; faithfulness and betrayal; and movement and stillness. For Ovanessian, death is not the end of life but the continuation of it. Tilting up the camera to film a giant tree is a metaphor for life and continuity. The inherent tragedy of the film's tale comes as a result of the conflict between love and the oppressive forces it must overcome, desires which ultimately lead to ruinous consequences due to the traditions, morals and values held by the society. Ovanessian's inclinations towards Armenian culture and Christian iconography make this universal story uniquely interesting amongst Iranian films.

In terms of iconography, every single frame of the film has been designed with precision and a stylistic and minimalist approach. There are scenes that allegorically refer to biblical figures, such as Judas Iscariot and Mary Magdalene and the influences of Carl Theodor Dreyer and Robert Bresson are keenly felt here. Ovanessian's basic technique was to lock the camera in place in a meticulously planned frame to achieve an entrancing level of harmony and balance and to let the scenes play out. As well as complementing the drawn-out tempo, the camera manages to create various atmospheres. On the notable occasion where the camera does move, it tilts up to a big tree in the clear sky, accompanied by operatic Armenian music. It features a linear narrative and static long-take shots of the everyday lives of characters with little regard for the dramatic conventions on which the plot hinges. Like Bresson and Dreyer, Ovanessian uses transcendental means of communicating his Christian theology as well as his Armenian orthodox heritage. With its slow pace, Ovanessian has tried to capture the real rhythm of life of the village, the actual time which a certain act takes in real life and the memories of the past which remain with the characters. *Cheshmeh* (The Spring) is a masterwork and a remarkable debut film from a highly disciplined and determined figure. Unfortunately he never had the opportunity to recapture the same artistic success again, as he was disappointed with the cold public and critical reception to *The Spring*, and became disillusioned filmmaking in Iran to an extent and instead he opted to pursue theatre directing.

When he emigrated to France, whilst he did make attempts to create films, he did not have access to the same resources and opportunities to be able to maintain the status he had in Iran for his work on film and stage.

Khosrow Haritash was another outstanding figure of the movement. A graduate of the USC School of Cinematic Arts in Los Angeles in 1966, Haritash made only four feature films, namely *Adamak* (The Dummy, 1971), *Berehneh ta Zohr ba Sorat* (Naked until Noon with Speed, 1976), *Soraydar* (The Janitor, 1976) and *Malakout* (Divine One, 1976), of which only *The Janitor* survives to this day whilst the others have been destroyed. He paid his dues by serving as the assistant to Samuel Khachikian, the veteran director known as the Iranian Hitchcock, working on some of the most technically competent films

Figure 7.7 Arby Ovanessian's *Cheshmeh* (The Spring, 1972), a stylistic New Wave film.

which would still fall under the *Filmfarsi* classification. In his directorial debut *Adamak*, Haritash addressed issues such as modernism and the gap between different generations. His second film *Berehneh ta Zohr ba Sorat* (Naked until Noon with Speed, 1976) was an erotic film banned for its nudity. Heritash's *The Janitor* was an adaptation of the novel *Komedi Heivani* (The Animal Comedy) written by Hassan Ali Sharifi Mehr. It was made with a neorealist approach and was about the life of an impoverished family living in the suburbs of Tehran.

Apart from Forough Farrokhzad, Marva Nabili is the other female filmmaker of the New Wave movement. She made just one film, *Khaak-e Sar Beh Morh* (The Sealed Soil, 1976), which was never given a chance to be shown in Iran because of censorship. Nabili studied cinema in London and New York before returning to Iran in the mid 1970s. She worked with Fereydoun Rahnema as an actor and appeared in his *Siavash in Persepolis* (1965). Nabili's *The Sealed Soil* is one of the rare feminist films in the movement with a female protagonist (the other one is Hajir Dariush's *Bita*) that focused on Iranian women's problems in a traditional society. Like most *Mowj-e No* films, the main theme of *The Sealed Soil* is focused on the dichotomy between tradition and modernity. The film is focused on a young village girl named Rooy-Bekheir (Flora Shabaviz) and her persistent refusal of proposals for her hand in marriage by various suitors. The old village that is surrounded by a newly built sprawling city encroaching upon their town, metaphorically embodies the main theme of the film. Rooy-Bekheir is caught between the traditional values of her small village and her own desire for independence and individuality. She has not yet been directly impacted by any form of modern life or modern ideas. In a further bout of stubbornness, she refuses to go into the new town that is being constructed near her village. This, coupled with her rejection of traditional values, makes her an outcast. Rooy-Bekheir's controversial behaviour causes alarm amongst the villagers who believe that she has become possessed by a demon and needs to be cured by an exorcist. There are no close-ups within the film and the main character is usually seen in medium shots or long shots from a distance, the visual language of the film is simple and placid in some ways, and the camera is used as a simple tool of observation. Like Shahid-Saless, Nabili rarely uses camera movement and tracking shots except in a few scenes but instead she establishes a visual style composed of static shots and an observational camera which again is reminiscent of Bresson and Akerman's aesthetic.

The Sealed Soil was smuggled out of Iran by Nabili and taken to the United States, where she completed her final cut. A restored copy of the film was shown

Figure 7.8 Marva Nabili's *Khake Sar Beh Morh* (The Sealed Soil, 1976) which focused on the dichotomy between tradition and modernity in Iran.

at the London Feminist Film Festival at the BFI Southbank in September 2017 which Nabili attended for a Q&A session. During the Q&A she explained that *The Sealed Soil* was made clandestinely because the Shah regime would not allow people to film villages and only 'progress' was allowed to be shown when it came to rural Iran.

Hajir Dariush, an influential critic and a film graduate from IDHEC in Paris, had a significant role in organizing the Tehran International Film Festival before the Islamic Revolution. Like Arby Ovanessian, Mohammad Reza Aslani and Kamran Shirdel, he made just one feature-length film, *Bita* (1972). After making a documentary film called *Goud-e Moghadas* (Sacred Arena), Dariush made his first short fiction film *Jeld-e Maar* (Serpent's Skin) in 1964 loosely based on D. H. Lawrence's *Lady Chatterley's Lover*. Dariush then made his first and last feature-length fiction melodrama *Bita* in 1972, based on a short story by Goli Taraghi, which was a feminist *Mowj-e No* film dealing with the problems of a modern woman in a traditional society. Bita, a young lonely woman, struggles to come to terms with social barriers in her life. She is a simple and beautiful girl who, after the death of her mentally ill father and rejection by her boyfriend, becomes depressed and frustrated.

Like Nasser Taghvai in *Tranquility in the Presence of Others*, Dariush shows the moral decline of middle-class Iranians on the verge of transforming to modernism. Bita is humiliated by her intellectual boyfriend and is forced to marry a man she does not love, and is eventually left alone and helpless on the streets of Tehran. Influenced by Antonioni's film style, Dariush uses empty spaces and silence to convey the loneliness and despair of his central character.

Social realism and the street film genre

According to Susan Hayward, social realism in film

> refers as it does in literature, to a depiction of social and economic circumstances within which a particular echelon of society (usually the working and middle classes) find themselves. The earliest examples of this tradition in sound cinema, however, date back to the 1930s and it is John Grierson and his work in documentary that is generally credited with the introduction of the social-realist aesthetic into narrative cinema.
>
> (Hayward 2000, p. 331)

The movements that the *social problem* film is closely associated with are national cinemas during certain periods of time, notably Italian neorealism of the 1940s, but also Free British Cinema of the 1950s and the British New Wave of the 1960s as well as France's *Cinéma vérité* of the 1960s.

Social realism is a prominent trend in Iranian *Mowj-e No* and national cinema to this day, and one that was keenly embraced by the generations of filmmakers that came after the first wave. These were creatives who were primarily left-leaning and deeply concerned with the social and political entanglements of Iranian society – from class divisions, poverty and social injustice to political tyranny – and deeply influenced by Italian neorealism and Latin American political cinema. These filmmakers made stories resonating with the lives of ordinary people, raising powerful questions as well as introspecting on the most deprived sections of society. They portray sympathetic and under-dramatized elements of everyday life and the struggle for survival. Their stories centre around characters' interactions with social institutions.

With the continuation and amplification of the state's efforts to enforce modernization, foreign interference transforming burgeoning popular rule into oppressive government control at an all-time high with the prevalence of secret police and domestic spying campaigns, as well as turbulent economics booming for some whilst leaving many behind, the conflict between modern and traditional values became established as a theme that trickled over into cinematic form. This occurred long before the New Wave and was a recurrent theme and staple genre within *Filmfarsi*. In the late 1960s, the same conflict allowed for a new form of crime thriller to take hold in Iranian New Wave cinema, which was darker and more pessimistic than the earlier, more hollow efforts.

What could perhaps be viewed as an early offshoot of this type of storytelling, one with a much more visceral approach, came to be known as the '*Film-e Khiabani*' (street film genre). These were vengeance-driven tales which were a simulacrum of works by Italian political and post-neorealist directors such as Francesco Rosi, Elio Petri and Giuliano Montaldo – displaying their desire to denounce the powerful status quo. Thus, the Iranian imitators would follow the same story beats in an effort to scratch the itch for protest, whilst developing political consciousness and expressing resentment and tacitly advocating for the breakdown of structures of inequality and suppression Iranians were facing at a time of strict crackdowns on dissent, particularly of leftist partisans.

Ramin S. Khanjani speaks of the street film genre thus:

> Kimiai's last two films in particular could be viewed as part of a larger phenomenon of a desire to revive elements of a trend of filmmaking in the Iranian cinema of the 70s, often discussed under the self-revelatory term of 'Street films/*film-haye khiabani*'. The down-and-out, bitter (anti)heros of these films – basically a sub-category of 'tough-guy/jaheli' genre – wandered through the streets of the city which rejects and spits out their worthless existence as a nuisance disturbing the glitz of modernizing urban areas. As such, the setting and character attracted high-profile filmmakers such as Amir Naderi, Fereydoun Goleh and Kimiai (in *Reza the Motorcyclist*, 1970) to prepare a subversive vision of the urban life, striking a note of dissidence, de rigueur for the time, by defying the state-propounded image of progress and divulging its contradictions.
>
> (Khanjani 2014)

In the street genre, for instance film noir or Hollywood New Wave films, there is a close connection between the city and the characters. These filmmakers encourage the viewer to sympathize with indomitable – and ultimately doomed – anti-heros who have become sickened by their current situation and commit acts of self-destruction. The city is like a warden that imprisons the characters and they, captivated by a certain destiny, await for their fate whilst wandering its streets. Oftentimes, such films would take place in the streets of modern Tehran, which the isolated characters of the film wander through; they are then shot dead by police or urban mobsters on the cold asphalt of these streets and their tragic ends are dignified as a form of martyrdom for a noble cause, just like the character of Hank McCain (played by John Cassavetes) in Giuliano Montaldo's *Machine Gun McCain* (1969). The most emblematic and prototypical of such films is Masoud Kimiai's *Qaysar* (1969), the tale of an anti-hero taking justice into his own hands and exacting a revenge that comes with fatal consequences.

Before such films the prevalence of urban poverty and the alienation of characters with a neorealist approach was rarely encountered in Iranian cinema. Whilst the overt elements of protest in such films would be suppressed – one can never go against the authorities and win – the strong moral indignation that existed, particularly in the representation of the protagonist, had sent a loud and clear message of individual injustice, just as with the social realist dramas albeit with more of a crowd-pleasing element. The notion of martyrdom is one that was greatly resonant within Iranian (and most other Islamic) cultures and the breakout of such tales was almost an inevitability. Such a fervorous call to action, I believe, is inexorably linked to real-life protests and upheavals which took place leading to the revolution, a movement featuring many dissatisfied and disenfranchised young males.

Among this group of *Mowj-e No* filmmakers, Masoud Kimiai was strongly influenced by American film noir, gangster and western films. Having been brought up in the working-class south of Tehran at a time when it was rapidly sprawling into a crowded and urban environment, he was familiar with and thus able to effectively represent a starkly realistic depiction of life under such deprived and squalid conditions. In his films such as *Qaysar* (1969), *Reza Motori* (Reza the Motorcyclist, 1970) and *Gavaznha* (The Deer, 1974), the portrayal of graphic realistic violence had pretty much never been seen in Iranian cinema before. Kimiai began work as an assistant director, which led to his familiarity with the *Filmfarsi* derivatives of this genre; also, as a former assistant of Samuel Khachikian (referred to as the 'Iranian Hitchcock' and regarded as the master of the crime thriller in Iranian cinema), he was an innovative forerunner and a key figure in the development of *Mowj-e No*. Kimiai was similarly fascinated by American film noirs and passionate about the portrayal of rebellious anti-heroes and disaffected people plagued by poverty and crime.

Kimiai set his cinematic gaze on the criminal element, a niche which he continued to pursue throughout his career. Friendship, betrayal and revenge are the most common thematic elements of Kimiai's films. The characters in his films are from the lower rungs of society such as soldiers, day labourers, street hoodlums and peasants. Relying on the noble savage trope so commonly found in cinema, he made use of people who were suffering from poverty and saw no real means of escape from their precarious situations. In Kimiai's male-dominated portrayals we find merciless clashes in a society wherein masculinity takes precedence over all else. Women often play a minor role in his films; they exist usually beneath the heavy shadow cast by men and rely on their support to survive in such a patriarchal society. The focus often lies on highlighting brutality and what motivates it. Whilst his protagonists are contemporary in their appearance, they look to the past with lamentation and regret (a past that is always with them and which they cannot break away from).

With his rebellious and anarchic attitude and a yearning for justice, Qaysar is the first true anti-hero in Iranian cinema and a prototypical one. The film combines the protagonists of revenge-seeking American westerns and the dark desperation of film noir. It is the story of a young, alienated traditional man who attempts to avenge his sister's rape and his brother's murder by a

Figure 7.9 Behrouz Vosoughi as an iconic figure and a rebellious character in Masoud Kimiai's *Qaysar* (1969).

villainous gang. Unlike the pivotal characters of previous Iranian crime dramas, Qaysar is less driven by want of money or love, almost entirely by a thirst for vengeance. *Qaysar*'s gruesome realism, graphic violence and doomed characters were a strong shock to the system for Iranian cinema but it was well received by audiences; they were most impressed by the main character's values and sympathized with him because of the visceral realness of his situation.

In traditional Iranian crime genres, a moralistic ending was an uncompromising formula; but in the new crime films such as *Qaysar*, the rebellious character's criminal acts and anti-social behaviour were glorified by the filmmaker. Qaysar was the victim of injustice in a world rife with violence, rage and despair. The boundary between good and evil was blurred and the new heroes bore more similarity to and fewer distinctions from the villains.

Spurred on by the popularity of Masoud Kimiai's *Qaysar* (1969) and ever-rising societal tensions, the next generation of *Mowj-e No* were much more brazen in their social criticisms and used darker, grittier themes, violence and noir elements, most notably the trope of rebellious anti-hero who resorts to seeking justice outside of the law.

Like Kimiai, this group of filmmakers, including Amir Naderi, Nasser Taghvai, Fereydoun Goleh and Kamran Shirdel, with their socio-political concerns and neorealist approach, inspired by the setting and character of *Qaysar*, pointed to injustices, class contradictions and poverty in Iranian society in a dramatic and exciting fashion.

After the ban of *Tranquility in the Presence of Others*, Taghvai made *Sadegh Kordeh* (Sadegh the Kurd, 1972), a crime thriller based on a true story with a vengeful protagonist and a rebellious character seeking revenge after his wife was raped and murdered by an unknown lorry driver. This rape and revenge theme became one of the main themes of Iranian films after Kimiai's *Qaysar*. Like *Qaysar*, Taghvai's *Sadegh the Kurd* addressed issues such as defence of honour and the death of the hero by the police, although their film styles were completely different. *Sadegh the Kurd* was one of the outstanding films of *Mowj-e No* due to its good characterization, powerful suspense and dramatic structure, and its tragic ending.

Amir Naderi, a self-taught filmmaker and photographer who began his career in cinema with still photography for New Wave films (*Panjareh* and *Hassan Kachal*), is one of the most important figures of the second generation of Iranian New Wave filmmakers concerned with social realism. Naderi was influenced by the style and aesthetics of Italian neorealist cinema and the

French New Wave in his pre-revolutionary films such as *Tangna* (Deadlock, 1973), *Khodahafez Rafigh* (Goodbye Friend, 1971), *Saz Dahani* (Harmonica, 1973), *Tangsir* (1974) and *Marsieh* (The Requiem, 1978). Growing up in a poor family and experiencing poverty and unemployment, he took a neorealist approach to the lives and plight of the underprivileged and marginalized people. Naderi used similar themes, characters and narrative structures in his films. His anti-hero characters, like the characters of the French New Wave or the doomed characters of the French and American film noirs, have a bitter and tragic fate. His debut film, *Khodahafez Rafigh* (Goodbye Friend, 1971), a crime thriller inspired by Jules Dassin's acclaimed film *Rififi* (1955), is the story of a few friends who set out to rob a jewellery store; after the robbery, they fight over the money and kill each other. In his second film *Tangna* (Deadlock, 1973), Naderi and his co-scriptwriter Mohammad Reza Aslani (another New Wave filmmaker) focused on revenge and violence and took their frustrated and wounded anti-hero to the streets of Tehran. After arguing in a billiard hall, Ali Khoshdast (played by Saeed Raad), an honest man from the slums of Tehran, gets into a heated confrontation and inadvertently kills a member of a gang of thugs and then runs away. A mob pursues him through the claustrophobic alleys of Tehran, seeking vengeance; eventually they are able to trap him and beat him to death. The film takes place between a dismal morning and a gloomy sunset on a miserable day, a day when Ali is wounded and alone in his predicament and tries to escape the inevitable, but in the final shot of the film we see him dying on the asphalt. The fatal and tragic ending became a signature element of Naderi's later films. As per convention followed by so many crime tales, Naderi's anti-heroes have their unfortunate fate of death and defeat already sealed. *Tangna* is one of the best examples of street films in Iranian cinema and often ranks highly in *Film Magazines* top film polls, appearing twice in the top 10 best films of all time by Iranian film critics in 1988 and 2009 (Rahimian 2009).

Naderi's *Marsieh* (The Requiem, 1978) was the last film he made before the revolution. Like his other films, *The Requiem* is a bitter and murky social drama about the lonely existence of a convict released from prison after eight years to find that his mother has died whilst he was away; he is ostracized from society and is forced to prowl the streets of Tehran, unemployed, destitute and without the means to support himself. He joins two hucksters and is able to gain some sense of belonging, meagre though it may be.

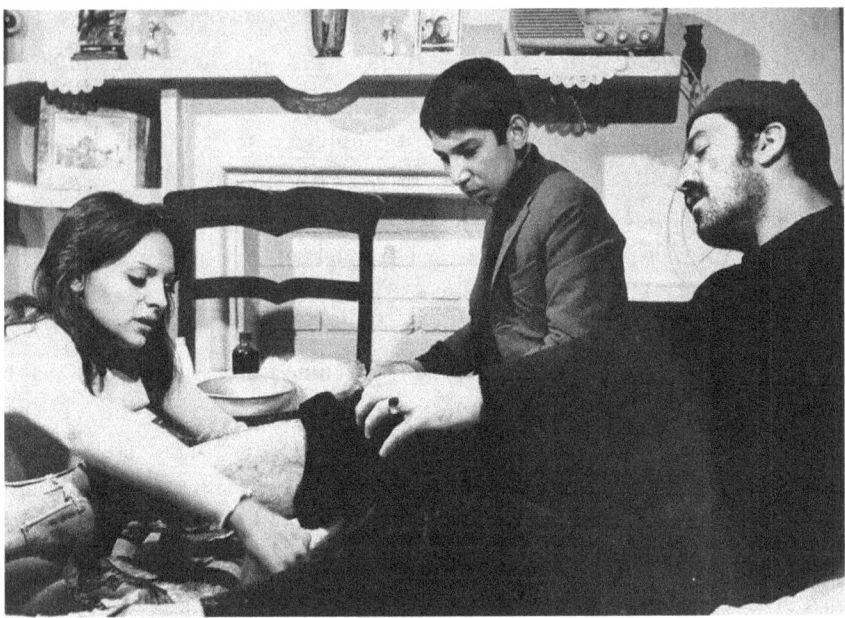

Figure 7.10 Saeed Raad, the anti-hero of Amir Naderi's *Tangna* (Deadlock, 1973).

Fereydoun Goleh (1941–2005) studied film directing in the United States and started to make films upon his return to Iran in the late 1960s. Goleh was initially involved in the Iranian film industry as a scriptwriter, prolifically writing screenplays for *Filmfarsi* including *Donya-ye Abi* (Blue World, directed by Saber Rahbar, 1969), *Khashme Oghabha* (Wrath of Eagles, directed by Iraj Ghaderi, 1970) and *Koocheh-mardha* (Alley of Valiants, directed by Saeed Motalebi, 1970). He also made his first film *Shab-e Fereshtegan* (Night of Angels, 1968), which was made to the standards that were in line with *Filmfarsi* in order to conform to the dominant film industry practice, similar to the early efforts of Dariush Mehrjui, who made his first film in Iran, *Almaas 33* (Diamond 33, 1967), a spy thriller taking heavy inspiration from the James Bond series as a proof of concept for his viability as a skilled director who can work within the industry and produce financial success with his films.

Influenced by the French *Nouvelle Vague* and the American New Hollywood cinema, he made bitter urban dramas within the street film mould featuring antihero characters such as *Kafar* (The Infidel, 1972), *Deshneh* (The Dagger, 1972), *Zir-e Poost-e Shab* (Under the Skin of the Night, 1974) and *Kandu* (Beehive, 1975). In an interview conducted in 2001, Goleh cites American and European New Wave filmmakers as his influence:

When I was studying in the United States in the 1960s, the New Wave of American cinema was just forming and affecting us. In Europe, Fellini and Antonioni were the giants of cinema, and the French *Nouvelle Vague* had just begun, and Godard had just started making films. All these had an impact on film students like me. Or John Cassavetes, who worked hard and independently to make films.

(Goleh 2001, p. 84)

Goleh's later productions stood out from the norm and were of high quality; however, there are still similarities between his films and *Filmfarsi* in terms of characters and atmosphere. The characters in his film were often from the same class and social strata, mainly on the outskirts of Tehran, as the typical *Filmfarsi* characters were, but the way they were represented in Goleh's films was totally different to the way they were pictured in *Filmfarsis*. They were lonely and helpless people struggling to survive in a society that systematically neglected and marginalized them. In the opening shot of *Under the Skin of the Night*, a dung beetle is shown rolling a ball of manure which is representational of the characters' endless toiling within an unjust society.

Goleh's films followed the same path as the films of Naderi and Kimiai, and are among the best examples of *Cinema-ye Khiabani* (street cinema) in Iranian cinema. Goleh's *The Infidel*, influenced by Kimiai's *Qaysar*, with its gloomy atmosphere, follows an anti-hero character involved in robbery and his tragic fate. Goleh portrays Tehran as a terrible city that swallows its victims like a monster. In Goleh's *Beehive* and *Under the Skin of the Night*, Tehran is a city with deep class divisions that alienate the lonely, helpless characters of the film and push them to a tragic end, despite its bright and glamorous nights. In *Under the Skin of the Night*, Qassem Siah is an unemployed young man, a passerby, and a suburban dweller who wanders the streets of Tehran; he desires to find a safe place to sleep with an American tourist woman and to quench his lust, but he does not succeed. Inspired by Frank Perry's *The Swimmer* (1968), Goleh's *Beehive* is about an ostracized convict, Ebi (played by Behrouz Vosoughi), who after his release from prison, has no place to sleep except for a remote coffee shop on the outskirts of Tehran. He takes part in a high-stakes bet in order to escape from his grim circumstances; after losing the bet, he agrees to eat without paying in all the cafés and restaurants of the city which are adorned with glittery and colourful neon lights. In a sequence near the end of the film,

Ebi lashes out against the indifferent city and high society by smashing all the mirrors at a five-star hotel's restaurant and is severely beaten by hotel security. As Goleh said in an interview with Nader Takmil Homayoun, people like the characters of *Beehive* 'live in such poverty that they've lost all notion of belonging to society. As though a bee leaving the hive to sting the people of the city' (Homayoun 2007).

Figure 7.11 Fereydoun Goleh's *Kandu* (Beehive), one of the best examples of street cinema in Iran.

Goleh's observational camera, like the camera of a documentary filmmaker, follows Ebi on his nightly strolls in the streets and cafés of Tehran, and shows how he succumbs to his bleak destiny by taking part in a self-destructive game that is imposed on him. Ebi's arrest by the police and his return to prison at the end of the film closes the circular loop of the narrative.

Zakaria Hashemi started his film career by acting in New Wave films such as *The Night of the Hunchback* and *Brick and Mirror*. He made his directorial debut with the New Wave film *Se-Ghap* (Three Taps) in 1971, which is about a professional gambler who sets out to stake everything on one final gamble to raise money for his friend's sister's wedding. Hashemi, like Kimiai, was raised in a poor, working-class family in the south of Tehran and was closely acquainted with the culture and lifestyle of the people of the area. Like nearly all instances of the street film genre of the *Mowj-e No*, *Three Taps* was made with a neorealist approach and the signature tragic ending.

Hashemi later made *Tooti* (The Parrot, 1977) based on his own naturalistic novel, which not only shows the violent thuggish underside but also the world of prostitution. The film mainly takes place in the neighbourhood of the chain of brothels in Tehran (*Shahr-e Nou*), a type of red light district and the location of many *Filmfarsi*. *Filmfarsi* depictions of *Shahr-e Nou* were done so in a leering way purely for the purposes of objectification. But the way Hashemi pictured this world defamiliarizes us with that trope and presents these women as more realistic. The film is about two childhood male friends who frequent the neighbourhood and try to help the titular character Tooti, a prostitute of Jewish origin, escape from the clutches of her vicious pimp. The film had limited screenings and was banned before the 1979 revolution for its dark portrayal of the capital of Iran.

In Jalal Moghaddam's *Farar az Taleh* (Escape From the Trap, 1971), we can see traces of *Qaysar* with the same narrative style and familiar anti-hero character played by Behrouz Vosoughi. It is about a man who is released from prison and strikes a deal with the husband of a girl he loves so that he will divorce her and they can be together; in order to raise these funds he must resort to criminal acts and it ends poorly for him, as expected.

Kamran Shirdel, a prominent figure in Iranian documentary cinema, studied film direction at the *Centro Sperimentale di Cinematografia* in Rome, Italy and, inspired by Italian neorealism, created socio-political documentaries about issues such as the class divide, injustice and corruption in Iranian society for the Ministry of Culture and Arts, but unfortunately most of his films were banned for their critical intonations. Shirdel then made his first and last feature film

Sobh-e Rooz-e Chaharom (On the Morning of the Fourth Day, 1972), which was a remake of Jean-Luc Godard's *À bout de souffle* (Breathless, 1960), with the help of Mohammad Reza Aslani, as a co-scriptwriter.

Like Golestan's *Brick and Mirror*, Shirdel's film can be regarded as an example of an early *Mowj-e No* film that was made under the direct influence of Italian neorealism and the French New Wave. It is about Amir (played by Saeed Raad, New Wave's usual anti-hero actor), a car thief and a rebellious character (like Michel in Godard's *À bout de souffle*) who accidentally kills a man in Abadan and escapes to Tehran where he tries to convince his girlfriend to run away with him to the south of Iran. But, like the character of Patricia in *À bout de souffle*, she ends up betraying him and exposing him to the authorities. At the end of the film, like Michel in *À bout de souffle*, Amir is shot down by the police.

Afterword

The impetus for this book has been to help close the gaps in knowledge when it comes to our understanding of the origins of New Wave (*Mowj-e No*) cinema and its dynamic connection to concurrent theatrical and literary developments in Iran between 1958 and 1968.

It is a historical as well as analytical investigation of this extremely significant cinematic movement, an artistic and intellectual venture which took hold in Iran from 1958 and continued in its scope and structure until 1979. As the movement has a long and intricate history, my main focus was to outline the emergence and development of this cinema covering the late 1950s to 1968 in as much detail as possible including the context of cultural, social and political shifts occurring in Iran during this period. Laying out the research in order to identify the elements which gave rise to this movement, I tried to define the degree to which these different elements, including the influence of Italian neorealism and French New Wave (*La Nouvelle Vague*), contributed to the formation of this cinema.

Although influenced by Italian neorealism and French *Nouvelle Vague*, the Iranian *Mowj-e No* emerged within the context of the cultural and intellectual climate of 1950s and 1960s Iran. Therefore, it was primarily the outcome of internal rather than external factors. Like their French and Italian counterparts, the core intention of Iranian New Wave filmmakers was to liberate Iranian cinema from its mainstream and conventional practices in bright and original ways.

I attempted to investigate the movement thematically and stylistically in the context of the larger social, political, cultural and cinematic discourse of the time. As discussed in Chapters 2 and 3, the 1960s was a period in which cinematic, dramatic and literary discourse crossed and enriched one another in Iran. This strong interaction between the modern literature, theatre and cinema of the time is an important and underexplored feature of the movement.

So, in my research I attempted to describe the interactive relationship between the New Wave movement and its literary and dramatic sources.

A large section of the research is dedicated to analysis of the life and works of three intellectual figures and influential filmmakers of the 1960s: Ebrahim Golestan, Farrokh Ghaffari and Fereydoun Rahnema, who I consider to be the pioneers of *Mowj-e No* in Iran. These three artists were united in their desire to further a cinema that created a connection between modern Iranian society and its cultural, historical and mythological roots. In addition, I analysed the formal and aesthetic elements of the major, controversial films that have been made by other forerunners. Although it was not an integrated movement and its filmmakers were not following a set style, ideology or cinematic approach, there were undoubtedly common elements and similarities in their films in terms of form and content. Realism, poetic vision, alienated characters and ambiguous atmosphere, episodic narrative and documentary style were the most important common elements.

Typically, New Wave cinematic movements are considered as a 'split-flow', but there are filmmakers from the intellectual community who have never been a part of the dominant cinema (*Filmfarsi*), and made their films independently. So this is not a split from the *Filmfarsi* flow, but a distinctive and distinguishable cinema. In its first phase, intellectual cinema tried its best to build up new aesthetic standards to contrast with the thematic and stylistic characteristics of typical *Filmfarsi*, such as reconciliation between the classes, heroism, shallow characters, simple narratives and happy endings. Through a close study of Iranian cinema within the context of modernity I came to the conclusion that the idea of setting up a prestigious intellectual cinema occupied the minds of Iranian intellectual filmmakers for years but did not come to fruition until the early 1960s. That was a remarkable time in the history of Iranian cinema when the idea of cinema as an artform became a reality, and this was followed by the next generation of motivated filmmakers in the 1970s.

Although modern Iranian literature began earlier than Golestan with the works of Sadegh Hedayat (in particular *The Blind Owl*, 1936), Bozorg Alavi and Sadegh Chubak, the works of Golestan are distinct from the writings of these other writers due to his deep acquaintance with classical Persian literature, on the one hand, and modern American and European literature, on the other. Meanwhile his experiences in documentary cinema reinforces the visual aspects of his stories, which can be seen in his collection of stories, *Azar, Maah-e Akher-e Pa'eez* (Azar, the Last Month of Autumn, 1948), *Shekar-e Sayeh* (Shadow-Hunting, 1955) and *Juy-o Divar-o Teshneh* (The

Stream, the Wall and the Thirsty One, 1967). Golestan was operating from a critical framework in his literary work that he continued to develop through his filmmaking process.

This is illustrative of the desire for 'the new' and its ineluctability, arising from a much broader social and cultural renewal process. It was a necessity for change that persisted in the minds of its purveyors long before they had the means to realize it. It can be postulated that this applies to Rahnema's efforts to insert the characteristics of modern poetry into his films, as well as Ghaffari's urge to bring forth the ideas of Western modernism he learned from film scholars in Paris, and apply them to distinctly Persian stories and folklore. It was amidst such a literary and cultural environment that these young filmmakers came on the scene with new ideas about what can be created by applying alternative approaches to cinema.

I tried to shed some light on the unexplored corners of *Mowj-e No* and its forerunners. These were the ones who laid the foundations for the *Mowj-e No*, a cinematic movement wherein each of its filmmakers had their own approach and style, but in total and alongside each other, were part of a campaign and a cinematic stream that was the spirit of the time. The spirit that connects artistic, thoughtful and independent cinema of yesterday to the Iranian independent cinema of today with its much broader reach and acceptance. Whilst such filmmaking is still far from easy, their work was proof of concept for what was possible for those who came after.

Perhaps the original proponents of the New Wave were not quite able to reach the full cinematic potential of this movement, or to reach the levels that Iranian literature was able to achieve within that same period. But what had come out of this phenomenon was a provocative foray into a completely exciting and unexplored realm.

This was the spark that was needed to alight the incredibly rich, fiery heritage of Iranian filmmaking, which went beyond an intellectual movement and shaped generations of cinema and cultural identity, the fruits of which artists and serious film lovers are able to enjoy today and onwards.

Bibliography

(In English)

Adorno, Theodor and Max Horkheimer, *Dialectic of Enlightenment*, Stanford, CA: Stanford University Press, 2002.
Agamben, Giorgio, *Stanzas: Word and Phantasm in Western Culture,* trans. Ronald L. Martinez, Minneapolis: University of Minnesota Press, 1993.
Akrami, Jamsheed, 'The Blighted Spring. Iranian Cinema and Politics in the 1970s', in J. D. H. Downing (ed.), *Film and Politics in the Third World*, New York: Praeger, 1987.
Armes, Roy, *Third World Film Making and the West*, Berkeley and Los Angeles: University of California Press, 1970.
Astruc, Alexandre, *The Birth of a New Avant-Garde: La Caméra-Stylo*, ed. Peter Graham, London: Secker and Warburg, 1968.
Avery, Peter, *The Cambridge History of Iran*, vol. 7, Cambridge: Cambridge University Press, 1991.
Aycock, Wendell and Michael Schoenecke, *Film and Literature: A Comparative Approach to Adaptation*, Lubbock: Texas Tech University Press, 1988.
Bayman, Louis, *Directory of World Cinema*, Italy, University of Chicago Press, 2011.
Bazin, André, *What Is Cinema?*, University of California Press, pp. 39–40, 1967.
Bickerton, Emilie, *A Short History of Cahiers du Cinéma*, London: Verso, 2009.
Bordwell, David and Kristin Thompson, *Film History: An Introduction*, 1st edn, New York: McGraw Hill, 1994.
Boroujerdi, Mehrzad, *Iranian Intellectuals and the West: The Tormented Triumph of Nativism*, Syracuse, NY: Syracuse University Press, 1996.
Cardullo, Bert (ed.), *André Bazin and Italian Neorealism*, Continuum International Publishing, p.19, 2011.
Close-Up Film Centre. '18 November – 16 December 2017: Sohrab Shahid Saless: Exiles', November and December 2017. Available online: https://www.closeupfilmcentre.com/film_programmes/2017/sohrab-Shahid-saless (accessed 22 January 2022).
Cook, David, *A History of Narrative Film*, 3rd edn, New York and London: W. W. Norton & Company, 1996.
Cronin, Paul, *Sar-e Kelas ba Kiarostami / Lessons with Kiarostami*, trans. Sohrab Mahdavi, Tehran: Nazar Publication, 2017.
Dabashi, Hamid, *Close Up: Iranian Cinema: Past, Present and Future*, London: Verso, 2001.
Deleuze, Gilles, *Cinema 1: The Movement-Image*, trans. Hugh Tomlinson and Barbara Habberjam, London: Athlone Press, 1986.
Deleuze, Gilles, *Cinema 2: The Time-Image*, New York: Bloomsbury Publishing, 2005.

Ebert, Roger, 'Caravans', *Roger Ebert* January 30, 1979. Available online: https://www.rogerebert.com/reviews/caravans-1979 (accessed 16 January 2020).

Elena, Alberto, *The Cinema of Abbas Kiarostami*, London: Saqi Books, 2005.

Fitting, Peter, What Is Utopian Film? An Introductory Taxonomy. *Utopian Studies* 4 (2) (1993): 1–17.

Freud, Sigmund, *The Standard Edition of the Complete Psychological Works of Sigmund Freud*, vol. 11, London: Hogarth Press, 1961.

Geist, Dan, 'Fereydoun Hoveyda: The Provocateur', 7 November 2020. Available online: https://tehranbureau.com/fereydoun-hoveyda-the-provocateur (accessed 22 January 2022).

Gheissari, Ali, *Iranian Intellectuals in the Twentieth Century*, 1st edn, Austin: University of Texas Press, 1997.

Gunning, Tom, *Night and Day in The Big City*, Lecture at the Gene Siskel Film Center at Northwestern University, 4 May 2007.

Hayward, Susan, *Cinema Studies: The Key Concepts*, 2nd edn, London: Routledge, 2000.

Homayoun, Nader, *Takmil*, (Film) *Iran: A Cinematographic Revolution*, 2007.

Issari, Mohammad Ali, *Cinema in Iran, 1900–1979*, Metuchen, NJ: Scarecrow Press, 1989.

Jahed, Parviz, (ed.), *Directory of World Cinema: Iran, Vol. 1*, London: Intellect Books, 2012.

Jahed, Parviz, (ed.), *Directory of World Cinema: Iran, Vol. 2*, London: Intellect Books, 2017.

Kamshad, Hassan, *Modern Persian Prose Literature*, Bethesda, MD: Iranbooks, 1996.

Khanjani, Ramin S., 'The Crime That Has to Be Tried on the Street: The Films of Masoud Kimiai'. *Off Screen* vol. 18 (9) (September 2014). Available online: https://offscreen.com/view/the-crime-that-has-to-be-tried-on-the-street (accessed 22 January 2022).

Kuhn, Annette and Guy Westwell, *Oxford Dictionary of Film Studies*, Oxford: Oxford University Press, 2012.

Lang, Robert, 'An Interview with Fereydoun Hoveyda'. *Screen*, vol. 34 (4) (Winter 1993): 392–400.

Marie, Michel and Richard Neupert, *The French New Wave: An Artistic School*, Malden, MA: Blackwell Publishing, 2002.

Mirsepassi, Ali, *Political Islam, Iran, and the Enlightenment: Philosophies of Hope and Despair*, Cambridge: Cambridge University Press, 2010.

Monaco, James, *The New Wave, Truffaut, Godard, Chabrol, Rohmer, Rivette*, 1st edn, New York: Harbor Electronic Publishing, 1976.

Mulvey, Laura, 'Afterward', in Richard Tapper (ed.) *The New Iranian Cinema: Politics, Representation and Identity*, London: I.B. Tauris. 2002.

Naficy, Hamid, 'Iranian Feature Film: A Brief Critical History'. *Quarterly Review of Film Studies* (Autumn 1979): 443–64.

Naficy, Hamid, *A Social History of Iranian Cinema, Volume 2: The Industrializing Years*, Durham, NC: Duke University Press, 2011.

Ostrowska, Dorota, *Reading the French New Wave*, London: Wallflowers Press, 2008.

Powrie, Phil and Reader, Keith, *French Cinema: a Student's Guide*, Arnold, 2002.
Queenan, Joe, We'll Always Have Paris. *The Guardian*, 27 March 2009. Available online: https://www.theguardian.com/film/2009/mar/27/french-new-wave-cinema (accessed 22 January 2022).
Rosenbaum, Jonathan, *Ebrahim Golestan (Three Capsule Reviews and One Essay)*. Personal Blog, 14 April 2021. Available online: https://jonathanrosenbaum.net/2021/04/ebrahim-golestan (accessed 22 January 2022).
Sadr, Hamidreza, *Against The Wind, Politics of Iranian Cinema*, Tehran: Zarrin Publishing 2002.
Schrader, Paul, *Transcendental Style in Film*, Oakland: University of California Press, 2018.
Shaya, Gregory, 'The Flâneur, the Badaud, and the Making of a Mass Public in France, circa 1860–1910'. *The American Historical Review*, vol. 109 (1) (2004): 41–77.
Siskel, Gene, 'Caravans: Sandlot drama'. *Chicago Tribune*, Section 2, p. 5, 1 February 1979.
Sorlin, Pierre, *European Cinemas, European Societies, 1939–1990*, London: Routledge, 1991.
Stam, Robert and Randal Johnson, 'Brazil Renaissance, Beyond Cinema Novo'. *Jump Cut* vol. 21 (November 1979): 13–18.
Talajooy, Saeed, 'Bahram Beyzaie's Ragbar (Downpour)', in Parviz Jahed (ed.), *Directory of World Cinema: Iran. Vol. 1*, London: Intellect Books, 2012.
Talajooy, Saeed, 'The Literary and Dramatic Roots of the Iranian New Wave'. *The Middle East in London*, vol. 15 (2) (February–March 2019): 7–8.
Tester, Keith, 'Introduction', in Keith Tester (ed.) *The Flâneur*, London and New York: Routledge, 1994.
Totaro, Donato, 'Gilles Deleuze's Bergsonian Film Project'. *Off Screen*, vol. 3 (3) (March 1999).
Truffaut, François, '*Une certaine tendance du cinéma français*' ('A Certain Tendency of French Cinema'). *Cahiers du Cinema*, vol. 1 (1954): 211–19. Republished in F. Truffaut, *Le Plaisir des yeux*, Paris: Flammarion, 1987.

(In Persian)

Al-e-Ahmad, Jalal, *Yek Chal-o Do Chaleh* (One Well and Two Ditches), Tehran: Ravagh Publications, 1964.
Al-e-ahmad, Jalal, *Gharbzadegi / Westoxication*, Tehran: Mazda Publication, 1997.
Amini, Najafi, Ali, Chekhov and Shahid-Saless. DW Radio website (2010). Available online: https://www.dw.com/fa-ir/%DA%86%D8%AE%D9%88%D9%81-%D9%88-%D8%B3%DB%8C%D9%86%D9%85%D8%A7%DA%AF%D8%B1-%D8%A7%DB%8C%D8%B1%D8%A7%D9%86%DB%8C/a-5171819 (accessed 22 January 2022).
Aslani, Mohammad Reza, *Film va Cinama* (Film and Cinema), 6, April 1998.

Assadi, Ali, An Introduction to Sociology of Cinema in Iran. *Farhang va Zendegi* (Culture and Life), 13–14 (1973): 13.

Assadi, Ali, Daramadi bar Jame'ah-shenasi-ye Cinama dar Iran (An Introduction to the Sociology of Cinema in Iran). *Farhang va Zindigi* (Culture and Life), 13–14 (Winter 1973–Spring 1974).

Bahar, Shamim, *Dar bare-ye Yek Tajrobeh Cinemayee* (About a Cinematic Experience), *Andisheh va Honar*, May 1966.

Baharlou, Abbas, *Tarikh-e Tahlili-e Sad Saal Cinamay-e Iran* (An Analytical History of a Century of Iranian Cinema), Tehran: Daftar-e Pazhohesh-ha-ye Farhangi (Cultural Research Bureau), 2001.

Barzin, Saeed, Sakhtar-e siasi,tabeghati vajameeyati dar Iran (The Political, Class and Populational Structure in Iran). *Etela'at-e Siasi* vol. 81–2 (1994).

Behnam, Jamshid, *Iranian va Andishe-ye Tajaddod* (Iranians and and the Idea of Modernism), Tehran: Farzan-e Rooz Publishing, 1375 (1996).

Beyzaie, Bahram, *Arash Magazine*, no. 5 (1962).

Dariush, Hajir, Omid Iran journal. Vol. 43, 1, p. 23, April 1954.

Dariush, Hajir, Review of *Shab-e Quzi* (*The Night of the Hunchback*). *Honar va Cinema*, 7 (2 February 1964).

Dariush, Hajir, Ayandegan. 141, June 1968.

Davaei, Parviz, *Ferdowsi*, February 1965.

Davaei, Parviz, *Setareh Cinema* (Cinema Star). 666, 4 May 1969.

Davaei, Parviz, *Setareh Cinema* (Cinema Star). 722, October 1970.

Eshghi, Behzad, Kashefan-e Forotan-e Almas (The Sincere Discoverers of the Diamond). *Film Magazine*, No. 62. 1988. p.35.

Eslami, Maziar and Morad Farhadpour, *Paris-Tehran: The Cinema of Abbas Kiarostami*, Tehran: Rokhdad-e Nou, 2008.

Ghadimi, Houshang, *Setareh Cinema* (Cinema Star). 24, 1954.

Ghaffari, Farrokh, *San'at-e Cinema dar Iran* (The Film Industry in Iran). *Setareh Solh* 1, July–August 1950.

Ghaffari, Farrokh, *Setareh Solh* (Monthly Magazine), vol. 5, pp. 46–50, August 1951.

Ghaffari, Farrokh, Sadaf. Vol. 2, November 1954, pp. 121–7.

Ghaffari, Farrokh, *Zendegi va Cinama dar Iran* (Life and Cinema in Iran). Talash No.2, September 1966.

Ghaffari, Farrokh, *Goftego ba Farrokh Ghaffari* (Interview with Farrokh Ghaffari). *Farhang va Zendegi* vol. 2, June 1970.

Ghaffari, Farrokh, *Farhang va Zendegi*. Vol.18, Summer 1975.

Goleh, Fereydoun, *The Life and Films of Fereydoun Goleh: Interview with Reza Dorostkar, Javad Tousi, Saeed Aghighi and Tahmaseb Solhjou*, Tehran: Naghsh-o-Negar Publication, 2001.

Golestan, Ebrahim, *Kayhan International* (newspaper) no.3, December 1964.

Golestan, Shahrokh, *Fanoos-e Khial* (The History of Iranian Cinema), Tehran: Kavir, 1993.

Golshiri, Houshang, *Tarikhcheh-ye Eghtebas Adabi dar Cinema-ye Iran* (The short History of Literary Adaptation in Iranian Cinema), Faslname-ye Farabi (Farabi Quarterly), No 64, 2009.

Hajjarian, Saeed. *Jaryanhay-e Roushanfekri dar Iran –e Mo,aser* (Intellectual movements in contemporary Iran). Fekr-e Nou. No. 6. May 2000.

Heidari, Gholam, *Cinema-ye Iran, Bardasht-e Natamam* (Iran's Cinema, Incomplete Take), Tehran: Chakameh Publisher, 1991.

Hosseini, Hassan, Interview with Hassan Hosseini. *Convention and Disorder, Daily Bulletin, Seminar on different cinema in Iran* 27 (10) (2002): 7.

Jahed, Parviz, Ganjineh-haye Kargah-e Film-e Golestan (The Treasures at Golestan Film Company), *BBC Persian*, 19 June 2004. Available online: https://www.bbc.com/persian/arts/story/2004/07/printable/040719_pm-pj_fire_golestan.shtml (accessed 22 January 2022).

Jahed, Parviz, *Neveshtan ba Doorbin* (Writing with a Camera), Tehran: Nashr-e Akhtaran, 2005.

Jahed, Parviz, Eghtebas Adabi dar Cinama-ye Iran (Literary Adaptation in Iranian Cinema), *BBC Persian*, December 2006. Available online: http://www.bbc.com/persian/programmes/story/2006/11/061113_she-lit-adapt1.shtml (accessed 22 January 2022).

Jahed, Parviz, Khesht va Ayeneh Yek Shahkar ast (Brick and Mirror is a Masterpiece), *Radio Zamaneh*, 12 August 2007. Available online: www.zamāneh.com/jahed/2007/08/post_161.html.

Jahed, Parviz, Az Cinémathèque Paris ta Kanoon-e Film-e Tehran (From Paris Cinémathèque to Tehran Film Club) (Interview with Farrokh Ghaffari), Tehran: Nashr-e Ney, 2014.

Jahed, Parviz, *Hamchon dar Yek Ayeneh* (Through the Dark Glass), Tehran: Nashre Afraz, 2018.

Kashi, Sabereh, Khakestar va Almas (Ash and Diamond), in Hossein Moazezinia, *Filmfarsi Chist?* (What is *Filmfarsi?*), Tehran: Saghi Publication, 2001.

Kashi, Sabereh, *Eshtebahat-e Tarikhi* (Historical Mistakes). Gozaresh-e Film (a film journal), 2000, p. 55.

Kavoosi, Houshang, *Ferdowsi* 152, August 1954.

Kavoosi, Houshang, *Naghdi bar Shab-e Ghuzi* (Review of The Night of the Hunchback). *Ferdowsi* 372, 25 November 1958.

Kavoosi, Houshang, *Honar va Cinama* 3, April 1961a, p. 32.

Kavoosi, Houshang, *Honar va Cinama* 18, November 1961b.

Kavoosi, Houshang, Negin. Vol. 39, August 1968, p. 11.

Kavoosi, Houshang, Film-e Irani va Filmfarsi (Iranian Film and *Filmfarsi*). *Negin* 57, January 1969.

Kavoosi, Houshang, Yek Gooftego (A Conversation). *Setareh Cinema* (Cinema Star) 726, November 1970: 17.

Kavoosi, Houshang, *Farhang va Zendegi*. Vol. 18. Summer 1975.
Khalaji, Mehdi, Enghelab-e Iran va Soghot-e Padeshahi (Iranian Revolution and the Fall of the Monarchy). *Nimrooz Newspaper*, no. 763, December 2003, p. 15.
Khoshnam, Mahmoud, Enghelab-e Iran va Soghot-e Padeshahi (Iranian Revolution and the Fall of the Monarchy), *Nimrooz Newspaper*, no. 762, December 2003, p. 30.
Mehrabi, Masoud, *Tarikh-e Cinema-ye Iran* (The History of Iranian Cinema), Tehran: Film Publication, 1984.
Mehrabi, Masoud, *Farhang-e Filmha-ye Mostand Cinema-ye Iran* (Directory of Documentary Films in Iran), Tehran: Pajzhoheshgah-e Farhangi Publishing, 1996.
Mir Ehsan, Ahmad, Zibayee Shenasi-e 100 Sal Cinemay-e Iran (The Aesthetic of 100 Years of Iranian Cinema). *Faslname-ye Farabi* 37 (2000).
Mir Ehsan, Ahmad, Interview with the author, 2002.
Moazezinia, Hossein, *Filmfarsi Chist?* (What is *Filmfarsi?*), Tehran: Saghi Publication, 2001.
Moghaddam, Jalal, *Gooftego* (Interview). *Talash* 11, 1968.
Mohammadi, Majid. Cinama-ye Emrooz-e Iran (The New Iranian Cinema), Tehran: Jameh-ye Iranian Publication. 2001.
Nouriala, Esmail, Film va Honar. Vol. 34. April 2. 1969.
Omid, Jamal, *Tarikh-e Cinema-ye Iran, 1279–1357* (The History of Iranian Cinema, 1900–1978), Tehran: Entesharat-e Rowzaneh, 1995.
Rahimian, Behzad, *Behtarin Film-haye Zendegi Ma* (The Best Films of Our Life). Monthly Film Magazine Poll, vol. 400, August 2009. Available online: https://www.film-magazine.com/archives/articles.asp?id=74 (accessed 22 January 2022).
Rahnema, Fereydoun, Cinema dar Iran. *Sokhan* 6, August 1955.
Rahnema, Derakht-e Hezar Shakh-ye Cinema (Rahnema and the Thousand Branch of Cinema). *Talash* 10, June 1968.
Rahnema, Fereydoun, Goftegoo ba Parviz Eslampour (Interview with Parviz Eslampour). *Film va Honar* (Film and Art), n.s. 34, 2 April 1969.
Rahnema, Fereydoun, A Conversation with Rahnema. *Negin* 82 (March 1971): 72.
Rahnema, Fereydoun, *Vagheiat Gerayee Film* (Film Realism), Tehran: Boof Publishing, 1972.
Rahnema, Fereydoon, *Rastakhiz* (newspaper), No 87, 12 August 1975.
Rezaei, Ehsan, *Tarikhche-ye Momayyezi dar Cinemay-e Iran* (The Short History of Censorship in Iranian Cinema), Majaleh-ye 24, No 55, pp 32–4, September 2010).
Saghafi, Morad, *Roshanfekran dar Iran* (Iranian Intellectuals). Goftegoo (periodical journal).Vol. 30. Winter 2000.
Sarfaraz, Hossain, *Setareh Cinema* 667, April 1969.
Sattari, Jalal, Farhang va Zendegi. Vol. 18, summer 1975.
Shamlou, Ahmad, *Hamchoun Kocheh-ee Bienteha* (Like a Never Ending Alley), Tehran: Negah Publication, 1995.

Shayegan, Dariush, *Asia dar Barabar-e Gharb* (Asia Versus the West), Tehran: Amirkabir Publication, 1977.

Shoa'ee, Hamid, *Farhang Cinema-ye Iran* (Directory of Cinema in Iran), Tehran: Herminco Co., 1975.

Shoa'ee, Hamid, *Naam Avaran-e Cinema dar Iran: Fereydoun Rahnema* (Outstanding Figures of Iranian Cinema), Tehran: no pub., 1976.

Tahaminejad, Mohammad, *Cinema-ye Roya Pardaz-e Iran* (Iran's Dream-making Cinema), Tehran: Aks-e Mo'aser Publication, 1986.

Tahaminejad, Mohammad, *Risheyabi Ya'as* (Finding the Roots of Disappointment). In *Vijeh Cinema va Teatre* (For Cinema and Theatre), vols. 2–3, Tehran: Babak Publications, 1976–7, p. 116.

Tahaminejad, Mohammad, *Cinema-ye Iran dar Dahe-ye Chehl* (Iranian Cinema in the 1960s).

Talebinejad, Ahmad, *Yek Etefagh-e Sadeh* (A Simple Event), Tehran: Moa'sese-ye Farhangi Honari Sheyda, 1993.

Index of names

Abbas, Baharlou 70, 91–2, 132, 221
Adorno, Theodor 30, 218
Afghani, Ali Mohammad 123–5
Afrasiab 176, 179
Agamben, Giorgio 86, 218
Ahmadi, Taji 106, 147, 149, 150
Akbari, Ali-Akbar 30
Akerman, Chantal 190, 202
Akhavan-e Saless, Mehdi 99
Akrami, Jamsheed 46, 218
Al-e Ahmad, Jalal 3, 18, 31, 32–3, 48, 69, 77, 81, 84, 97, 139, 182, 220, 86–7, 89, 140
Antonioni, Michelangelo 50, 71, 77, 118, 187, 192, 204, 211
Apick, Mary 151, 135
Armen, Megreditch 199
Armes, Roy 5–6, 114–16, 218
Aseyed Ali Mirza 87, 89
Asgari-Nasab, Manoochehr 85
Aslani, Mohammad Reza 14, 45, 48, 49, 74, 85, 87, 119, 160, 170, 174, 193, 198–9, 203, 209, 214, 220
Astruc, Alexandre 110, 119, 121–2, 218
Avery, Peter 175, 177, 218
Ayyari, Kianoush 1

Baba'i, Kurous 93
Bafghi, Vahshı 91
Bahar, Shamim 70, 148, 221
Baudelaire, Charles 187
Baygan, Fazlullah 93
Bayman, Louis 104, 218
Bazin, André 103–4, 111–12, 116, 122, 156, 218
Beckett, Samuel 98
Behnam, Jamshid 33, 221
Belmondo, Jean-Paul 112
Benet, Stephen Vincent 140
Benjamin, Walter 187

Bergman, Ingmar 45, 77, 97, 116, 118, 127, 159, 167
Bickerton, Emilie 111, 119, 218
Bijan 175
Bingham, Adam 188–9
Bond, James 210
Bordbar, Barham 10
Bordwell, David 13, 114–15, 218
Boroujerdi, Mehrzad 2, 18, 33, 69, 218
Bresson, Robert 183, 190–1, 198–9, 200, 202
Byron, Lord 11

Camus, Albert 77, 98, 122, 129
Capra, Frank 49, 173
Cardullo, Bert 102–4, 218
Cassavetes, John 39, 211, 206
Castellani, Renato 104
Ceylan, Nuri Bilge 192
Chabrol, Claude 111–12, 116, 219
Chaplin, Charlie 50, 118, 173
Chekhov, Anton 122, 134–5, 140, 192, 220
Cholokhov, Mikhail 98
Chubak, Sadegh 3, 96, 99, 129, 130, 216
Clair, Rene 50
Clement, Rene 173
Clouzot, Henri-Georges 132
Cooper, Merian C. 21
Coutard, Raoul 112
Crane, Stephen 140
Cronin, Paul 109, 196, 218

D'Arcy, William Knox 89
Dabashi, Hamid 18, 23–4, 218
Daneshvar, Hossein 29
Dariush, Hajir 48, 53, 60–1, 72, 116, 150, 164, 168, 174, 202–4, 221
Dariush, Parviz 123
Darvish Khan (Esfandiarpur) 88–9
Daryabaigi, Ali 29

Dassin, Jules 209
Davaei, Parviz 9, 10, 11, 52, 63–4, 68, 70–2, 149, 173, 221
De Santis, Giuseppe 102
De Sica, Vittorio 13, 98, 102–4, 107, 147, 173
Deleuze, Gilles 4, 101–3, 105, 107, 115, 117, 186, 188, 218, 220
Douchet, Jean 145
Dowlatabadi, Mahmoud 3, 97, 129, 130
Dreyer, Carl Theodor 23, 198–200
Dulac, Germaine 178
Duras, Marguerite 112, 186

Ebert, Roger 37, 219
Elena, Alberto 46, 193, 195–6, 219
Entezami, Ezzatolah 20, 49, 118
Epstein, Jean 175
Eshghi, Behzad 17, 221
Eslami, Maziar 86

Fannizadeh, Parviz 15, 78
Fardid, Ahmad 31
Fardin, Mohammad Ali 65
Fargo, James 37
Farhadi, Asghar 1
Farhadpour, Morad 86
Farmanara, Bahman 3, 12, 14, 49, 50, 129, 168
Faroughi Kadjar (Qajar), Ahmad 116, 179
Farrokhzad, Forough 7, 45, 97, 139, 141–4, 146, 202
Fatemi, Nezam 53
Faulkner, William 77, 98, 122, 138, 140
Fellini, Federico 50, 108, 118
Ferdowsi, Abul-Qâsem 27, 92, 221–2
Fischinger 173
Fitting, Peter 79, 84, 85, 87, 219
Flaherty, Robert 173
Ford, John 77, 112, 173
Forouzan 53, 65
Forsi, Bahman 98
Freud, Sigmund 86, 219

Galeta, Robert 101
Ganjavi, Nizami 91

Garsivaz 176
Geist, Dan 120, 219
Geloin, Ghislaine 122
Gerami, Mehdi 93
Germi, Pietro 102
Ghaderi, Iraj 210
Ghaffari, Farrokh 1, 4, 8, 10, 12, 14–15, 17, 29, 33, 39, 42, 44, 45, 47, 48, 49, 52, 53, 63, 66, 67, 71–4, 76, 80, 81, 84, 91, 97, 104–7, 116–17, 120, 135, 137, 148, 153, 154–69, 173, 185, 216–17, 221–2
Gharib, Shapour 53
Gharibian, Faramarz 44
Ghazi, Mohammad 123
Gheissari, Ali 31, 219
Ghotbi, Reza 44, 47, 168
Giroud, Francois 109
Godard, Jean-Luc 12, 77, 108, 111–14, 116–17, 122, 146, 182, 185, 197, 211, 214, 219
Goethe, Johann Wolfgang Von 11
Goleh, Fereydoun 14, 205, 208, 210–13, 221
Golestan, Ebrahim 1, 4, 7, 8, 9, 12, 14–17, 36, 45, 52–3, 58, 70–6, 81, 97–9, 104–7, 116–17, 120–3, 125, 135, 137, 138–49, 150–4, 156, 159, 162, 164, 174–5, 185, 187, 194, 198, 214, 216–17, 220–2
Golestan, Shahrokh 36, 139
Golshiri, Houshang 3, 98, 100, 123, 129, 131, 222
Gorky, Maxim 98

Haanstra, Bert 49
Haghighi, Nemat 76
Hajjarian, Saeed 69, 222
Hangwall, Mahmoud 139
Haritash, Khosrow 8, 49–50, 131–2, 201–2
Hashemi, Zakaria 123, 145–7, 150, 213
Hatami, Ali 9, 12, 14, 39, 87, 93, 94, 117, 132–5
Hawks, Howard 112
Hayward, Susan 109, 204, 219
Hedayat, Sadegh 10, 77, 86–9, 129, 132, 216

Index of Names

Heidari, Gholam 11, 12, 58, 222
Hejazi, Mohammad 93
Hemingway, Ernest 77, 98, 122–3, 125, 138, 140
Hill, Arthur 49
Hitchcock, Alfred 10, 61, 111–12, 132, 165, 201, 206, 185
Hitler, Adolf 157
Homayoun, Dariush 37, 41
Horkheimer, Max 30, 218
Hosseini, Hassan 8, 12, 222
Houshang, Azadivar 85
Hoveyda, Amir Abbas 151
Hoveyda, Fereydoun 113, 119–21, 161, 219

Iscariot, Judas 200
Issari, Mohammad Ali 24, 27, 29, 36–8, 40, 47, 57–9, 92, 107, 168, 219
Ivens, Joris 173

Jafari, Mohammad Ali 29
Jahed, Parviz 10, 27, 29, 65, 71, 82, 91, 92, 121, 128–30, 132, 139, 140–1, 144, 146, 150–1, 154–5, 157–9, 161–4, 168, 174, 189, 219–20, 222
Jairani, Fereydoun 30
Jalili, Aboulfazl 1
James Monaco 111, 219
Jami, Abdolrahman 91
Jancsó, Miklós 49, 50

Kafka, Franz 81, 98, 122–3, 129
Kaheh, Kambiz 6
Kamshad, Hassan 124, 219
Karimi, Nusrat 108
Karman, Roman 98
Kashi, Sabereh 7, 8, 12, 57, 222
Kavoosi, Houshang 9, 11, 53–4, 63, 60, 66, 70, 116, 163
Kay Kavus 179
Keaton, Buster 50
Kermani, Arvenaghi 93
Keshavarz, Mohammad Ali 15, 165–6
Khalaji, Mehdi 41, 223
Khanjani, Ramin S. 205, 219
Khatibi, Parviz 93
Khomeini, Ayatollah 32, 35, 81–2

Khorvash, Fakhri 15
Khoshnam, Mahmoud 40, 223
Khrushchev 157
Kiarostami, Abbas 1, 46–7, 109, 186, 189–90, 192–6, 218–19, 221
Kimiai, Masoud 3, 9, 12–17, 38, 44, 50, 73, 76, 80, 99, 117, 119, 129–30, 133, 193, 205–8, 211, 219
Kimiavi, Parviz 12, 14, 43, 48–50, 77, 84–9, 168, 174, 186, 196–7
Koushan, Esmail 29, 91, 93–4, 158
Kubrick, Stanley 88

Lang, Fritz 97
Langdon, Harry 173
Langlois, Henri 153, 158–9, 177, 180, 183
Lattuada, Alberto 49
Lawrence, D. H. 203

Magdalene, Mary 200
Maggiorani, Lamberto 118
Mahmoud, Ahmad 97
Makhmalbaf, Mohsen 1, 20
Malak Motie, Naser 53
Malle, Louis 113
Manijeh 175
Mann, Delbert 49
Marie, Michel 114, 219
Marker, Chris 112, 182
Marx, Karl 30
Mashayekhi, Jamshid 15
Mason, James 49
Masoumi, Parvaneh 133
Mastaan, Iraj 93
Maupassant, Guy de 123
McCain, Hank 206
McLaren, Norman 173
Mehrabi, Masoud 16, 21, 91, 223
Mehrjui, Dariush 1, 3, 8–10, 12, 14–17, 37, 43, 45, 76–7, 80, 82, 100, 104, 118, 123, 127–9, 160, 185, 210
Menzel, Jiří, 49
Meshkin, Akbar 15, 126
Mikhalkov, Nikita 49
Minassian, Herand 139
Minassian, Soleyman 9, 76, 139, 143, 150
Mir Ehsan, Ahmad 17, 23–5, 28, 92, 104, 107, 116, 223

Mirsepassi, Ali 32–3, 84, 219
Moazezinia, Hossein 30–1, 52, 54–6, 65, 222–3
Moezi Moghadam, Fereydoun 11
Moghaddam, Jalal 9, 39, 74, 76, 153, 161, 163, 174, 223
Moghaddam, Q. 22
Mohammadi, Majid 35, 38, 223
Mohseni, Majid ix, 29, 55, 80, 171
Mohtasham, Nosratollah 63
Mollapour, Davoud ix, 82, 100, 123–5
Monaco, James 111
Monfaredzadeh, Esfandiar 76
Monroe, Marilyn 61
Montaldo, Giuliano 206
Mosadegh, Mohammad 32
Mosta'an, Hosseingholi 93
Motalebi, Saeed 210
Mulvey, Laura 196, 219

Nabili, Marva 202–3
Naderi, Amir 1, 8, 11, 14, 38, 96, 99, 105, 129, 130, 205, 208, 210
Naficy, Hamid 5, 6, 16–17, 115, 174, 219
Najafi, Ali Amini 192, 220
Nancy, Jean-Luc 196
Naraghi, Ehsan 84
Naser al-din Shah Qajar 20
Nasibi, Nasib 85, 178
Nassirian, Ali 49
Neupert, Richard 114, 219
Nichols, Mike 10
Nouri, Parviz 52
Nouriala, Esmail 72–3, 223

Ohanian, Ovanes 24–6
Olcott, Sidney 23
Omid, Jamal 8–11, 15, 22, 27, 45, 50, 156, 159, 223
Ostrowska, Dorota 111, 114, 220
Ovanessian, Arby 14, 123, 146, 150, 183, 186, 198, 199, 200–3
Ozu, Yasujiro 190, 198

Pahlavi (Diba), Farah 36, 46, 49, 168
Pahlavi, Mohammad Reza 19, 32
Pahlbod, Mehrdad 151

Panahi, Jafar 1
Pasolini, Pier Paolo 50, 108, 167
Paterson, Christine 53
Pejman, Ahmad 76
Pendry, Alan 139, 141
Penn, Arthur 10
Perry, Frank 211
Pirasteh 58
Powell, Michael 156
Powrie, Phil 109
Pressburger, Emeric 156
Proust, Marcel 98

Queenan, Joe 113–14, 220

Ra'ais Firouz, Mehdi 29, 93
Raad, Saeed 38, 209–10, 214
Rahbar, Saber 210
Rahimian, Behzad 209, 223
Rahnema, Fereydoun 1, 4, 7–10, 12, 14–17, 45, 47–8, 52–3, 72, 74, 77, 85–7, 91, 104, 107, 116–17, 137, 156, 158, 159–60, 162, 164, 166, 169–85, 196, 198, 202, 216–17, 223–4
Ray, Satiajit 49
Reader, Keith 109
Reed, Carol 156
Renoir, Jean 25, 62, 109
Resnais, Alain 97–8, 112–13, 117
Reypour, Bahram 52
Reza Khan 19
Reza Shah 21–3, 27, 36, 41, 92
Ricci, Antonio 118, 103, 147
Riva, Emmanuelle 49
Rivette, Jacques 111–12, 219
Robbe-Grillet, Alain 49, 112–13
Rohmer, Eric 111–12, 121, 219
Rosenbaum, Jonathan 145, 220
Rossellini, Roberto 13, 102–3, 107, 127, 147, 173
Rostam 175–6
Royaee, Yadollah 170

Sa'edi, Gholamhossein 3, 97–100, 125–9, 188
Saberi, Pari 15, 166
Sadeghi, Bahram 98, 131–2
Sadoul, Georges 154–7, 166

Index of Names

Safarian, Robert 31
Saghafi, Morad 69, 223
Sahami, Khosrow 166
Sami-Nejad, Roohangiz 26-7
Samuel Khachikian 9, 29, 171, 201, 206
Sartre, Jean Paul 77, 129
Sattari, Jalal 65-6, 223
Sayyad, Parviz 39, 133-4, 151, 152, 190
Schoedsack, Ernest 21
Schrader, Paul 198, 220
Scorsese, Martin 199
Seberg, Jean 112
Sepanta, Abdolhossein 26-8, 91-2, 171
Shahid-Saless, Sohrab 1, 12, 14-15, 39, 47, 49-50, 105, 117-18, 135, 150, 168, 186, 188-196, 202, 218, 220
Shamlou, Ahmad 97, 99, 170-71, 223
Shariati, Ali 84, 86
Shaw, Bernard 138
Shayegan, Dariush 3, 32, 48, 84, 85, 223
Shirazi, Ahmad 9, 29
Shirdel, Kamran 14, 45, 49, 98, 104, 108, 123, 125, 160, 198, 203, 208, 213-14
Shirvanlu, Firuz 45-6
Shoa'ee, Hamid 175-9 184, 224
Siavash 172, 176, 179
Siskel, Gene 37, 219-20
Sohrab 175
Sorlin, Pierre 103-4, 147-8, 220
Stalin, Joseph 157
Sudabeh 172, 179
Sultan Mahmoud Qaznavi 92
Szabó, István 49

Tabari, Manouchehr 85
Taghavi, Ebrahim 138
Taghvai, Nasser 1, 3, 12, 14, 16, 38, 47-8, 76, 83, 85, 100, 117, 123, 125, 126-7, 129, 135, 150, 168, 174, 188, 193, 204, 208

Tahaminejad, Mohammad 25, 62, 224
Taheridoost, Gholamhossein 85
Taji, Ahmadi 106, 147, 149, 150
Takmil Homayoun, Nader 212, 219
Talajooy, Saeed 78-9, 98, 123, 143, 220
Talebinejad, Ahmad 5, 6, 15-16, 73, 97-9 108, 117-19, 123, 126, 224
Tamimi, Farrokh 170
Tarr, Béla 190-1
Tati, Jacques 173
Tayab, Manouchehr 85, 174
Thompson, Kristin 13, 114-15, 218
Tomlinson, Hugh 101, 218
Tourani, Behrouz 27
Truffaut, Francois 12, 50, 110-12, 114, 116, 119-20, 122, 185, 219-20
Turgenev, Ivan 138

Vadim, Roger 109
Vafa, Nezam 29
Vahdat, Nosratollah 34
Varda, Agnes 112
Vedadian, Mehri 124
Vidor, King 50
Visconti, Luchino 13, 102, 199
Vosoughi, Behrouz 38, 96, 207, 211, 213

Wajda, Andrzej 97
Waltari, Mika 127
Wayler, William 50
Welles, Orson 45, 118, 159, 186
Wiene, Robert 132

Yasemi, Siamak 9, 29, 33, 61, 65-6, 91-3
Youshij, Nima 97, 99, 146, 170

Zamani, Manouchehr 175
Zavattini, Cesare 106-7, 103
Zhian, Reza 182
Zurlini, Valerio 37

Index of films and books

17 Days to Execution (*17 Rooz be E'daam*) 163
1984 84
2001: A Space Odyssey 88

A Clockwork Orange 84
A Fire (*Yek Atash*) 138, 141, 144
A World Full of Hope (*Donya-ye Por Omid*) 9
Agha Mohammad Khan Qajar 63
Ahl-e Hava 89
Ahu Khanoom's Husband (*Shohar-e Ahu Khanoom*) 9, 82, 99–100, 123–5, 186
Alley of Valiants (*Koocheh-mardha*) 210
Ancient Poems (*Poems Anciens*) 170
And God Created Woman (*Et Dieu Crea La Femme*) 109
Animal Comedy, The (*Komedi Heivani*) 202
Arabian Nights 10, 80, 105, 163
Ashamed (*Sharmsar*) 29, 158
Ashes and Diamonds 97
Asia Versus the West (*Asia dar Barabar-e Gharb*) 32, 84, 224

Baba Shamal 94
Ballad of Tara (*Charike-ye Tara*) 14, 78, 133, 197
Bashu, The Little Stranger (*Bashu, Gharibe-ye Koochack*) 15, 78
Beehive (*Kandu*) 210, 212
Bicycle Thieves 101–5, 107, 118, 147, 173
Bijan and Manijeh (*Bijan o Manijeh*) 175
Bita 47, 150, 202–4
Black Eyes (*Cheshman-e Siah*) 27
Blind Owl, The (*Boof-e Koor*) 10, 132, 216
Blood Moon, The (*Mahtab-e Khonin*) 169
Blue World (*Donya-ye Abi*) 210
Bonnie and Clyde 10
Book of Kings, The (*Shahnameh*) 91–3, 172, 175–6, 179
Brazil 85

Bread and Alley (*Nan-o-Kocheh*) 46, 193
Breathless (*À bout de souffle*) 108, 112–13, 146, 214
Brick and Mirror (*Khesht va Ayeneh*) 9, 15, 17, 39, 52, 70, 75, 81, 99, 105–8, 120, 125–6, 137, 142, 145–50, 152, 162, 164, 186–8, 194, 213–14
Broken Ships (*Kashti Shekasteh-ha*) 140

Cabinet of Dr. Caligari, The 132
Canterbury Tales, The 168
Captain Khorshid (*Nakhoda Khorshid*) 125
Caravans (*Carvan-ha*) 37, 219, 220
Chess of the wind, The (*Shatranj-e Baad*) 43, 186, 198–9
Cow, The (*Gav*) 3, 9–11, 14–17, 37, 42–3, 79, 82, 98–9, 118–19, 123, 127–9, 185–7
Crossroads of Accidents, The (*Chahar-rah-e Havades*) 170, 171
Crow, The (*Kalagh*) 44, 132, 196
Cry of the Storm, The (*Nare-ye Toofan*) 9
Curse, The (*Nefrin*) 125, 127
Cycle, The (*Dayereh-ye Mina*) 14, 43, 47, 79, 99, 127, 129, 185, 187

Dagger, The (*Deshneh*) 210
Dash Akol 38, 99, 129
Deadend (*Bonbast*) 10, 134–5
Deadlock (*Tangna*) 38, 209–10
Decameron, The 167
Deer, The (*Gavaznha*) 38, 43–4, 50, 206
Desert of the Tartars, The (*Sahra-ye Tatarha*) 37
Diamond 33 (*Almaas 33*) 210
Divine One (*Malakout*) 50, 99, 201, 131–2
Don Quixote 167
Downpour (*Ragbar*) 14, 50, 78, 118, 132–3
Dummy, The (*Adamak*) 201

Earth Trembles, The 102
Eclipse 187
End of Suffering (Payan-e Ranjha) 170
Escape from the Trap (Farar az Taleh) 9, 73, 213
Europe '51 101

Far From Home (Dar Ghorbat) 47, 135, 190
Farhad o Shirin 91
Ferdowsi 91–2
Foreign Bride, The (Aroos Farangi) 34, 70
From a Drop to the Sea (Az Ghatreh ta Darya) 140

Germany, Year Zero 101
Ghalandar 134
Goodbye Friend (Khodahafez Rafigh) 8, 11, 209
Graduate, The 10
Grass, The 21
Guilty, The (Gonahkar) 93

Haft Orang 91
Haji Agha, the Cinema Actor (Haji Agha, Actor-e Cinema) 24–6
Harmonica (Saz Dahani) 209
Hassan Kachal (Hassan the Bald) 9, 93–4, 133, 135, 208
Hassanlou Cup (Jaam-e Hassanlou) 198
Hills of Marlik, The (Tappeh-haye Marlik) 138, 145
Hills of Qaytariyeh, The (Tapeh-haye Qaytarieh) 86–7, 89
Hiroshima Mon Amour 97, 113
Hossein Kord-e Shabestari 93
House Is Black, The (Khaneh Siah Ast) 10, 70, 141, 143

Ilakhchi 89
Infidel, The (Kafar) 210–11
Iran of Yesterday and the Iran of Today, The 91
Iran Is My Homeland (Iran Sara-ye Man Ast) 89
Iran's Railroad 21
Iran's Son Has No News of His Mother (Pesare Iran az Madaresh bi Etella' Ast) 48, 177–84

Janitor, The (Soraydar) 201
Joan of Arc 23
Journey, The (Safar) 14
Journey of the Stones (Safar-e Sang) 80

Kharg Island, The Unique Pearl of the Persian Gulf 89
Killing Mad Dogs (Sag Koshi) 44, 132, 196

L'immortelle 113
La Notte 187
Lady Chatterley's Lover 203
Land of Iran (Iran Zamin) 48, 85, 174, 198
Last Station, The 98
Last Year at Marienbad 113
Leily and Majnoun (Leily va Majnoun) 27
Leyli o Majnun 91
Liberation (Rahayee) 125
Like a Never Ending Alley (Hamchoun Kocheh-ee Bi-enteha) 171, 223
Lonely Hearts, The (Sooteh Delan) 134
Long Shadows of the Wind, The (Sayeh-haye Boland-e Baad) 99
Lor Girl, The (Dokhtar-e Lor) 26–8, 91
Lord of the Flies 84
Lost Horizon 84

M 97
Machine Gun McCain 206
Madness of the Power, The (Jonoun-e Hokoumat) 93
Maybe Some Other Time (Shayad Vaghti Digar) 196
Maziar 78
Metropolis 84
Miracle in Milan 118
Mongols, The (Mogholha) 39, 43, 47, 50, 79, 88–9, 186, 196–7
Monsieur Beaucaire 23
Mourners of Bayal, The (Azadaran-e Bayal) 127–28
Mourning and Melancholia 86
Mr Twentieth Century (Aghay-e Gharn-e Bistom) 34
My Uncle Napoleon (Daei Jan Napoleon) 135

Naked Until Noon with Speed (*Berehneh ta Zohr ba Sorat*) 42, 201–2
Nameless Fear (*Vaheme-haye Binam o Neshan*) 126
Nassim-e Ayyar 93
Night It rained, The (*An Shab ke Baroon Omad*) 108
Night of Angels (*Shab-e Fereshtegan*) 210
Night of the Hunchback, The (*Shab-e Quzi*) 10, 15, 17, 33, 52, 80, 99, 105, 148, 153–4, 162–8, 186, 213
Nightingale of the Farm, The (*Bolbol-e Mazraeh*) 80
Nights of the Temple, The (*Shabha-ye Ma'bad*) 56
November, the End of Fall (*Azar Maah-e Akhar-e Payeez*) 138

O.K. Mister 47, 79, 80, 84, 89, 169, 186
Oh Guardian of Deers (*Ya Zamen-e Ahu*) 86
On the Morning of the Fourth Day (*Sobh-e Rooz-e Chaharrom*) 108, 214
One Thousand and One Nights (*Hezar-o-Yek Shab*) 10, 80, 91, 105, 163, 166
Orazan 89
Ossessione 102

P for Pelican (*P Mesle Pelican*) 87–9
Paisan 102
Parichehr 93
The Parrot (*Tooti*) 213
The Prisoner of the Emir (*Zendani Amir*) 29
Parvin Daughter of Sasan (*Parvin Dokhtar-e Sasan*) 78
Persepolis (*Takht-e Jamshid*) 85, 174
Perspective (*Cheshmandaz*) 139, 141
Pierrot le Fou 113
Prince Ehtejab (*Shazdeh Ehtejab*) 3, 47, 50, 98–9, 129, 131, 186

Qarun's Treasure, The (*Ganj-e Qarun*) 9, 13, 33, 37, 58, 60–1, 65–6
Qaysar 9–11, 13, 15–17, 38, 72, 117, 119, 133–4, 186, 206–8, 211, 213

Realism of Film (*Vagheiatgrayee-ye Film*) 169
Red Desert 187, 192

Renowned Amir Arsalan, The (*Amir Arsalan-e Namdar*) 93
Report (*Gozaresh*) 195
Requiem (*Marsieh*) 209
Reza Motorcyclist (*Reza Motori*) 9, 38
Rififi 209
Ring-necked Dove, The (*Towghi*) 133
Rivalry in the City (*Reghabat dar Shahr*) 42, 106, 161
River, The 62
Rome Open City 102
Rostam and Sohrab (*Rostam o Sohrab*) 175
Rooster, The (*Khoroos*) 153
Ruler For a Day (*Hakem-e Yek Rooz-e*) 93
Rules of the Game, The (*La règle du jeu*) 109
Running Canon, The (*Zanburak*) 47, 106, 135, 154, 167–8

Sacred Arena (*Goud-e Moghadas*) 203
Sadegh Kordeh 125
Sadegh the Kurd (*Sadegh Kordeh*) 38, 125, 208
Samad and the Steel Armoured Ogre (*Samad va Foolad Zereh Div*) 39
Samak-e Ayyar 93
Sattar Khan 39, 134, 135
Sea, The (*Darya*) 99
Sealed Soil, The (*Khak-e Sar be Mohr*) 202, 203
Secrets of the Treasure of the Jinn Valley, The (*Asrar-e Ganj-e Darre-ye Jenni*) 43, 79, 80, 99, 135, 137, 145, 150–2
Serpent's Skin (*Jeld-e Maar*) 203
Shadow-Hunting (*Shekar-e Sayeh*) 140
Shirin and Farhad (*Sfhirin o Farhad*) 27, 93
Siavash in Persepolis (*Siavash Dar Takht-e Jamshid*) 9, 17, 52, 74, 162, 173, 175–9, 186, 202
Sign of Leo, The (*Le signe du lion*) 121
Soil, The (*Khaak*) 10, 129–30
Song of Freedom, The (*Chants de Deliverance*) 170
Song of the Village, The (*Ahang-e Dehkadeh*) 80
South of the City (*Jonub-e Shahr*) 29, 42, 70, 79, 106–7, 148, 153, 162–3

Spring, The (*Cheshmeh*) 39, 47, 50, 150, 183, 198–9, 201
Spring of Heghnar 199
Still Life (*Tabiat-e Bijaan*) 39, 47, 135, 150, 188–92
Stone Garden, The (*Bagh-e Sangi*) 47, 187
Storm of Life (*Toofan-e Zendegi*) 29, 76
Stranger and the Fog, The (*Gharibeh va Meh*) 14, 39, 78, 82, 133, 186
Stream, the Wall and the Thirsty One, The (*Juy-o Divar-o Teshneh*) 216
Stromboli 101
Suitor, The (*Khastegar*) 134, 135
Summer of the Same Year (*Tabestan-e Haman Saal*) 125
Sunrise (*Tolou*) 9
Swallows Return to Their Nest, The (*Parastuha be Laneh Barmigardand*) 80
Swamp 127
Swimmer, The 211

Tale of Baba Sobhan, The (*Owsane-ye Baba Sobhan*) 10, 129–30
Tangsir 3, 38, 96, 99, 129–30, 186, 208
Taste of Cherry (*Ta'm-e Guilass*) 192
Tat People of Block-e-Zahra (*Tat Neshinan-e Bouin-Zahra*) 89
Three Taps (*Se-Ghap*) 213
Through the Glass Darkly 97, 127
To Catch a Thief 111
To Have and Have Not 125
Toghi 9

Tranquility in the Presence of Others (*Aramesh dar Hozour-e Digaran*) 3, 16, 39, 42, 47, 79, 83, 98–9, 119, 125–6, 129, 150, 186–8, 204, 208
Trans-Europ Express 113
Trouble with Harry, The 10, 165
Two Cents' Worth of Hope 104

Umberto D 104, 107
Under the Skin of the Night (*Zir-e Poost-e Shab*) 210
Utopia 190
Uzak 192

Vivre sa vie 16

Water and Heat (*Aab va Garma*) 141
Wave, Coral and Stone (*Mowj, Marjan, Khara*) 138, 140, 144
Westoxification (*Gharbzadegi*) 18, 33, 84, 220
Wheel Circulation (*Gardesh-e Charkh*) 141
When the Sea Became Stormy (*Vaghti Darya Toofani Shod*) 99
Which One Is the Bride? (*Arus Kodum-e?*) 163
Window, The (*Panjareh*) 9
Wrath of Eagles (*Khashme Oghabha*) 210

Youssef o Zolaikhah 93

www.ingramcontent.com/pod-product-compliance
Lightning Source LLC
Chambersburg PA
CBHW062141300426
44115CB00012BA/2004